Understanding
Singapore
Politics

Understanding
Singapore
Politics

Bilveer Singh
NUS, Singapore

World Scientific

NEW JERSEY · LONDON · SINGAPORE · BEIJING · SHANGHAI · HONG KONG · TAIPEI · CHENNAI · TOKYO

Published by

World Scientific Publishing Co. Pte. Ltd.
5 Toh Tuck Link, Singapore 596224
USA office: 27 Warren Street, Suite 401-402, Hackensack, NJ 07601
UK office: 57 Shelton Street, Covent Garden, London WC2H 9HE

Library of Congress Cataloging-in-Publication Data
Names: Singh, Bilveer, 1956– author.
Title: Understanding Singapore politics / Bilveer Singh.
Description: [Hackensack], New Jersey : World Scientific, [2017] |
    Includes bibliographical references and index.
Identifiers: LCCN 2017003572| ISBN 9789813209220 (hardcover) |
    ISBN 9789813209237 (softcover)
Subjects: LCSH: Singapore--Politics and government.
Classification: LCC DS610.7 .S575 2017 | DDC 320.95957--dc23
LC record available at https://lccn.loc.gov/2017003572

British Library Cataloguing-in-Publication Data
A catalogue record for this book is available from the British Library.

Copyright © 2017 by World Scientific Publishing Co. Pte. Ltd.

All rights reserved. This book, or parts thereof, may not be reproduced in any form or by any means, electronic or mechanical, including photocopying, recording or any information storage and retrieval system now known or to be invented, without written permission from the publisher.

For photocopying of material in this volume, please pay a copying fee through the Copyright Clearance Center, Inc., 222 Rosewood Drive, Danvers, MA 01923, USA. In this case permission to photocopy is not required from the publisher.

Desk Editor: Jiang Yulin

Typeset by Stallion Press
Email: enquiries@stallionpress.com

Printed in Singapore by Mainland Press Pte Ltd.

Key Personalities in Singapore's Politics		vii
Chronology of Key Political Developments		xv
List of Tables		xxi
Abbreviations		xxiii
Key Terms		xxvii
Acknowledgements		xxxiii
Preface		xxxvii
Introduction		xxxix
Chapter 1	The Key Determinants of Singapore Politics	1
Chapter 2	The Political History of Singapore and the Continued Relevance of the Past	11
Chapter 3	The Singapore Political System — A Hybrid Westminster Model?	21
Chapter 4	Political Parties — The Resilience of the One-Party Dominant State	31
Chapter 5	Para-Political Organisations in Singapore	41
Chapter 6	Nation Building and National Identity	59
Chapter 7	Political Leadership and the Challenge of Renewal	73
Chapter 8	Rise of Civil Society Politics and Democratisation	93
Chapter 9	Rise of New Issues in Singapore's Politics	113
Chapter 10	Elections in Singapore — Is the Hegemony Being Challenged?	127
Chapter 11	Singapore in the Post-Lee Kuan Yew Era	145
Chapter 12	Linkage between Singapore's Domestic and Foreign Policy	153
Conclusion: Whither Politics in Singapore?		159
Select Bibliography		167
Index		179

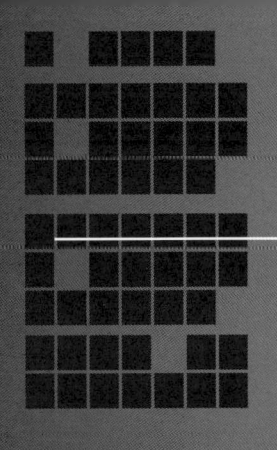

Key Personalities in Singapore's Politics

Chiam See Tong (1935-present)
A trained lawyer and an Opposition veteran, Chiam See Tong was first elected to Parliament in 1984 as the Member of Parliament (MP) for the Potong Pasir constituency. Until 2011, he was the longest-serving Opposition MP. He founded the Singapore Democratic Party (SDP). Later, he was forced to leave the party following a challenge from Chee Soon Juan. In 1996, he joined the Singapore People's Party (SPP). He spearheaded the formation of the Singapore Democratic Alliance (SDA), being the *de facto* Opposition leader until 2011. In March 2011, the SPP withdrew from the SDA and Chiam contested the 2011 General Elections in a Group Representation Constituency (GRC) in Bishan-Toa Payoh where he lost. Ill-health has, however, prevented him from being active in politics even though he remains a respected and popular political figure nationally.

David Marshall (1908–1995)
David Marshall was Singapore's first Chief Minister and one of the pioneer nationalists who pushed for Singapore's independence. His act of resignation in 1956 following his inability to help Singapore gain its independence, though often viewed as impulsive and irrational, signified the birth of nationalism for the small state. Despite his resignation, he left his mark as a charismatic leader that inspired others to think in terms of Singapore's nationalism and independence.

Devan Nair (1923–2005)
Devan Nair was a leading and famous trade unionist in Singapore. After the Second World War, in the midst of rising nationalism in Singapore, he joined the communist-led Anti-British League. Later in 1954, he became a founding member of the PAP and supported Lee Kuan Yew against the communists. He was the founder of the non-communist National Trades Union Congress (NTUC) in 1961 that largely sealed Singapore's victory against the communists. In 1964, he founded the

Democratic Action Party and won a parliamentary seat in the Malaysian elections. On his return to Singapore in 1969, he continued to lead the NTUC and was elected to the Singapore Parliament from 1979 to 1981. He served as Singapore's third president from 1981 to 1985. He controversially resigned as Singapore's president following Lee Kuan Yew alleging that he needed to be treated for alcoholism. Nair, however, claimed it was due to the clash of political views that led to the acrimony and clash between the Head of State and Head of Government.

Goh Chok Tong (1941-present)
Despite not being Lee Kuan Yew's first choice as successor, Goh Chok Tong became Singapore's second Prime Minister. Prior to this appointment, Goh served as Senior Minister for Trade and Industry, Finance, and Health, and became the Deputy Prime Minister in 1985. His consultative style contrasted Lee's hard authoritative stance, which made him popular among liberal-oriented Singaporeans. He first entered politics in 1976 and also contested the 2015 General Elections, making him the longest-serving MP in Singapore's politics today. Though not in cabinet, he has held the honorary title of Emeritus Senior Minister since 2011.

Goh Keng Swee (1918–2010)
Goh Keng Swee was involved in the Malayan Forum that mulled over the independence of Malaya. In 1959, he won the Kreta Ayer seat and joined the first government under then Prime Minister Lee Kuan Yew's leadership as Minister of Finance. He was known as being the key driver of the Singapore economy and also a fervent supporter of merger with Malaysia due to economic considerations. Two years after independence, he became Minister of Interior and Defence, handling Singapore's military and security policies. He also contributed to the reform of Singapore's education system through the 1979 'Goh Report' that introduced streaming. He retired in 1984.

J. B. Jeyaretnam (1926–2008)
Joseph Benjamin Jeyaretnam, the former leader of the Workers' Party (WP) from 1971 to 2001, epitomised the ability of the Opposition to succeed against all odds against the pre-dominant one-party dominant state of Singapore. In the 1981 Anson by-election, he defeated the PAP candidate, Pang Kim Hin, to become the first member of an Opposition party to get elected to the Singapore Parliament, thus ending the PAP's complete domination of Parliament since 1968. He was re-elected in the 1984 General Elections but lost his seat in 1986 for being convicted of falsifying his party's accounts. His conviction was quashed by the Privy Council. Following the 1997 General Elections, he returned to Parliament as a Non-Constituency Member of Parliament

(NCMP) but was stripped of his parliamentary seat for being declared a bankrupt in 2001. He left the WP in 2001 and in 2008 founded the Reform Party (RP).

Lee Hsien Loong (1952-present)
Lee Hsien Loong, the current Prime Minister, was educated in Cambridge and Harvard, and is the eldest son of Lee Kuan Yew, Singapore's first Prime Minister. He was groomed for political office for a long time and at the age of 32 entered politics by winning a parliamentary seat in the 1984 General Elections. Two years later, he was elected into the PAP's Central Executive Committee (CEC) and in 1990 became one of two Deputy Prime Ministers. In 1992, he was diagnosed with cancer. In 2004, he became Singapore's third Prime Minister and led the party to victory in the 2006, 2011, and 2015 General Elections.

Lee Kuan Yew (1923–2015)
By any measure, Lee Kuan Yew is the 'father' of modern Singapore. A lawyer by training, he and his close comrades-in-arms founded the PAP in November 1954. He held the position of PAP Secretary-General from November 1954 to November 1992 except for a short interim in 1957. Lee entered politics as an assemblyman in April 1955 and served as a parliamentarian till his death in March 2015, making him one of the longest serving parliamentarians in a functioning democracy. He was Singapore's Prime Minister from 1959 to 1990, and saw Singapore through as a British colony, a state in Malaysia and as an independent nation. In November 1990, he became a Senior Minister in the cabinet of Goh Chok Tong. In 2004, he was appointed as Minister Mentor in the cabinet of Lee Hsien Loong. Following the 2011 General Elections, even though he won a parliamentary seat, he refused to take up any cabinet position, opting to be a backbencher. Lee Kuan Yew led his party to eight electoral victories from 1959 to 1988 and his *imprimatur* can be seen in almost every aspect of national politics in Singapore right to this day.

Lim Chin Siong (1933–1996)
Often regarded as the primary nemesis of Lee Kuan Yew, Lim Chin Siong was the co-founder of the PAP in 1954. Later in 1961, he was the key architect in the formation of the *Barisan Sosialis* (BS), which was made up of breakaway core members of the PAP's left-wing. A Chinese-educated union leader, believed to be the 'open' united front leader of the Malayan Communist Party, he was elected into the Legislative Assembly at the age of 22 in 1955. He was the key instigator of many violent riots and strikes in Singapore in the 1950s including the infamous 1955 Hock Lee Bus Riots. He was detained, first by the Lim Yew Hock government from 1956–1959 and

later by the Lee government from 1963–1969. Till today, he remains a controversial figure in Singapore politics.

Lim Yew Hock (1914–1984)
Lim Yew Hock was Singapore's second Chief Minister from 1956 to 1959. Lim, then Minister for Labour and Welfare, replaced David Marshall and headed a new coalition government. As Chief Minister, he took firm actions to suppress anti-colonial activists and communists. From 1956 to 1958, Lim led an all-party delegation to negotiate with the British in a series of *Merdeka talks*, and won Singapore internal self-rule. Lim's hardline approach towards communism alienated a large portion of the Chinese-speaking electorate from him and his Labour Party, which enabled the PAP to win the 1959 General Elections.

Low Thia Khiang (1956-present)
Today, he is the *de facto* leader of the Opposition in Parliament. He is also the longest-serving Opposition member in Parliament today, having been first elected to his seat in Hougang in 1991. He participated in seven elections and won on six occasions. A very charismatic leader, he is seen as the key to the WP's parliamentary success and the person behind the Opposition's ability to dent the PAP's electoral dominance. After defending his Hougang seat in four general elections, he led the WP team that defeated the PAP in Aljunied GRC in the 2011 and 2015 General Elections. He has been the WP's Secretary-General since 2001. In May 2016, his leadership of the party was challenged for the first time by Chen Show Mao, a fellow member of Aljunied GRC. Low successfully defended his position but this also indicated that there may be trouble ahead in the WP as far as internal unity is concerned, something that has characterised all Opposition parties in Singapore.

Othman Wok (1924-present)
In 1954, amidst rampant communist threats and the fight for independence, Othman Wok joined the PAP. In the general elections nine years later, he managed to win a parliamentary seat as a representative of Pasir Panjang. He subsequently assumed the responsibilities of Minister of Social Affairs, a post he held for the next 14 years. Othman is remembered for his handling of the racial riots that struck Singapore in 1964 on the birthday of Prophet Mohammad and up until today, he continues to fervently promote the need for racial harmony. He was Singapore's Ambassador to Indonesia for three years (1978–1981), after which he served on the Singapore Tourism Board and Sentosa Development Board for another couple of years. Old age and ill-health have kept him away from public life even though he remains a highly respected political figure in Singapore. He also prides himself as being from the 'Orang Laut' community, the original inhabitants of Singapore.

S. R. Nathan (1924–2016)

Mr S. R. Nathan began his career as a civil servant and went on to become an eminent politician. He was Singapore's sixth president from 1999 to 2011, the longest-serving Head of State of Singapore to date. He served with distinction in the Ministry of Foreign Affairs and the Ministry of Home Affairs, and also became the Director of the Security Intelligence Department, Singapore's external intelligence agency, in the Ministry of Defence. In January 1974, when terrorists from the Japanese Red Army and the Popular Front for the Liberation of Palestine threatened to bomb petroleum storage tanks on Pulau Bukom off Singapore's southern coast, known as the 'Laju Incident', Nathan volunteered to be held hostage to secure the civilians that were being held hostage. He was a highly popular figure, preferring to maintain a low profile. He died on 22 August 2016 and was given a state funeral.

S. Rajaratnam (1915–2006)

S. Rajaratnam was one of Singapore's pioneering political leaders. A founding member of the PAP, his political career was characterised by his fervent anti-colonial stance. In 1959, he resigned from journalism to campaign for the Legislative Assembly seat in Kampong Glam. In 1965, he became Singapore's first foreign minister. He is remembered for believing that Singapore's small size was not an impediment to making it an influential member internationally. On the domestic level, he is known for his emphasis on creating a harmonious and multiracial society, as indicated by his contribution to the Singapore pledge: "one united people, regardless of race, language or religion". The height of his political career was as a Deputy Prime Minister (1980–1985) and as the first Senior Minister in the Republic (1985–1988).

Teo Chee Hean (1954-present)

A President's Scholar, he served with distinction both academically and in the Singapore Armed Forces. After various senior staff appointments, he became Chief of the Republic of Singapore Navy in 1991 with a rank of Rear Admiral. In 1992, he entered politics as part of a GRC under the then Prime Minister, Goh Chok Tong. Since then, he has held various senior ministerial portfolios, including being Acting Minister for the Environment, Minister of Education and various stints in the Ministry of Defence. Presently, he is a key minister in the cabinet of Prime Minister Lee Hsien Loong. In addition to being the First Assistant Secretary-General of the PAP CEC, he is the Co-ordinating Minister for National Security and the Deputy Prime Minister.

Tharman Shanmugaratnam (1957-present)

Tharman Shanmugaratnam came to prominence from his association with the Monetary Authority of Singapore (MAS), where he eventually became Managing

Director. In 2001, he entered politics, becoming the Minister of State for Trade and Industry, and Education. Following the 2006 General Elections, he became the Minister of Education and the Second Minister of Finance. He joined the CEC of the PAP in 2002 and is currently the Second Assistant Secretary-General of the CEC. Presently, he is the Co-ordinating Minister for Economic and Social Policies and Deputy Prime Minister.

Toh Chin Chye (1921–2012)
Toh Chin Chye's political career began with his involvement in the Malayan Forum, with Malayan nationals such as future Prime Ministers Lee Kuan Yew and Tun Abdul Razak, to deliberate on the independence of Malaya. He was one of the founding members of the PAP and was its chairperson from its formation in 1954 to 1981. In the 1959 General Elections, Toh was elected as a PAP MP for Rochor. Thereafter, there was a contest between Lee and Singapore's only mayor, Ong Eng Guan for the premiership and it was Toh's vote that swung the fight in Lee's favour. Toh was Deputy Prime Minister from 1959 to 1968, Minister of Science and Technology from 1968 to 1975 and Minister of Health from 1975 to 1981. He stepped down from the cabinet and party leadership in 1981 but remained a critical voice in Parliament for two terms, often criticising government and party policies. He retired in 1988.

Singapore's Key Fourth Generation Political Leaders

Chan Chun Sing (1969-present)
Holder of the President and Singapore Armed Forces scholarships, Chan Chun Sing is currently a Minister in the Prime Minister's Office and the Secretary-General of the NTUC. He entered politics in the 2011 General Elections as part of the GRC team led by Lee Kuan Yew in Tanjong Pagar and entered Parliament through a walkover. He contested and won in the 2015 General Elections. Prior to this he was the Chief of Army from 2010 to 2011. He has held a number of ministerial positions including Acting Minister for Community Development, Youth and Sports; Minister of State, Ministry of Information, Communications and the Arts; Senior Minister of State, Ministry of Defence; Acting Minister, Ministry of Social and Family Development; and Second Minister for Defence.

Chee Hong Tat (1973-present)
Chee Hong Tat has been a civil servant most of his adult life until he was elected into Parliament in 2015. He was part of the winning team at the Bishan-Toa Payoh GRC. He was appointed as Minister of State for Health and Minister of State for Communications and Information. He was the Principal Private Secretary to Minister

Mentor Lee Kuan Yew from 2008 to 2011. Following this, Chee became the Chief Executive Officer at the Energy Market Authority and later, the Second Permanent Secretary at the Ministry of Trade and Industry.

Heng Swee Keat (1961-present)
Heng Swee Keat is currently the Minister of Finance. He entered politics in the 2011 General Elections as a member of the Tampines GRC. He also won in the 2015 General Elections. Prior to entering politics, he served as the Permanent Secretary at the Ministry of Trade and Industry, and Managing Director of the Monetary Authority of Singapore from 2005 to 2011. He also served as the Principal Private Secretary to the then Senior Minister Lee Kuan Yew in 1997. Following the 2011 General Elections, Heng was appointed as the Minister of Education. On 12 May 2016, Heng suffered a stroke during a cabinet meeting. By late August 2016, Heng had fully recovered and resumed his duties as an MP and Minister of Finance even though another minister was also appointed as the Second Finance Minister. Heng is also known for having chaired the 'Our Singapore Conversation' and SG50 Steering Committees.

Lawrence Wong (1972-present)
Currently, Lawrence Wong is the Minister for National Development and the Second Minister for Finance. He entered politics in the 2011 General Elections as part of the West Coast GRC. In the 2015 General Elections he anchored the PAP's team for the Marsiling-Yew Tee GRC. Previously, he has held appointments in the Ministry of Defence, Ministry of Education, Ministry of Communications and Information, and the Ministry of Culture, Community and Youth. Prior to entering politics, he had served as the Principal Private Secretary to Prime Minister Lee Hsien Loong from 2005 to 2008.

Ng Chee Meng (1968-present)
Ng Chee Meng is currently the Minister for Education (Schools) and Second Minister for Transport. He entered politics following the 2015 General Elections. Prior to entering politics he had served as the Chief of the Republic of Singapore Air Force and the Chief of Defence Force, Singapore Armed Forces.

Ong Ye Kung (1969-present)
Ong Ye Kung is currently the Minister for Education (Higher Education and Skills) and Second Minister for Defence. He entered politics in the 2015 General Elections, as a member of the Sembawang GRC. Prior to entering politics, he held an array of appointments at Keppel Corporation, NTUC and the Singapore Workforce Development Agency. He has also served as the Press Secretary to former Prime

Minister Lee Kuan Yew from 1997–2003 and Principal Private Secretary to Prime Minister Lee Hsien Loong (2003–2005). Prior to contesting the 2015 General Elections, he was part of the PAP's Aljunied GRC that lost to the WP in 2011. Ong's father was Ong Lian Teng, a BS's Member of the Legislative Assembly/MP from 1963 to 1966 for the Bukit Panjang Constituency.

Tan Chuan-Jin (1969-present)
Tan Chuan-Jin is currently the Minister of Social and Family Development. He entered politics in the 2011 General Elections as part of the Marine Parade GRC. He also won in the 2015 General Elections. Prior to entering politics, he served in the Singapore Armed Forces, holding the rank of a Brigadier General. He has also served as the Minister of State at the Ministry of Manpower, and Ministry of National Development. In May 2014, he became the Minister of Manpower.

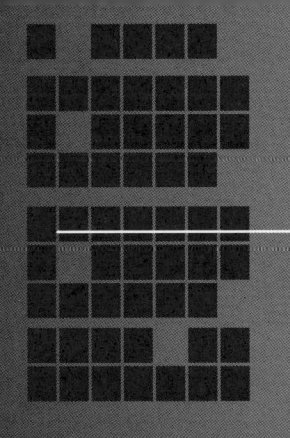

Chronology of Key Political Developments

1819: Stamford Raffles of the East India Company, together with William Farquhar, establishes a trading post in Singapore after securing an agreement with Sultan Hussein of Johore and Temenggong Abdul Rahman. Farquhar becomes Singapore's first Resident.

1824: Singapore is ceded to the British by Sultan Hussein in exchange for payments and recognition as the legitimate ruler of the Johore Sultanate. British control over Singapore was internationally recognised under the Anglo-Dutch Treaty of 1824 where the Dutch withdrew all objections to British occupation of the territory.

1826: Together with Penang and Malacca, Singapore becomes part of the British Straits Settlements.

1830: Singapore is administered under the Presidency of Bengal in India.

1832: Singapore becomes the administrative centre of the Straits Settlements.

1867: Administration of the Straits Settlement is transferred from the Residency of Bengal to the British Colonial Office, thus becoming a Crown Colony.

1867: The Suez Canal is opened, linking Singapore directly with the industrial centres of the world, thereby increasing its trade.

1915: The Indian Mutiny breaks out with British Muslim *Sepoys* rising against the British, fearing that they will be sent to Turkey for war.

1922: Singapore becomes the main British naval base in East Asia.

1941: In December, Japanese planes begin bombing Singapore.

1942: In January, Malaya falls to the Japanese and the Causeway is blown up. Water supply from Johore to Singapore is cut and Lt. Adnan from the Malay Regiment puts up a brave fight. The British forces under Lt-Gen. Arthur E. Percival surrender to the Japanese and Singapore is renamed *Syonan-to*, Light of the South.

1945: Japan surrenders unconditionally after the bombings of Hiroshima and Nagasaki. Allied forces return to Singapore and the administration of Singapore is taken over by the British Military Administration.

1946: After the Straits Settlements is dissolved, Singapore is administered as a separate crown colony.

1948: When the Malayan Communist Party launched an insurgency, the British declares a State of Emergency in Malaya and Singapore. In March, Singapore's first limited election is held for six seats in the Legislative Council with the Singapore Progressive Party winning three.

1950: The Maria Hertogh riots break out in December, killing 18 people.

1951: The second limited election for the Legislative Council is held with the number of seats increasing from six to nine.

1953: The British Government appoints the Rendel Commission to make recommendations on self-government in the colony.

1955: The first local government elections are held under the Rendel Constitution with 25 out of 32 members of the Legislative Assembly to be elected. David Saul Marshall becomes the Chief Minister of Singapore.

1956: David Marshall demands full self-government, failing which he resigns and Lim Yew Hock, his deputy, becomes the second Chief Minister of Singapore.

1957: While Malaya gains independence from the British, Lim Yew Hock succeeds in gaining full self-government from the British.

1959: Elections for the first fully elected Legislative Assembly were held in May with the People's Action Party winning 43 out of 51 seats. Lee Kuan Yew becomes Singapore's Prime Minister. Yusof bin Ishak becomes the Head of State (*Yang Dipertuan Negara*) and the National Anthem, *Majulah Singapura* is presented for the first time.

1961: Tunku Abdul Rahman, Malaya's Prime Minister proposes merger between Malaya and the British territories of Singapore, Sabah, Sarawak and Brunei.

1962: Singapore holds a referendum on merger and the PAP's option is preferred.

1963: 'Operation Coldstore' is launched in February, arresting 107 left-wing leaders. Singapore merges with the Federation of Malaya and together with Sabah and Sarawak, to form the Federation of Malaysia. The PAP wins the state elections by defeating the *Barisan Sosialis* (BS) and United Malays National Organisation. Indonesia's launches *Konfrontasi* against Malaysia, including Singapore.

1964: Devan Nair wins the only PAP seat in the Malaysian federal elections, outraging UMNO. Two racial riots break out in Singapore in July and September.

1965: Indonesian saboteurs bomb 'MacDonald House' killing three people. Malaysia expels Singapore from the Federation of Malaysia and Singapore emerges as an independent state.

1966: With Suharto at the helm in Indonesia, *Konfrontasi* ends.
1967: The National Service Bill is passed, allowing for compulsory conscription of all males above 18 years. The first batch is conscripted in July.
1968: Britain decides to withdraw its troops from Singapore. The PAP wins all seats in the elections, which is boycotted by the BS.
1969: Racial riots break out in Malaysia and there is a minor spillover into Singapore.
1970: Yusof Ishak dies and Benjamin Sheares is made Singapore's second President.
1971: The last British forces leave Singapore.
1972: The PAP wins all seats in the elections.
1973: The Presidential Council for Minority Rights is established to safeguard minorities from being discriminated against.
1974: The 'Laju Incident' occurs when four international terrorists hijacked a ferry and threatens to blow up petroleum tanks at Pulau Bukom.
1976: The PAP wins all 69 seats in the elections.
1980: The PAP wins all 75 seats in the elections.
1981: Devan Nair becomes Singapore's third President. J. B. Jeyaretnam of the Workers' Party (WP) wins the Anson seat at a by-election, breaking the PAP's 16-year monopoly of Parliament.
1984: The PAP's record of complete victories in the general elections (1968, 1972, 1976 and 1980) comes to an end as the WP and the Singapore Democratic Party (SDP) manage to win one seat each in Anson and Potong Pasir constituencies at the 1984 General Elections. The PAP won 77 out of the 79 seats in Parliament.
1988: Group Representation Constituencies (GRCs) are introduced and the PAP wins 80 out of 81 seats in the general elections. Chiam See Tong is the sole Opposition member in Parliament from Potong Pasir.
1990: Lee Kuan Yew steps down as Prime Minister and is succeeded by Goh Chok Tong. Lee Kuan Yew remains in cabinet as Senior Minister.
1991: The Constitution is amended to introduce the Elected Presidency (EP).
1993: Ong Teng Cheong, the former Deputy Prime Minister, becomes the first directly elected President of Singapore.
1998: The Asian financial crisis breaks out. Singapore's economy slips into recession for the first time since 1985 along with the other Asian economies.
1999: S. R. Nathan becomes the second directly elected President. He wins without contest.
2000: The Speaker's Corner is introduced at Hong Lim Park.
2001: In November, Goh Chok Tong announces that the 2001 General Elections will be his last as Singapore's Prime Minister. The PAP wins 82 out of 84 seats with 75.3% of the popular votes. In December, the government arrests 15 members of the *Jema'ah Islamiyah* that were planning to undertake acts of terrorism in the Republic.

2003: Outbreak of the Severe Acute Respiratory Syndrome (SARS) virus in Singapore. Singapore signs free trade agreement with the United States of America, the first Asian state to do so.

2004: Goh Chok Tong steps down as the Prime Minister and is succeeded by Lee Hsien Loong, the eldest son of Lee Kuan Yew. Goh Chok Tong remains in the PAP cabinet as Senior Minister and Lee Kuan Yew is appointed to the newly created post of Minister Mentor.

2005: Despite objections from religious and social groups, and many Members of Parliament (MPs), the PAP government approves plan to build two integrated resorts in Singapore. S. R. Nathan begins his second term as an Elected President as he is the only eligible candidate to be nominated.

2006: Lee Hsien Loong contests his first general elections as Prime Minister. The PAP receives 66.6% of the popular vote, winning 82 of the 84 seats in Parliament. Low Thia Khiang and Chiam See Tong remain the two sole Opposition candidates, successfully holding on to their seats in Hougang and Potong Pasir respectively.

2007: In May, Singapore is given the right to host a leg of the Formula One 2008 World Championship. In November, Singapore hosts the 13th ASEAN Summit and the Third East Asian Summit.

2008: In February, the International Olympic Committee awards Singapore the right to host the inaugural 2010 Summer Youth Olympics. In May, the International Court of Justice awards *Pedra Branca* to Singapore and Middle Rocks to Malaysia, settling a 29-year territorial dispute between the two neighbours.

2009: In June, Singapore celebrates 50 years of self-governance, coinciding with 50 years of PAP rule in Singapore.

2010: In May, Prime Minister Lee Hsien Loong and Malaysian Prime Minister Najib Tun Razak announce the resolution of the dispute over the Malaysian Railway Station at Tanjong Pagar. In October, Madam Kwa Geok Choo, the wife of Lee Kuan Yew, dies at the age of 89.

2011: In May, the PAP wins the general elections with the Opposition making major inroads by winning a GRC at Aljunied. The PAP wins 81 seats with the Opposition capturing six. Two important ministers, George Yeo and Lim Hwee Hua, are defeated in the elections. In August, former Deputy Prime Minister Tony Tan wins the presidential election over Tan Cheng Bock, a former PAP MP, by a mere 0.34%.

2012: In February, WP's MP for Hougang, Yaw Shin Leong, is sacked by the party for ethical reasons. In the by-election held in May, the WP's candidate, Png Eng Huat, defeated the PAP's candidate, Desmond Choo.

2013: PAP MP Michael Palmer resigns from his parliamentary seat of Punggol East on ethical grounds in December 2012. In the January by-election, WP's Lee Li Lian wins the seat from the PAP's candidate, Koh Poh Koon. In December, Singapore experiences its first major riot in 44 years in 'Little India' following a death of an Indian foreign worker.

2014: In April, Singapore and Malaysia announce their intention to build a third link, dubbed the 'Friendship Bridge', to improve land transport between Singapore and the Malaysian mainland.

2015: In March, at the age of 91, Singapore founding Prime Minister Lee Kuan Yew dies of illness. After seven days of state mourning, Singapore witnesses a massive funeral on 29 March with more than half a million people paying their respects at the Old Parliament Building and en route to his cremation at Mandai Crematorium. In the September General Elections, the PAP retained its massive majority in Parliament with the Opposition suffering a dent in its support even though the WP won six parliamentary seats.

2016: In March, PAP MP David Ong resigns from his parliamentary seat in Bukit Batok on ethical grounds. A by-election was held in May, where the PAP candidate Murali Pillai defeats Chee Soon Juan, the SDP candidate. This marks the first time since 1992 that the PAP wins a by-election. In August, Singapore's sixth President, S. R. Nathan passes away and is given a state funeral. Following the Prime Minister proposing changes to the EP to ensure minority representation, a Constitutional Commission is appointed to discuss the issue and in September, the White Paper on the EP is released. In November, the new Bill amending the Constitution is passed with the 2017 presidential election reserved for a candidate from the Malay community.

2017: In January, the PAP announced the co-option of four additional members for the party's 34th Central Executive Committee (CEC). These were Masagos Zulkifli, Ong Ye Kung, Sitoh Yih Pin and Murali Pillai. Ong became one of the three organising secretaries of the party alongside Chan Chun Sing and Gan Kim Yong. In February, the government announced that the EP's election would be held in September 2017, unlike in the past, when it was held in August. Chan also stated that if a minority candidate left a GRC, no by-election would be called.

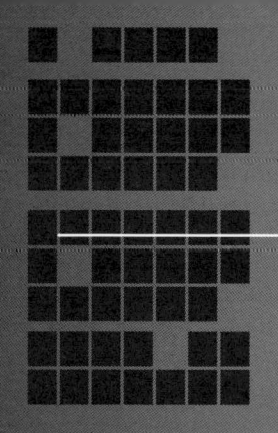

List of Tables

Table 4.1:	Functioning Political Parties in Singapore	33
Table 10.1:	Local Elections from 1948 to 1965	129
Table 10.2:	Parliamentary Elections since Independence	130
Table 10.3:	Singapore — Single Member and Group Representative Seats in Parliament	131
Table 10.4:	2011 General Elections Results	138
Table 10.5:	2015 General Elections Results	138
Table 10.6:	Parliamentary By-Elections	139
Table 10.7:	Singapore's Electoral Power: 1948–2015	141
Table 10.8:	Singapore's Presidential Election Results	142

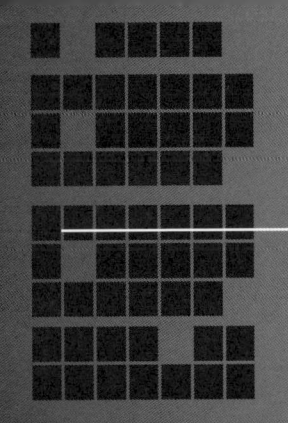

Abbreviations

ACB	Anti-Corruption Branch
AMP	Association of Muslim Professionals
ASEAN	Association of Southeast Asian Nations
AWARE	Association of Women for Action and Research
AWSJ	Asian Wall Street Journal
BMA	British Military Administration
BS	*Barisan Sosialis*
BTO	Built-To-Order
CAAS	Civil Aviation Authority of Singapore
CASE	Consumers' Association of Singapore
CCC	Citizens' Consultative Committee
CCMC	Community Club Management Committee
CDAC	Chinese Development Assistance Council
CDC	Community Development Councils
CEC	Central Executive Committee
CID	Criminal Investigation Department
CIQ	Customs, Immigration and Quarantine
COV	Cash-over-Valuations
CPA	Council of Presidential Advisers
CPF	Central Provident Fund
CPIB	Corrupt Practices Investigation Bureau
CPM	Communist Party of Malaya
CSO	Civil Society Organisation
DBS	Development Bank of Singapore
EDB	Economic Development Board
EDC	Economy Drive Committee
EIC	East India Company
EP	Elected Presidency

ExCEL	Excellence through Continuous Enterprise and Learning
FEER	Far Eastern Economic Review
FT	Foreign Talent
FW	Foreign Worker
GIC	Government Investment Corporation
GLC	Government-Linked Company
GRC	Group Representation Constituency
HDB	Housing and Development Board
HOME	Humanitarian Organisation for Migration Economics
ICJ	International Court of Justice
ICTC	Infocomm Technology Committee
IHT	International Herald Tribune
IMF	International Monetary Fund
IRA	Inland Revenue Authority
IRCC	Inter-Racial and Religious Confidence Circles
ISA	Internal Security Act
KBE	Knowledge-Based Economy
KTM	Malayan Railway
LM2011	Labour Movement 2011
MAS	Monetary Authority of Singapore
MBS	Marina Bay Sands
MCA	Malayan Chinese Association
MCCY	Ministry of Culture, Community and Youth
MCP	Malayan Communist Party
MCYS	Ministry of Community, Youth and Sports
MIC	Malayan Indian Congress
MICA	Ministry of Information, Communications and the Arts
MM	Minister Mentor
MOP	Minimum Occupation Period
MP	Member of Parliament
MSF	Ministry of Social and Family Development
MUIS	*Majelis Ugama Islam Singapura* (Singapore Islamic Religious Council)
NCMP	Non-Constituency Member of Parliament
NEC	National Education Committee
N-ETF	NTUC-Education and Training Fund
NMP	Nominated Member of Parliament
NPPA	Newspaper and Printing Presses Act
NS	National Service
NSP	National Solidarity Party
NSS	Nature Society of Singapore

NTUC	National Trades Union Congress
NWC	National Wages Council
OB Markers	Out-of-Bounds Markers
OEC	Organisational Excellence Committee
PA	People's Association
PAC	Presidential Advisory Committee
PAP	People's Action Party
PAYM	People's Association Youth Movement
PEC	Presidential Election Committee
PEER	Panel for Employee Engagement and Recognition
PERDAUS	A Muslim voluntary organisation
PERGAS	*Persatuan Ulama dan Guru-Guru Agama Islam Singapura* (Singapore Islamic Scholars and Religious Teachers Association)
PKMS	*Pertubuhan Kebangsaan Melayu Singapura* (Singapore Malay National Organisation)
PM	Prime Minister
PMO	Prime Minister's Office
POCA	Prevention of Corruption Act
PRC	People's Republic of China
PSC	Public Service Commission
PSO	PS21 Office
PUB	Public Utilities Board
RCs	Residents' Committees
REACH	Reaching Everyone for Active Citizenry @ Home
RP	Reform Party
RWS	Resorts World Sentosa
SAF	Singapore Armed Forces
SARS	Severe Acute Respiratory Syndrome
SATU	Singapore Association of Trades Union
SBA	Singapore Broadcasting Authority
SCCC	Singapore Chinese Chamber of Commerce
SCV	Singapore Cable Vision
SDA	Singapore Democratic Alliance
SDP	Singapore Democratic Party
SEF	Singapore Electronic Forum
SFCCA	Singapore Federation of Chinese Clans Association
SFSWU	Singapore Factory and Shop Workers' Union
SFTU	Singapore Federation of Trade Unions
SGLU	Singapore General Labour Union
SIF	Singapore International Foundation

SILS	Singapore Institute of Labour Studies
SINDA	Singapore Indian Development Association
SJER	Southern Johor Economic Region
SLF	Singapore Labour Foundation
SMC	Single Member Constituency
SPH	Singapore Press Holdings
SPP	Singapore People's Party
SPUR	Skills Programme for Upgrading and Resilience
SRC	Smart Regulation Committee
SS	Straits Settlements
STUC	Singapore Trades Union Congress
TWC2	Transient Workers Count Too
UMNO	United Malays National Organisation
UN	United Nations
UNCLOS	United Nations Convention on the Law of the Sea
UNF	United National Front
UPF	United People's Front
WB	World Bank
WDA	Workforce Development Authority
WEC	Women's Executive Committee
WIN	Women Integration Network
WP	Workers' Party
WSC	Women's Sub-Committee
YEC	Youth Executive Committee
YOG	Youth Olympic Games

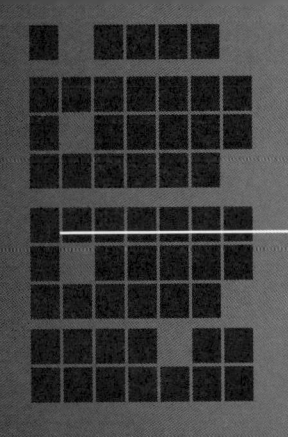

Key Terms

Alliance: Political coalition of UMNO, MCA, MIC.

Allied Forces: Forces organised against the Axis Coalition in the Second World War.

'ASEAN *Kecil*': Describing Singapore, Malaysia, Indonesia as ASEAN's core.

Bicameral House: The existence of two chambers in the assembly.

Bureaucracy: Literally, rule by officials; the administrative machinery of a country.

By-Elections: Elections conducted in between general elections.

Cabinet: The executive body consisting of ministers appointed by the Prime Minister.

Cadre System: A group of elite members of a party, distinguished by their ideological commitment and loyalty to the political party.

Civil Service: The administrative machinery of the state characterised by its hierarchical organisation and a highly specialised division of labour.

Civil Society: The realm of autonomous groups and associations; a private sphere independent from public authority.

Chief Minister: The Chief Executive during the period of Singapore's limited self-government from 1955–1959.

Communal Parties: Political parties whose membership are drawn from particular ethnic groups.

Consociational Democracy: A form of democracy that operates through power sharing amongst a number of parties or political formations.

Crown Colony: A British colony placed under the direct administration of the British Parliament.

Decentralisation: The expansion of local autonomy through the transfer of powers and responsibilities away from national bodies.

Decolonisation: The granting of independence to former colonial territories.

Democracy: Rule by the people; this implies popular participation and government in the public interest, and can take a wide variety of forms.

Democratic Socialism: A variant of socialist ideology that treats greater egalitarianism as its primary goal and operates under a democratic system.

Dictatorship: Rule by a single individual; the arbitrary and unchecked exercise of power.

Executive: The branch of government that is responsible for implementing law and policy.

Federation: A political system in which there is a constitutional division of power and functions between a central government and a set of regional governments, usually known as states, provinces or cantons.

Feedback Unit: A unit established by the government in 1985 to garner feedback on all issues in Singapore.

First Past-the-Post Electoral System: An electoral system where the candidate that first attains the most number of votes is declared the winner. It is also known as a 50 + 1 system.

First World Economy: An economy driven by capitalist and democratic values.

Free Press: A press not controlled by government censorship regarding politics or ideology.

General Election: An election usually held at regular intervals for the majority or all public offices.

Global Terrorism: The proliferation of terrorism affecting the international community.

Governance: The various ways in which social life is coordinated, of which government is merely one.

Government: The mechanism through which ordered rule is maintained; the machinery for making and enforcing collective decisions in society and elsewhere.

Government-Linked Company (GLC): A corporate entity in which the government has a stake.

Grassroots Organisations: Groups of ordinary citizens who are highly involved in the collective social, political and economic action, whose activities are usually spontaneously organised and lack a centralised administration.

Ideology: A more or less coherent set of ideas that provides the basis for some kind of organised political action.

Imagined Community: The assumed commonality shared by all members of a community.

Interest Groups: An organised association that aims to influence the policies or actions of government; interest groups may have a sectional or promotional character.

Islamic State: A terrorist organisation that came to prominence in 2014.

Islamist Terrorism: Terrorism justified on grounds of Islamic tenets.

Jema'ah Islamiyah: A key terrorist group active in Southeast Asia.

Judiciary: The branch of government that is empowered to decide legal disputes and adjudicate on the meaning of the law.

Landlocked State: A state which has no direct access to the sea.

Left-Leaning Groups: A broad ideological disposition characterised by sympathy for principles such as liberty, equality, fraternity and progress.

Legislation: The passing of laws by the legislative system.

Legislative Assembly: The legislative body introduced into Singapore after the Second World War to incorporate local leaders into the administration.

Malayan Union: The British proposal for the amalgamation of the former Federated and Unfederated States of Malaya.

Malaysian Malaysia: The concept of a multiracial state proposed by the PAP during the period of merger.

Mass Media: Societal institutions concerned with the production and distribution of all forms of knowledge and entertainment.

Merger and Separation: The period of political union and eventual departure of Singapore and the Federation of Malaysia from September 1963 to August 1965.

Meritocracy: Rule by the talented; the principle that rewards and positions should be distributed on the basis of ability.

Multiculturalism: The belief that it is important to include people or ideas from many different countries, races or religions.

Multiracialism: Equality of political representation and social acceptance in a society made up of various races.

Nation: Unique sense of unity by the people within a particular territory.

Nation Building: An ongoing process of constructing or structuring a nation using the power of the state.

National Education: State-sanctioned education aimed at imbuing students with values that would strengthen national cohesion and resilience.

National Identity: A shared identity based on commonly accepted values, myths and symbols.

National Service: The compulsory service of able-bodied male citizens in the armed forces, police force and civil defence force.

OB Markers: Subjects the government has deemed unacceptable for public debate.

Old Guards: First generation of the PAP leaders who oversaw the decolonisation and independence of modern Singapore.

One-Party Dominant System: A hegemonic party system which is one party-centred but does not preclude the existence of other political parties.

Parliament: A forum for debate and deliberation; parliament is equivalent to assembly or legislature.

Pedra Branca: Also known as *Pulau Batu Putih* whose ownership was contested by Singapore and Malaysia.

Plural Society (Pluralism): A belief in, or commitment to, diversity or multiplicity; or the theory that power in modern societies is widely and evenly distributed.

Political Culture: A pattern of psychological orientations towards political objects; a people's political attitudes, beliefs, symbols and values.

Political Socialisation: Institutions that propagate and cultivate political attitudes, opinions and expectations of the individual.

Politicisation: The process through which individuals acquire political beliefs and values, and by which these are transmitted from generation to generation.

Politics: The activity through which people make, preserve and amend the general rules under which they live.

Polity: A society organised through the exercise of political authority; for Aristotle, rule by the many in the interest of all.

Praetorian Culture: Public's acceptance of the military leaders as national political figures.

Premiership: A system of government in which executive power is concentrated in the Prime Minister's hands.

Presidency: A system of government in which executive authority is disengaged from parties or other government bodies, in the manner of an executive president.

Pro Bono Publico: For the good of the public

Public and Private Spheres: The public sphere refers to the state: apparatus of government; or public realm including politics, commerce, work, art and culture. The private sphere refers to civil society; and the personal realm, comprising of the family and domestic life.

Republic (Republicanism): The principle that political authority stems ultimately from the consent of the people; the rejection of monarchical and dynastic principles.

Reformasi (Reformation): Social movement for democratisation in Indonesia and Malaysia after the 1997 Asian financial crisis.

Rendel Constitution: Published in February 1954, the Rendel Constitution allowed for internal self-government in Singapore for the first time.

Siege Mentality: The perception of being surrounded by more powerful and threatening political entities.

Sovereign State (Sovereignty): Absolute and unlimited power; sovereignty can imply either supreme legal authority or unchallengeable political power.

Statutory Boards: Semi-independent agencies that specialise in carrying out specific plans and policies of the various ministries.

'Stayer versus Quitter': An expression describing the social divide between Singaporeans who stay in Singapore and those who have chosen to migrate.

Syonan-to: Singapore's name during the Japanese Occupation; literally means 'Light of the South'.

Tudung: Headscarves worn by Muslim women.

Unicameral House (Unicameralism): The concentration of legislative power in a single chamber assembly.

United Nations General Assembly: The main deliberative body of the United Nations; composed of representatives of all member states.

Westminster Parliamentary System: A system of government in which the executive is drawn from, and (in theory) accountable to, the Assembly or Parliament.

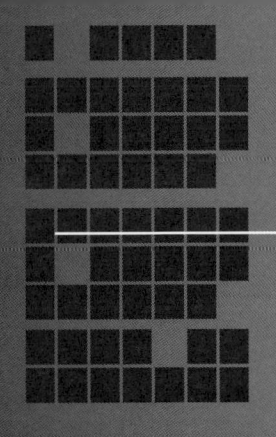

Acknowledgements

I wish to express my heartfelt thanks and gratitude to the many people who assisted me in one way or another in completing this study. In many ways, this monograph is a follow-up to the two earlier editions that were published by McGraw-Hill Education (Asia) titled *Politics and Governance in Singapore: An Introduction*. The first edition was published in 2006 and the second edition in 2012. I wish to thank McGraw-Hill Education (Asia) for its assistance in the earlier publications and for the understanding shown in encouraging the publication of this particular edition with World Scientific. In particular, I wish to thank Ms. Leong Li Ming for all the help and assistance that was provided in this endeavour.

I also would like to place on record my sincere thanks and appreciation to World Scientific, especially Mr. Jiang Yulin, in assisting in bringing out this study, which was professionally undertaken with patience and great support.

For this study, I would like to thank my Research Assistant, Isis Iskandar for the meticulous work that was done in the collection and collation of data.

Finally, I am extremely grateful to my family for all the blessings and support that was provided in seeing through this study. The love, affection and understanding of my wife, Gurdial Kaur, my sons, Jasminder Singh and Prabhinder Singh, my daughter-in-law, Malwina Kaur and the new addition to the family, my grandson, Karanveer Singh, whose infectious smile sustained me in the travails of this project.

I, however, take full responsibility for the views and for any error that may occur in the book.

Bilveer Singh
March 2017

Dedication

*To Gurdial Kaur, Jasminder Singh,
Malwina Kaur, Prabhinder Singh and Karanveer Singh*

Preface

There is every need to understand what is going on in Singapore, especially its politics. Singapore's politics is a concern for everyone who lives and has a stake in the Republic. The aim of the book is not to create a political stirring. Far from it, it is aimed at providing students and those interested in Singapore's politics with an academic compass that will allow them to follow the essence of Singapore's politics. While it is impossible to cover every aspect of Singapore's politics, the main substance that is to be examined in this study is important for any foundational understanding of Singapore's politics. In a way, it is to understand what makes up the 'bones' of Singapore and how, over the years, 'flesh' has been added to make it the type of 'person' Singapore is today. In the same vein, what is the 'scaffolding' that makes up Singapore? What is its 'roof', the number of 'pillars' it has and how have the different 'bedrooms', 'doors' and 'windows' been constructed to end up with what has come to be known as the 'Singapore House'? After years of 'tutelage' as part of the Malay World, then as a British colony, experiencing the hardship and brutalities of Japanese occupation, post-Second World War semi and full self-government under British colonialism, a state in the Malaysian Federation and independence since August 1965, is Singapore today a 'house', 'home' or 'hotel'? How is this structure called Singapore surviving in the midst of regional and international turbulences?

While it has been a common view that Singaporeans find politics 'distasteful', at the same time, it is something that cannot be ignored. To describe a population of immigrant origins living in a highly urban setting and with close interactions with the outside world as apolitical does not really capture reality. This is because political decisions impinge on the lives of Singaporeans on a daily, almost 7/24/365 basis. Others have described Singaporeans as essentially 'spectators', a political culture that stems from their fear of the 'tiger's world' or sense of inadequacy that has led the majority to simply live with what is being decided for them by the political elites. This is the 'nanny state' syndrome at its best. While these descriptions may have some truth, what cannot be ignored is that a typical Singaporean is increasingly sophisticated in the political sense. While one might not want to 'dabble' in politics, there is a difference between being politically withdrawn and being apathetic about what is happening on the 'political front'. Even more, it is not the same as not knowing what is going on in the political arena. This is because Singaporeans, through education, mass media and personal experiences and exposure to the outside world, have come to realise the importance of politics and political decisions as they directly impact upon their lives on an almost daily basis. Through political socialisation, Singaporeans have been increasingly tuned to believe that 'correct politics' will determine their future. Hence, the increasing importance of politics in Singapore; a trend that is likely to continue with greater intensity in the coming years. Of course, political caution and a tendency not to rock a smoothly-sailing ship are also important characteristics of the Singaporean's approach to politics.

Against this backdrop, this study aims to expose the readers to the various facets of Singapore's politics. The reader is also invited to think through important questions that will be raised along the way: What are the fundamentals of Singapore's politics? What are the key determinants and how has Singapore's anatomy impinged upon the type of politics in the Republic? What are the key political structures and how have these interacted to shape the nature of politics in Singapore? Is Singapore a nation? At what stage of nationhood is Singapore at? What about the role of civil society? Is it a democracy? What about the state of political parties? What has led to the emergence of a one-party dominant state in the Republic? For how long can this endure? What about Singapore's future? Is it a 'little red dot' that can vanish like historical small states or is exceptionalism that defines Singapore? These questions, amongst other issues, will be discussed in the study.

Introduction

> The measure of a man is what he does with power.
> Plato[1]

In any given society, politics is always present and it is constantly affecting the daily lives of every individual in the community. Politics, simply described, is the contestation within society to decide on who is to lead the community and how the community should be led. However, to study politics, a much more specific definition is required. While the essence of politics is commonly known, the scholarly definition of politics is a contentious matter.[2] Derived from the Greek word *polis*, meaning city-state, politics is at times viewed as the art of governance. It deals with matters of state and issues that occur within a polity, which is a system of social organisation focusing on the element of a centralised decision-making entity. Since politics concerns all members in a society, it is also viewed as public affairs. This understanding of politics comes from the desire to distinguish between what is public and hence political, and what is private and nonpolitical. For example, when an individual decides on how much to spend on new electronic gadgets, it is a private decision and only requires the consent of the individual himself. However, when it comes to the decision on how much to spend on street lighting and walkways, it is regarded as a 'public' matter as it requires the consensus and agreement of the community since the expenses are borne by the public purse that is raised out of taxation. Since negotiations and bargaining are part and parcel of collective decision-making, politics is also at times seen as a function of compromises and consensus. Since resources are finite but desires and wants are not, the community must debate and arrive at a consensus on how to

---

[1] See "40 Famous Philosophical Quotes by Plato on Love, Politics, Knowledge and Power". Available at http://www.geckoandfly.com/18829/famous-philosophy-quotes-plato-love-politics-knowledge-power/
[2] See Andrew Heywood, *Politics* (London, England: Macmillan, 1997) pp. 3–12.

pursue a common good. Given that politics permeates all levels of society, another definition attempts to encapsulate this larger, if not, broader perspective of politics as a contestation for power not only in the central decision-making body of society but in all societal activities. As long as mankind lives in a community, there exist contestations amongst the individuals of the community to dominate one over another. Ranging from the power of decision-making to the power of agenda setting, individuals or groups of individuals compete for control of the various dimensions of power for the simple desire to achieve their own particularistic interests and goals. What is common to the various definitions of politics that have been discussed is that politics is and will always be at the centre of organised human existence. It is mainly because of this reason that one desires to study and understand the nature of what politics is.

Since the time of Aristotle, the analyses of politics have been centralised around the foundations of the polity, namely, the government. What is a government? In simple terms, a government "is any mechanism through which ordered rule is maintained".[3] While the government is represented by the various institutions and structures of the state which create and regulate policies, it should not be confused or made interchangeable with the notion of governance. A government is part of the larger concept of state and claims the "monopoly of legitimate physical violence".[4] Governance, however, is about how "governments and other social organisations interact, how they relate to citizens, and how decisions are taken in a complex world".[5] Therefore, the study of politics is not limited to the study of state institutions, but is much larger and includes the interaction and contestation between the government, societal actors and the ordinary citizenry. Thus, it is to the interest of any study of politics to include the study of government and governance of the state.

In the case of Singapore, the modern government and politics of the city-state can be said to have begun when Stamford Raffles established the first trading post for the British East India Company on the island in February 1819. Although the history of independent Singapore only begins in 1965, the contemporary government and politics of Singapore have been strongly influenced by the political events and developments that long preceded the Republic's independent existence. The study of the government and politics of Singapore is not confined to students and academics, but open to all who have a stake and interest in the island republic. It is important that the politics and governance of Singapore be given due attention so that one is better

---

[3] Ibid, p. 37.
[4] Max Weber, "What is a State" in Bernard E. Brown (ed.) *Comparative Politics: Notes and Readings*, 9th edition (Fort Worth: Harcourt College Publishers, 2000) p. 147.
[5] John Graham, Bruce Amos and Tim Plumpte, *Principles for Good Governance in the 21st Century: Policy Brief No. 15* (Ottawa, Canada: Institute of Governance, 2003) p. 1.

able to understand the complexities and challenges faced by the independent state. Only by doing so can one appreciate the achievements of Singapore since its independence and derive some predictions of what the future holds for Singapore.

The study of Singapore's politics and government has received fair coverage over the years. Literature from the 1980s such as Jon Quah's chapter, *Political Science in Singapore*, in Basant Kapur's *Singapore Studies: Critical Surveys of the Humanities and Social Sciences* provides a review of earlier works done by local and foreign academics attempting to study Singapore as a political entity.[6] Academic literature ranging from doctoral dissertations, journal articles and monographs cover a broad range of issues but each study is specific to a particular aspect of politics. For example, on national politics, the works of Michael Leifer and R. S. Milne focus on selected periods of political development.[7] On the aspects of political culture and leadership, scholars such as Chan Heng Chee have attempted to describe Singapore's political system in terms of authority and the distribution of economic and social goods.[8]

The first systematic study that provided an overview of the Singapore political system can be traced to Jon Quah, Chan Heng Chee and Seah Chee Meow's edited volume, *Government and Politics of Singapore*. Targeted at university students, this volume is organised in three parts, namely, the foundations of politics, the contemporary political system, and contemporary problems and issues. The various aspects of government and politics in Singapore are given fair coverage and tailored to the needs and demands of teaching the subject at the university level. In Ban Kah Choon, Anee Pakir and Tong Chee Kiong's *Imagining Singapore*, a different approach to the study of Singapore is employed.[9] Focusing on the power of imagination, this edited volume explores the internal landscapes of Singapore by asking pertinent questions such as "how it came about, was conceived of and conceptualised".[10] Reflecting on the "instinctual needs that are embedded in the imaginative assumption", this volume, covering a broad array of topics ranging from historiography, to security and public administration, evaluates how the conceptualisation of the various aspects of Singapore has been shaped and reshaped over the years. A second edition of the volume with two newly added chapters covering the notion of freedom and economic

---

[6] Jon S. T. Quah, "Political Science in Singapore" in Basant K. Kapur (ed.) *Singapore Studies: Critical Surveys of the Humanities and Social Sciences* (Singapore: Singapore University Press, 1986) pp. 83–146.

[7] See Michael Leifer, "Singapore in Malaysia: The Politics of Federation", *Journal of Southeast Asian Studies*, Vol. 6 No. 2 (September 1965), and R. S. Milne, "Singapore's Exit from Malaysia: The Consequences of Ambiguity", *Asian Survey*, Vol. 6 No. 3 (March 1966).

[8] Chan Heng Chee, "The Political System and Political Change" in Riaz Hassan (ed.), *Singapore Society in Transition* (Kuala Lumpur, Malaysia: Oxford University Press, 1976).

[9] Ban Kah Choon, Anne Pakir and Tong Chee Kiong (eds.), *Imagining Singapore* (Singapore: Times Academic Press, 1992).

[10] Ibid, p. 1.

developments in Singapore was published in 2004.[11] The chapters in the first edition were revised wherever possible to factor in the new domestic and external developments such as the financial crisis of 1997, the outbreak of the Severe Acute Respiratory Syndrome (SARS) epidemic and the rise of global terrorism.

A more recent trend in the study of Singapore focuses on explaining Singapore as a political and economic anomaly. A small island state with limited resources and surrounded by much larger neighbours, Singapore has managed to achieve what many others with similar limitations have failed to do. An example of such a trend is Arun Mahizhnan and Lee Tsao Yuan's *Singapore Re-Engineering Success*.[12] A compilation of essays contributed by political leaders such as Lee Hsien Loong, Lim Hng Khiang and Lim Swee Say, renowned academics Wang Gungwu and Michael Leifer, and prominent business personality, Y. Y. Wong of Singapore's WyWy Group and many others, this volume is a study of the challenges faced, surmounted and confronting Singapore to explain the future directions of the island state. The re-evaluation of the fundamentals of Singapore's success is argued to be important to ensure the continued growth and more importantly, the survival of Singapore as it approaches a new century. Following this line of approach to the study of Singapore, Linda Low's edited volume, *Singapore: Towards a Developed Status*, similarly attempts to understand Singapore by looking at its political and economic history to explain the enigma of its resilience.[13] This work is essentially a study of the changes occurring in Singapore as it moves from a newly independent nation to achieve the status of a developed state. From economic transitions to changing demographics, foreign policy considerations and security implications, this is a rich and diverse volume which attempts to uncover the prerequisites of attaining successful and lasting growth in Singapore.

Diane K. Mauzy and R. S. Milne's work, *Singapore Politics under the People's Action Party*, published in 2002 returned to the elite-centred approach of understanding politics.[14] An insightful and comprehensive overview of politics in Singapore since its independence, the book is a study of the rise of the PAP under the leadership of Lee Kuan Yew and its policies which have governed and brought Singapore to where it is today. Mauzy and Milne cover the limitations and challenges, including that of leadership succession facing the PAP and inadvertently, Singapore. The work also includes the study of the authoritarian aspects of the PAP government, elections and

---

[11] Ban Kah Choon, Anne Pakir and Tong Chee Kiong (eds.), *Imagining Singapore*, 2nd edition (Singapore: Eastern Universities Press, 2004).

[12] Arun Mahizhnan and Lee Tsao Yuan (eds.), *Singapore Re-Engineering Success* (Singapore: Institute of Policy Studies and Oxford University Press, 1998).

[13] Linda Low (ed.), *Singapore: Towards a Developed Status* (Singapore: Centre for Advance Studies, National University of Singapore and Oxford University Press, 1999).

[14] Diane K. Mauzy and R. S. Milne, *Singapore Politics under the People's Action Party* (London, England: Routledge, 2002).

electoral changes in Singapore as well as the marginalisation of the Opposition and the growth of civil society.

These works on the politics, government and governance of Singapore have contributed significantly to the understanding of independent Singapore. However, these studies have been broad-based. While interesting and thought-provoking, they have not systematically dealt with the politics, government and governance of Singapore. Since Quah, Chan and Seah's 1986 compendium, no one else has attempted to approach the subject matter in a similar way. This is where the current study enters to provide a comprehensive overview of politics, government and governance of Singapore that is tailored not only to students of politics but anyone who is keen to understand how the past and present continues to define Singapore's politics today. What is the pulse of Singapore politics like? What is Singapore's political anatomy? What are the fundamentals that continue to define politics in this small and compact state? This study attempts in part to answer these queries as the Republic has entered the new millennium for nearly two decades.

The literature on Singapore politics requires updating in light of the many changes to Singapore both internally and externally over the past few years. Since the late 1990s, the region has undergone many transformations and challenges. The Asian financial crisis beginning in the 1997 gave birth to the rise of *Reformasi* (Reformation) in Malaysia and Indonesia, leading to the downfall of Suharto's regime in Indonesia to be replaced by a nascent democratic government which has seen four presidents in the short span of less than a decade. Long-time Malaysian premier, Mahathir Mohamad stood down in 2003 to be replaced by his successor Abdullah Ahmad Badawi after the bitter experience of the purge of then Deputy Prime Minister and heir apparent to the premiership, Anwar Ibrahim, from both the government and United Malays National Organisation (UMNO). In turn, Badawi was replaced by Najib Tun Razak in 2009. In the face of mammoth changes in the region, Singapore is advertently required to change its political norms as it interacts with its neighbours.

The 11 September 2001 bombings of the World Trade Centre Towers and the subsequent 'war' on global terrorism have affected the governance of Singapore. Faced with a minority Muslim population and surrounded by much larger Muslim states of Indonesia and Malaysia, governance of a plural, multi-ethnic and multi-religious society has become more complex and complicated. With the Bali bombings in 2002 and 2005, and the discovery of the *Jema'ah Islamiyah* terrorist cells in Singapore, the presence of these threats is felt ever more closely to the primal chords of Singaporean society. Since 2014, the rise of the Islamic State has brought the threat level to a much higher level with the Singapore government now saying that it is only a matter of time when Singapore suffers a terrorist attack.

On the domestic front, Lee Hsien Loong's ascension to the office of Prime Minister in 2004 requires the current literature to be updated to reflect this new era of leadership. Since Lee Hsien Loong became the Prime Minister, the PAP government approved a controversial bill to legalise gambling (even though Singapore Pools has been managing some betting activities prior to this) by sanctioning the setting up of two major casinos, or what the Singapore government calls 'integrated resorts'. The National Kidney Foundation scandal uncovered in mid-2005 shocked Singaporeans on the size and degree of the mismanagement of one of the Republic's much-acclaimed health care charities, and also called into question how the PAP government should exercise its oversight function, and for some, take responsibility for the scandal. In the 2006 General Elections, when Lee Hsien Loong stood for the first time as Prime Minister, the PAP was denied, for the first time in many years to form the government on Nomination Day. Even though the PAP was returned to power and the Opposition continued to cling on to its 2 Single Member Constituency seats, approximately 33% of eligible voters cast their votes against the PAP. This has raised concerns about the voting behaviour and the likely trends among the younger electorate, compelling the PAP to launch the 'Post-1965 Generation' campaign to 'connect' younger voters with the ruling party.

Since then, many new developments have taken place. While the PAP was returned as the governing party in the 2011 General Elections, it also suffered its worst defeat since 1965. Following this, it lost two by-elections. Even the PAP's candidate for the presidential election won only by a whisker. However, in the 2015 General Elections, the PAP performed admirably, winning 70% of the valid votes. This, however, was partly due to a number of circumstances including the Republic's Silver Jubilee celebrations. However, the single most important factor was the sympathy vote the PAP garnered following the passing of Lee Kuan Yew in March 2015. In 2016, the PAP also won its first by-election since 1992.

These developments in Singapore justify the need for this current study as a complement to the existing literature by providing a systematic analysis of Singapore politics which incorporates internal and external developments with implications for the politics and governance of this island state. In addition to serving as a platform to understand contemporary politics, government and governance of Singapore, the study is also useful as it indicates some of the key challenges facing the polity as the Republic moves forward amidst new challenges from within and without.

Readers' Guide

This book attempts to answer the following queries:
a. It is organised along thematic lines covering issues ranging from political birth to challenges confronting Singapore's future.

b. Of particular importance is the chapter on political anatomy as it guides the reader to appreciate the realities confronting Singapore's politics. It is both a lens and a framework for exploring the various issues covered in this study.
c. It is also an update on recent developments which have important bearings on Singapore's politics.
d. At the end of each chapter, there will be a series of 'think questions' which aims to assist the reader to reflect on issues discussed and hopefully to inspire the reader to pursue the issue further as part of one's life-long learning.

Chapter One
The Key Determinants of Singapore Politics

Singapore cannot take its relevance for granted. Small countries perform no vital or irreplaceable functions in the international system. Singapore has to continually reconstruct itself and keep its relevance to the world and to create political and economic space.[1]

Singapore has been described in many ways. Some call it a political anomaly for its impressive stature in international politics despite being a small island republic. Others have labelled Singapore an economic success given its rapid transformation from a newly independent State dependent on manufacturing, services and trade into a First World economy; a leading financial, technological and medical centre in the region. The question to ask is, how did Singapore become what it is today?

To answer such an abstract question is to ask fundamentally what is the politics of Singapore? How do we explain or understand the policies and politics that have guided and shaped Singapore over the years? This study, besides providing an analysis of what is the island's politics, also attempts to equip its reader with the imperatives that form the framework to understand and study Singapore. It is hoped that armed with this toolkit, the keys to unlock the politics of Singapore, the readers themselves can rationalise their own daily observations and come to their own conclusions on what is Singapore and what is its politics.

Geography

Located at the southern end of the Strait of Malacca, one of the busiest sea lanes of the world, Singapore's fate and fortunes have been intimately tied to its geographical

---

[1] See Speech by Mr Lee Kuan Yew, Minister Mentor, at the S. Rajaratnam Lecture, 09 April 2009, 5:30 pm at Shangri-La Hotel. Available at http://www.pmo.gov.sg/mediacentre/speech-mr-lee-kuan-yew-minister-mentor-s-rajaratnam-lecture-09-april-2009-530-pm-shangri.

position. Singapore, being situated in the centre of Southeast Asia, has been the focal point of communications and entrepot trade for the region since the time of Stamford Raffles. First being an important port facility for the East-West trade in the 19th century, its importance to communications continues to grow as technology advances. Currently, Singapore is the leading telecommunications hub and gateway to the region for air travellers while maintaining its dominance over both local and international shipping.

Singapore's strategic location at the juncture of two of the world's greatest oceans, the Indian and Pacific oceans, has made it of interest to the leading world powers, especially maritime powers. During the colonial days, Britain had developed Singapore to be its chief naval port in the region to safeguard its strategic interests and dominate in the region. In the 1960s, at the height of the Vietnam War, the United States' presence in Singapore was greatly felt as Singapore became an important base for the gathering of military resources and the centre of deployment of American troops to Indochina. Moreover, the island also served as the 'rest and recreation' centre for troops returning from 'hot zones', an important contribution to Singapore's economy as well as the cause of the proliferation of 'red light' areas servicing foreign troops. Even though the last British soldiers left in 1971, American presence in Singapore has remained very strong. In recent years, Singapore has further developed its naval facilities to cater to visiting American vessels and it is the only location in Southeast Asia that has the ability to service American aircraft carriers and where aircraft carriers can berth onshore. Foreign military powers have and always will be interested in Singapore and this, in turn, affects the foreign policy of Singapore as well as the relationship between Singapore and its immediate neighbours, Indonesia and Malaysia, who have been critical of Singapore and its military relationship with external powers.

Malaysia, which lies to the north and east of Singapore, and Indonesia, which spans from the west to the south and to the east of Singapore, literally and physically surround the island republic, leading it to be described as a 'landlocked state'. The two traditional regional powers of largely Malay-Muslim descent have not always been friendly to Singapore. The centre of Southeast Asia is traditionally known as the Malay Archipelago, and Singapore's existence in this geographical area is a glaring anomaly as its population is pre-dominantly ethnic Chinese who are politically dominant, a resultant of British colonial immigration policies, and it remains the only state outside China (Taiwan and Hong Kong included) to be predominantly governed by ethnic Chinese. This has resulted in the perception that Singapore is a Chinese state, and when juxtaposed against its two very much larger Malay neighbours, is a 'juicy Chinese nut in a Malay nutcracker'.[2] This analogy is most apt as Singapore is persistently facing the pressures of bilateral relationships between Malaysia and Singapore.

---

[2] Tim Huxley, "Singapore and Malaysia: A Precarious Balance", *Pacific Review*, Vol. 4 No. 3, p. 210.

These border pressures although common to many countries, are particularly challenging and acute to Singapore. Not only is Singapore just a fraction of the size of Indonesia and Malaysia, Singapore also has a significant minority ethnic Malay population. The governance of this ethnic minority has to be of the utmost sensitivity as Singapore's neighbours are politically dominated by Malay-Muslims. Muslim ethnicity is a problem due to the potential for ethnic chauvinism in the region. Also, ethnic issues can be manipulated due to jealously concerning Singapore's progress. All these developments can threaten Singapore's security. These issues will be discussed in the following chapters. As thus, domestic politics and foreign policies with these two immediate neighbours are intertwined and inseparable.

Singapore also has several outstanding territorial contestations with its immediate neighbours. An example was Singapore and Malaysia's dispute over *Pedra Branca*. Since the early 1980s, Malaysia and Singapore had been in contestation over a rocky outpost in the intersection of the Singapore Straits and the South China Sea that hosts the Horsburgh Lighthouse, which was constructed by the British and administered by Singapore ever since.[3] In 2003, both Singapore and Malaysia filed their claims with the International Court of Justice (ICJ)[4] and in 2008, the court awarded sovereignty of *Pedra Branca* to Singapore.[5] While both parties agreed to accept the decision, Malaysia pledged to seek further evidence which it plans to bring to the court during the review process after 10 years.[6] Malaysia has also since accused Singapore of attempting to demarcate maritime boundaries in the latter's favour.[7] It is evident that the lighthouse will continue to be a thorn in Malaysia's side for some time to come. Moreover, the active reclamation of land by Singapore over the years has irked its neighbours. Land reclamation by Singapore in the Tebrau Straits separating Singapore and Malaysia has raised protests by Malaysia. Indonesia, on the other hand, has shown its disapproval of the sale of sand from Batam and Bintan for Singapore's reclamation works.

In recent years, Singapore's geographical location has posed even greater challenges and threats to the island state. The globalisation of Islamist terrorism has struck deep fear into the world community and Singapore has not been insulated from this menace. Indonesia, the world's largest Muslim state, has been the alleged base of operations for many extremist Islamist groups that have no qualms about using violence to pursue their objectives. Singapore has also become an important partner of Western powers, in particular the United States, who has been actively using force against terrorists in

---

[3] "Light of Reason", *The Straits Times*, 20 September 1991.
[4] "KL and Spore File Notices at ICJ on Island Row", *The Straits Times*, 25 July 2003.
[5] "Indonesia Bans Exports of Sand to Singapore", *The Straits Times*, 24 January 2007.
[6] *Singapore Resident Population, 1990–2006* (Singapore: Department of Statistics, Ministry of Trade and Industry, December 2006) p. 23.
[7] "Malaysia Tells Singapore to Stop Provocative Claims", *New Straits Times*, 18 August 2008.

reaction to the September 2001 bombings of the New York World Trade Center. Singapore's strategic position coupled with its predominantly Chinese population and strong support in the 'war on terror' makes it a promising ally of the Americans as a key base of operations against terrorist networks. Due to these factors which stem from Singapore's geographical location, Singapore has not been spared the attention of these terrorists. The uncovering of the *Jema'ah Islamiyah* terrorist cells and the bomb plots against US naval facilities and public transportation in Singapore in December 2001 were chilling reminders of the burden Singapore carries for its presence in the region. Since then, there has been continuous threats from Islamist terrorists, including plots from neighbouring parts of Malaysia and Indonesia to attack Singapore, including one from the island of Batam in 2016, some 30 km away in Indonesia.

Demography

According to Singapore's Department of Statistics, as of September 2015, Singapore residents, comprising of citizens and permanent residents, stood at about 3.9 million people, of whom 74.3% were ethnic Chinese, 13.3% ethnic Malays, 9.1% ethnic Indians and 3.2% of other ethnic minorities.[8] The breakdown of ethnic groupings or races in Singapore's context is an inheritance from British colonialism. As a result of economic needs and British immigration policies over the years, Singapore has become a plural society with the Chinese dominating both the politics and economy of Singapore since the Second World War, when the right to organise politically was sanctioned by the colonial authorities. This situation of Chinese dominance has become a potential focal point of ethnic conflagration because Singapore is located in the heart of the Malay World.[9]

The plurality and heterogeneity have created insurmountable challenges for Singapore's nation building and the construction of a national identity. With a relatively short history, there are few commonalities between the ethnic groups to facilitate the forging of a common identity. This has been an issue that perennially reiterates itself in many guises. Ranging from 'stayers vs. quitters' debates in recent times to the teaching of National Education, Singapore is always in the quest for a distinct identity that is associated with the construction of an 'imagined community' called the Singapore Nation or Singaporean Singapore.

However, the most pressing challenge of demography which bears heavily on Singapore is the governance of its ethnic groups. Given that it is not easy to govern a

---

[8] *Population Trends, 2015* (Singapore: Department of Statistics, Ministry of Trade and Industry, September 2015).
[9] See K. S. Nathan, "Malaysia-Singapore Relations: Issues, Problems and Prospects" in Kandalama Iskandar (ed.) *Management and Resolution of Inter-State Conflicts in Southeast Asia* (Penang, Malaysia: Southeast Asian Conflict Studies Network, 2003) pp. 149–159.

plural society, the situation has become even more challenging when the strategic minority of Singapore is the dominant majority of the larger neighbourhood in which Singapore is located. Due to its geopolitics, the Republic has to be extremely sensitive to external pressures and extraneous groups that have an innate interest in the Republic's domestic politics. The issue of ethnic management is not an imagined predicament but has real impact upon its domestic and external relations. From the racial riots in Singapore in 1950 and 1964 to Malaysia's violent 13 May racial riots in 1969 and the more recent uprising against ethnic Indonesian Chinese in May 1998, the question of ethnicity is a complex issue that requires careful and meticulous management and calibration. The social fabric in Singapore is extremely fragile and vulnerable to manipulation, with the ever-present insecurity that inter-ethnic violence can easily break out. Although Singapore's ruling government has constantly reiterated its position on the equality of all ethnic groups and promotion of individuals based on meritocracy, the realities of the situation do indicate that ethnic tensions have not dissipated as inter-ethnic and inter-religious divisions have remained deeply entrenched, with mutual suspicions and fears just beneath the political epidermis.

The core concern of the governance of ethnic relations in Singapore centres predominantly on the Chinese-Malay relationship. As Singapore is often regarded as a 'Third China' or worse, a state that was formerly a Malay island and where its rightful owners, the Malays, have been displaced, Chinese-Malay tensions have continued unabated and is something that cannot be taken for granted. Because of the geopolitical configuration of being surrounded by Malay neighbours, Singapore leaders have on many occasions expressed their fears of the 'dangerous, even irrational neighbourhood' and even publicly doubted the loyalties of Malay Singaporeans. An often quoted statement is Lee Kuan Yew's admittance that he does not trust a Malay officer to be in command of a machine gun crew[10] just as his son, Lee Hsien Loong, the current Prime Minister, had claimed that he does not want a Malay to be put in a position of difficulty due to his religion.[11] This clearly highlights the continued tensions between the Chinese and Malays within Singapore and this has regional implications in terms of difficult relations between Singapore and its neighbours, especially Malaysia. While things have improved, the ethnic peace cannot be taken for granted, especially against the backdrop of the threat posed by Islamist extremism and terrorism.

The recent resurgence of the complexities of ethnic management and cross-border relations has taken the form of a debate over the wearing of religious head garb by female Muslim students in Singapore national schools. The issue of the *tudung* or

---

[10] See "A Question of Loyalty: The Malays in Singapore", *The Straits Times*, 30 September 1999.
[11] See *The Straits Times*, 25 March 1987. Cited in Bilveer Singh, "A Small State's Quest for Security: Operationalising Deterrence in Singapore's Strategic Thinking", in Ban Kah Choon, Anne Pakir and Tong Chee Kiong (eds.), *Imagining Singapore*, Second Edition (Singapore: Eastern Universities Press (by Marshall Cavendish), 2004) p. 134.

head scarf began in January 2002 when four students were barred from attending classes while wearing the *tudung*.[12] A domestic issue with regard to Singapore's dress code in its educational system was easily transformed into an international one when several groups from Malaysia commented on the handling of the issue, accusing the Singapore authorities of being anti-Malay and anti-Islam.[13]

Any government in Singapore has a heavy responsibility to ensure that ethnic relations stemming from its plural society are handled with utmost sensitivity and importance. Singapore inherited this demographic composition upon its independence, and this has had a heavy impact on the policies that govern it. To understand Singapore, especially with regard to housing, religion and military security policies, it would be a mistake to ignore the importance of demography in the shaping of Singapore politics.

Economy

Economically, Singapore is a deficit territory as it is a small island which lacks natural resources and a hinterland to support its population. These concerns of Singapore were not raised during the colonial period as Singapore was administered together with Malaya. These limitations came to the foreground when Malaya was granted independence and Singapore was separated from it. The call for merger in the late 1950s and early 1960s centred on questions of whether Singapore would survive if it was independent. However, with the separation of 1965, Singapore had no choice but to venture on its own to ensure not only its political survival, but also its economic survival. In many ways, political survival was predicated on economic survival.

Since Stamford Raffles' successful negotiations to establish a trading post in Singapore, the island has been dependent on trade for its economic prosperity. With no natural resources to depend on, Singapore inadvertently focused its attention on the manufacturing sector. In the face of stiff competition, Singapore was quick to diversify its economic interests. Under the leadership of the PAP government, Singapore has been constantly venturing into the latest economic sectors dependent on skilled and professional workforce. The island republic cannot compete in terms of low labour costs with its surrounding neighbours but possesses, as a prized asset, a highly educated and disciplined workforce.

Singapore, being intensively linked to the world economy, is highly sensitive to the fluctuations of the open market. Over the years, Singapore has placed great importance on the management of its budget and never fails to accumulate surpluses which act as a buffer in times of need. The government has also taken the lead in

---

[12] Sandra Davie, "4 Still Wearing *Tudung* as Deadline Approaches", *The Straits Times*, 30 January 2002.
[13] Leslie Lau, "Politicians and Groups Criticize Spore over *Tudung*", *The Straits Times*, 31 January 2002.

ensuring the prudent handling of Singapore's financial assets by establishing government-linked companies and investment arms to diversify Singapore's economic nest. Hailed as a model for developmental states, Singapore's concern over its economy is driven not by desire for wealth, but the fact that it has no natural resources or hinterland to fall back upon. If the state is ever in threat, its primary line of defence is its economic linkages to the world market. It is to the benefit of all if Singapore remains economically vibrant as there is more to gain from cooperation than contestation. Furthermore, Singapore's reserves, which are among the world's largest, act as a safety net for the state.

The issue of the economy is arguably the source of political legitimacy for the PAP. Singapore has known no other government except a PAP government since 1959 when full internal government was thrusted to Singapore. Acknowledging the achievements of Singapore under PAP leadership, it has become an expectation of the PAP to provide and care for its citizens' economic welfare. The common adage in Singapore is that as long as the PAP can provide for Singaporeans, they will continue to accept PAP's rule. To a very large extent, the PAP government has managed to take care of the needs of its citizens by providing much needed largesse, be it financial assistance or through programmes such as Medishield.

Singapore's near total dependence on external trade has made it extremely vulnerable to the vagaries of the international market. Southeast Asian economies, Singapore's included, were badly affected by the so called "domino effect of the economic downturn that first began with the devaluation of the Thai *baht* in 1997".[14] Although Singapore was amongst the first economies to recover, the crisis revealed the degree of sensitivity of the contemporary international market upon which Singapore is dependent.

Singapore's preoccupation with economic performance has also spawned several debates over the need for foreign skilled workers. Given Singapore's limited talent pool, the PAP government has been actively opening the doors of Singapore to foreign talent (FT). Naturally, not all Singaporeans have agreed to the influx of foreigners taking up employment in Singapore as the latter have been viewed as taking opportunities away from the former. The debate intensified in the wake of the Asian financial crisis as many unemployed Singaporeans took issue with the government's persistent arguments for the need of FT. This debate still wages on and in the 2006 National Day Rally, Prime Minister Lee Hsien Loong reiterated the need to welcome more FT and more importantly, to entice these foreigners to stay and be a part of Singapore.

---

[14] Hussin Mutalib, "Malaysia's 1999 General Election: Signposts to Future Politics", *Asian Journal of Political Science*, Vol. 8 No. 1, p. 66.

The state of Singapore's economy is not the end point of policies; the economy is also used as a tool for the advancement of Singapore's foreign policy. Singapore's success has been marketed as a model for many developing states. Singapore shares its experience with these states, which in turn, helps to increase its prestige, which gives Singapore political leverage in international organisations. Singapore's preoccupation with the economy is the key to understanding the direction in which Singapore is heading. With such an understanding, one is able to rationalise the policies that have been in place and to a certain extent, be perceptive of the discourses in Singapore politics.

Political Experience and Heritage

The course of history has a tremendous impact on the development of Singapore politics. Societies do not come into being in a vacuum; rather, they are products shaped by the cumulative experiences of their members. History shapes the institutions of the day and functions as references that guide the thoughts and decisions of political leaders. The historical lessons from colonial rule to the turbulent period of merger and separation with the Federation of Malaysia have taught Singapore's political leaders to be cautious of their actions and inactions. The challenging era of the 1960s has caused Singapore to have deep-seated concerns regarding its immediate neighbours. While Singapore-Indonesia bilateral relations are of strategic importance, Singapore-Malaysia relations are of even higher importance, a 'special relationship' created from contentious experiences throughout the years.

Feeling 'isolated' from the Malay World, Singapore's leadership has developed a 'siege mentality' that views Singapore as being under constant threat from its neighbours. This in turn has motivated the political elite to constantly push Singapore forward in every aspect. There is no room for failure and unless Singapore is able to invent or innovate, it risks being wiped into oblivion. This mentality, imbued over the years, has been incorporated into the core of National Education, with phrases like "we can only depend on ourselves" and "the fate of Singapore is in our hands" being commonly used. While Singapore is unable to move away from the burden of its political experiences and heritage, it resorts to using them as tools to promote a sense of nationhood, portraying itself as a state that is eternally faced with crises. In a way, Singapore is a crisis state, as crises have erupted regularly and the government has been able to align the population behind it, leading in turn, with the crisis usually surmounted through wise policies. Despite this, the National Education programme has not been well-received by many students, who perceive it as nothing more than a propaganda of the PAP. Nonetheless, to study Singapore, one must constantly refer to critical junctures of history to extrapolate the lessons learnt, and how they continue to influence the course of Singapore politics. While the past remains relevant and has been a source of inspiration (against all odds), nevertheless, as long as Singapore leaders are unable to move out of the shadow of crisis mentality, they will always remain a prisoner of the past.

External Environment

Singapore has never and will never believe that it can be isolated from the rest of the world. To survive, Singapore must engage the international community. Even during its inclusion in the Federation of Malaysia, then Prime Minister Lee Kuan Yew was actively pushing for a vibrant foreign policy as opposed to the Federal Government's view, that is, if Malaysia left the world alone, the world would leave Malaysia alone. As the world continues to globalise at a rapid pace, Singapore has always been mindful of its position in the international community. What it lacks in physical size, it makes up for with a wealth of leadership, moral authority and a very healthy bank account. Singapore has played a key role in leading newly independent states in the United Nations (UN), forming a significant bloc of small states in the General Assembly. Moreover, Singapore has contributed tremendously to develop United Nations Convention on the Law of the Sea (UNCLOS), not only for the sake of better global governance, but to ensure its survival which depends heavily on unhindered access through the sea lanes of communications.

Being the richest state (with the exception of Brunei) in the region, Singapore has to be mindful of its neighbours. Unable to take up the helm of leadership of Association of Southeast Asian Nations (ASEAN) due to the presence of traditional leaders such as Indonesia and Malaysia, Singapore cautiously treads around in the neighbourhood. In recent years, the region has been struck with several natural calamities. In these natural disasters, Singapore has been quick to assist its neighbours. For example, in the wake of the 2004 tsunami that devastated the province of Aceh in Indonesia, Singapore was the first to land rescue personnel and deployed its armed forces to aid in the rescue and recovery of lives. Even though some may argue that Singapore's actions were altruistic, in reality, Singapore had no option but to assist as it was the only state amongst its immediate neighbours that was spared the effects of the tsunami. Also, it had the resources and expertise in terms of machinery, manpower and money to carry out the rescue missions. Given that these 'other than war' operations are valuable experiences for the Singapore Armed Forces (SAF), Singapore's inaction would have drawn criticisms from both Indonesia and Malaysia, demonstrating clearly how closely Singapore is intertwined with its immediate neighbourhood, referred in regional security parlance as the 'ASEAN Kecil' or 'Small ASEAN'. Since then, Singapore has always been in the forefront of helping its neighbours in calamities, natural or man-made, such as it did during the disappearance of Malaysian Airline MH 370 in March 2014. Singapore's sensitivity to external events is due to its interconnectedness with the world. With no natural resources nor a large territorial space to survive on, Singapore has looked beyond the traditional hinterland of Malaysia and into the much larger, vibrant, lucrative and yet, volatile international community.

Conclusion

The previous segments have examined the five 'keys', namely, geography, demography, economy, political heritage, and the external environment, which are crucial for understanding the anatomy of Singapore politics. These factors have perpetually impacted Singapore and only by understanding them can one 'unlock' the gateway to Singapore politics. The rules of politics, terms of engagement and the arena of political debate are defined, limited and fuelled by these imperatives that define Singapore's political anatomy.

Think Questions

1. What do you understand by the term 'anatomy of Singapore politics'?
2. How do the key factors affecting Singapore politics interact with each other, and how have these changed over the years?
3. Which element of the anatomy do you consider as the most vital?

Chapter Two

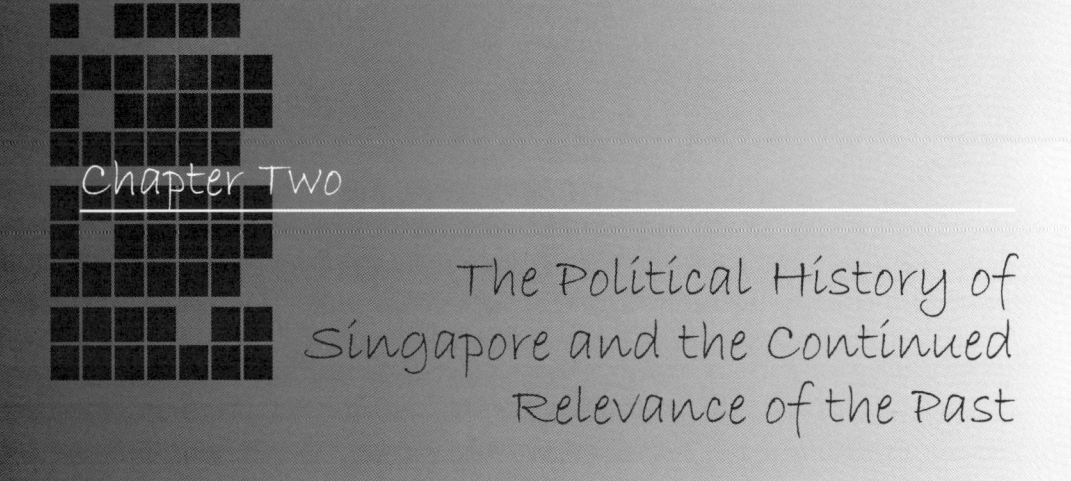

The Political History of Singapore and the Continued Relevance of the Past

> Not knowing the circumstance of Singapore's birth is a serious gap in knowledge. But this ignorance is not the fault of our pupils or teachers. It is the result of political circumstances ... If our young do not know our past, they will not understand how to hold multi-racial Singapore together, why we must give each ethnic community in Singapore an equal place, and why we must help one another to do better.[1]

Introduction

The importance of understanding the history of a state and society cannot be underestimated. History is not merely a collection of facts and figures but it is a recollection of events and experiences that reveal to the reader the contentions and struggles that have shaped, defined and persisted in influencing contemporary society. In Singapore's case, its history is closely intertwined with and inseparable from the history and developments of the PAP, as this largely explains the party's entrenchment in the Republic's politics and history.

Modern Singapore history can be divided into four important phases, namely, the British arrival in Singapore, the Japanese Occupation and the immediate post-war years, the period of merger and separation with Malaysia, and lastly, independent Singapore. Each of these phases is a critical turning point in history that has impacted and influenced the politics and governance of Singapore. By examining these critical junctures, one can view the legacies of political struggles and apply this knowledge to the understanding of the issues and factors that have persisted throughout Singapore's short history, and which continues to dominate political discourse and the very fundamentals of politics in Singapore.

---

[1] Prime Minister Goh Chok Tong's speech at the Teachers' Day Rally, 8 September 1996. See Contact (Singapore: Ministry of Education, Singapore). Special Teachers' Day Rally Issue, September 1996. At: www1.moe.edu.sg/contact/rally/index.html.

The 'Founding' of Singapore

Sir Stamford Raffles, an official of the British East India Company, arrived on the shores of Singapore on 26 January 1819 and by 30 January, had managed to conclude a preliminary treaty with the Temenggong of Johore to establish a trading post on the island. Thus this began the presence of the British in Singapore for the next 150 years. In the months that followed, Singapore expanded rapidly as a trading post and as its economic vibrancy grew, so too did its importance to British interests in the East. In the early days of the British presence in Singapore, the legal standing of its claim to the island was relatively weak. Traditionally, Singapore was recognised as part of Riau which was then under Dutch influence. It was feared by Raffles' superiors that his intrusion into Singapore may provoke Dutch hostility and "jeopardise the success of the entire Anglo-Dutch negotiations in Europe".[2] However, British presence in Singapore prevailed and by 1824, Singapore was ceded in perpetuity by Sultan Hussein of Johore to the British in exchange for payments and recognition as the legitimate ruler of the Johore Sultanate. British control over Singapore was internationally recognised under the Anglo-Dutch Treaty of 1824.

In 1826, Singapore, together with Penang and Malacca, was placed under a common administrative mechanism, known as the Straits Settlements (SS). The SS, which was initially established as a Presidency, was reduced in status due to administrative costs, to a Residency under the Presidency of Bengal. However, by the late 1860s, the SS was economically and strategically vital to British interests that in 1867, its administration was transferred directly from India to the British Colonial Office in London and the SS became a Crown Colony. Singapore continued to grow and develop as a British colony throughout the late 19th century and early 20th century. By 1922, after the conclusion of the Washington Naval Treaty of 1921, which limited British naval expansion from Hong Kong, Singapore became the most important naval base for the British.

The Japanese Occupation and Its Immediate Years

On 7 December 1941, the Japanese forces coordinated a well-planned strike on the American naval base in Pearl Harbor and simultaneously began landing troops at the Siamese-Malayan border. The Japanese forces under Lieutenant-General Tomoyuki Yamashita began their lightning campaign in the Malayan Peninsula and by February 1942, had forced the British and Australian forces to retreat to Singapore. The battle for Singapore was relatively brief and on 15 February 1942, Allied forces in Singapore

---

[2] Constance Mary Turnbull, *A History of Singapore 1819–1988*, 2nd edition (Singapore: Oxford University Press, 1989) p. 11.

under Lieutenant-General Arthur E. Percival surrendered to the invading Japanese Army at the Old Ford Factory in Bukit Timah. Singapore was renamed *Syonan-to* (Light of the South) and thus began the dark period of Japanese Occupation which saw the infamous massacre of Singapore's population in incidents like Sook Ching, where the occupying Japanese Army rounded up thousands of ethnic Chinese and summarily executed many of them. The Japanese Occupation lasted over three years and the British returned in September 1945 when Japan surrendered unconditionally after the bombing of Hiroshima and Nagasaki. Singapore was placed under the British Military Administration for a short while before civilian administration of Singapore was re-established.

The mood for decolonialisation was high after the war and fulfilling their promise, the British introduced a series of legislations that incorporated the local populace into the legislative process. In 1955, the first local elections were held in Singapore to implement the Rendel Constitution, with a total of 25 seats out of the 32-seat Legislative Assembly to be elected. David Marshall became Singapore's first Chief Minister when the Labour Party was successful in the 1955 elections. By 1959, Singapore had its first fully elected Legislative Assembly and the PAP under Lee Kuan Yew came to power when it won 43 seats out of a total of 51 seats in the Assembly. Even though Singapore moved towards self-government, nevertheless, it was short of total independence from the British as had been achieved by Malaya in 1957.

Merger and Separation, 1963–1965

The PAP government under leaders such as Lee, Goh Keng Swee and S. Rajaratnam sought merger with Malaya as a most urgent matter to achieve both political independence and economic survival.[3] Although the Malayan Prime Minister Tunku Abdul Rahman had his reservations towards the inclusion of Singapore into a federation with Malaya, by 1961, the Tunku had agreed to a partnership based on a federation of Malaysia, Singapore and the British Borneo territories. The Federation of Malaysia, consisting of Malaya, Singapore, Sabah and Sarawak, was to come into being on 31 August 1963 but was eventually pushed back to 16 September 1963 to accommodate the United Nations' survey on the people of Sabah and Sarawak to join the new political entity.

The period of merger saw much contestation between the political elites of the Alliance, the ruling party in Malaya, and the PAP. Disagreements ranging from the development of a common economy to Singapore's contribution to the federal treasury caused much enmity between the leaders of the Peninsula and Singapore. The most contentious issue between these two leaderships appeared to be related to the

---

[3] Ibid, p. 275.

very core of governance. After the merger, the PAP ventured into the Peninsula to contest the federal elections. Propagating a democratic socialist approach, the PAP called for the establishment of meritocracy and used the rallying cry of 'Malaysian Malaysia', posing a challenge to the politically communal concept of a 'Malay Malaysia'. Rather than accepting the political primacy of a particular ethnic race, the PAP advocated the equality of races which clearly irked the feelings of United Malays National Organisation (UMNO) towards Lee and the PAP. Tension between Lee and the UMNO leaders intensified and the overall unease of the Malay community over the challenge to the framework of a Malay-based nation state led to the eventual separation of Singapore from the Federation in 1965. Thus began Singapore's journey as a modern independent state.

Independent Singapore

The expulsion of Singapore from the Federation was sudden though not entirely unexpected. As R. S. Milne argued, the separation was a consequence of the ambiguities of merger. Nonetheless, Singapore after its exit from the Federation was a sovereign state and as a sovereign state, had to pay close attention to its immediate survival. It is arguable that Singapore did not start from ground zero. Singapore in the immediate period of independence had in its possession a sound system of administration inherited as part of its colonial legacy. The state institutions were not only present, but functioning efficiently and effectively. Moreover, Singapore over the years, had gained tremendously in terms of infrastructure that was built by the British in support of firstly, Singapore's importance as an economic hub and port of transit, but also as a military establishment of the British in the region. There were also many foreign missions located in the city-state, providing the basis of future foreign relations with these states.

Implications of Critical Historical Junctures to Contemporary Singapore

The colonial period was an important milestone for Singapore. Before the arrival of the British, Singapore though long known to many travellers and old empires, was merely a backwater locality. Raffles' stake in Singapore on behalf of the East India Company (EIC), was the first to reintroduce Singapore into the international mercantilist route. Raffles' move and the subsequent British action to preserve Singapore as part of its sphere of influence, as evident in the Anglo-Dutch Treaty of 1824, has ensured Singapore's place on the world map ever since. An important trading post and naval base, Singapore was the bastion of British presence in Southeast Asia as its development and importance quickly overshadowed those of older British settlements in the region, namely Penang and Malacca.

British colonialism left an indelible mark on Singapore which endures to this day. To the benefit of Singapore, the public administration of the island is based on the British system. An efficient, effective and uncorrupt civil service ensured the smooth administration of the island state even during transitional periods such as the periods of self-government, merger and eventual separation from Malaysia. Today, Singapore's civil service is rated as one of the best in the world. Transparency International, a global civil society organisation combating corruption, ranked Singapore as the eighth least corrupt state in the world in its 2015 report.[4]

British governmental influence has been so strongly embedded in its former colony that Singapore inadvertently adopted a Westminster parliamentary model of democracy upon achieving independence in 1965. Until the early 1990s, Singapore judiciary was still linked to the British Privy Council in London. Besides the physical institutions and the system of governance which the British bequeathed to Singapore, the British also developed Singapore's infrastructure to enable it to compete in the global economy. Excellent ports and supporting facilities were key to ensuring Singapore's commercial viability and economic survival throughout the years, especially in the immediate years following Singapore's independence.

However, colonial legacies have also contributed to contemporary challenges and issues. Singapore, although existing as a part of the Malay Archipelago, has a dominant ethnic Chinese majority. Colonial economic needs allowed the implementation of immigration policies that have resulted in the creation of a plural society. Singapore's ethnic composition significantly differs from its neighbours' and has persisted over the years to be a challenge of governance for Singapore. It also has implications for Singapore's foreign policy with its immediate neighbours, Malaysia and Indonesia. The governance of a plural society is never easy as the state attempts to accommodate the needs and aspirations of distinct ethnic communities. The issue is compounded in Singapore as ethnic Malays, though a minority group in Singapore, are the dominant ethnic community in Malaysia, Indonesia and Brunei, with a sizeable presence in Thailand and the Philippines. Ethnic relations are a sensitive and important issue in plural Singapore. Moreover, with the close association of Islam as a definitive characteristic of Malay ethnicity and Indonesia being the largest Muslim country, ethnic issues concerning the Malay community can and have been viewed in a religious context. Since the 11 September 2001 bombings of the World Trade Centre, the discovery of Islamist terrorist cells in Singapore in 2001 and the Bali bombings in 2002, the complexities of handling the ethnic issue have increased exponentially.

---

[4] The 2015 Transparency International Corruption Perceptions Index available at http://www.transparency.org/cpi2015#results-table, accessed 17 August 2016.

The period of the Japanese Occupation and the post-war years remain an important juncture of Singapore's history. Besides marking the beginning of the dismantling of colonialism, the Japanese Occupation instilled and awoke a sense of political awareness amongst the inhabitants of Singapore. Resulting from the brutal experiences of the *Syonan-to* years, the populace, in particular, the educated elites, both the English and Chinese educated, began to push for greater political participation. This juncture is crucial to contemporary Singapore politics as it was the beginning of political contestation by local elites that started out as a form of self-governance, then led to Singapore's independence, first as part of the Federation of Malaysia and later as an independent state. It was also during this period that saw the rise of the PAP under Lee, a development which continues to play a critical role in Singapore politics. This period of history has also been appropriated by the state as a reminder of Singapore's vulnerability as a small state and the perpetual need of its citizens to 'defend' the island state from all forms of aggression: militarily, economically and psychologically.

After the defeat of Japan, the Malayan Communist Party (MCP) was quick to capitalise on the post-war years in its attempt to establish a communist state in Malaya. The Malayan Emergency, which lasted from 1948 to 1960, had implications on the domestic politics of Singapore. It was during this period that political parties began to form to contest the series of local elections that were to be held. Mirroring the development of Western party systems, political parties in Singapore were formed along the lines of class and ideology. The leading political parties of the day such as the Labour Party and the PAP, were led by educated elites and trade unionists. Although the MCP was legally banned, socialist elements were present in Singapore, often working through Chinese educationists and some trade unions.

The PAP's experience during these years is key to understanding the current PAP's style of party organisation and governance. It must be remembered that the PAP at its origins was an umbrella of groups and individuals across the political spectrum. The internal strife within the PAP between the socialist-oriented group and the moderates between 1956 and 1961 was an important lesson for the PAP as a political party.[5] The PAP suffered severe defections from its rank and file in July 1961 when 13 Assemblymen defected to form the *Barisan Sosialis* (BS). Up to 20 to 25 branch Organizing Secretaries and branch committees left the PAP as well, leaving some entire branches decimated, including the physical destruction of the PAP's properties. This defection left the PAP with a single seat majority in the Legislative Assembly, and its hold over the government of Singapore was nearly lost. Although the PAP recovered by 1963 to defeat the BS in the watershed 1963 elections, the party has

---

[5] Diane K. Mauzy and R. S. Milne, *Singapore Politics under the People's Action Party* (London, England: Routledge, 2002) p. 38.

been wary of internal threats and has entrenched counter-measures to prevent the recurrence of similar defections that nearly once decimated it.

Since 1958, the PAP has instituted a cadre system in the hope of preventing any hostile takeovers from within. Cadres are carefully chosen and their numbers and identity have never been made public. Analogous to the Catholic Church's cardinals who are appointed by the Pope, who in turn elect the new Pope upon the passing of the former, this system was implemented by the PAP with the hope that the careful selection and screening of its party members can ensure the survival of the party in the face of internal threats. By 1998, it has been estimated that there were up to 1,000 PAP 'Cardinals' that elect the 'Pope'.[6]

In witnessing how the defection of branch leaders led to the complete loss of branches and facilities, the PAP has also learnt a painful lesson about the susceptibility of party branches to infiltrations. Since its experiences in the 1950s and early 1960s, the PAP has placed little reliance on party branches to be the backbone of its political machinery. The PAP party branches are usually small and hold little, if any, influence or decision-making capacity within the party. Instead, the PAP has directly cultivated its support amongst trade unions, in particular, through the establishment of the National Trades Union Congress (NTUC) and the use of para-political organisations such as the People's Association and the Citizens' Consultative Committees. Although these organisations portray themselves as separate from the PAP, the severe overlapping of these apolitical organisations and the PAP is "purely [a] technical one".[7]

Singapore's involvement in the merger and separation with the Federation of Malaysia can be said to be its most traumatic experience in its short history so far. This critical juncture of Singapore's history sheds crucial light on the ideology, constraints and limitations that persist in Singapore politics today. The implications of this period can be segregated into domestic and foreign policy implications. The formation of UMNO in 1946 as a response towards the Malayan Union plan and later, the formation of the Malayan Chinese Association (MCA) and Malayan Indian Congress (MIC), clearly demonstrate the origins of political participation in post-war Malaya as a reaction towards issues of citizenship qualifications and rights. Each ethnic community, in the desire to achieve its political goals, preferred to cooperate and negotiate with other ethnic communities at the elite level. Political parties were thus formed along communal lines. What first began as an electoral strategy of cooperation was consolidated in the multi-ethnic Alliance Party. Subsequently, with the onset of independence, the essence of a consociational democracy was sealed in the form of the Malayan Constitution of 1957. Bargaining between the communal parties,

---

[6] Koh Buck Song, "The 1000 PAP 'Cardinals' Who Appoint the 'Pope'", *The Straits Times*, 4 April 1998.
[7] Kenneth Paul Tan, "Democracy and the Grassroots Sector in Singapore", *Space & Polity*, Vol. 7 No.1, 2003, pp. 3–20.

especially between UMNO and MCA, centred on the exchange of political power for economic access. In return for recognising Malay political dominance, as well as the preservation of Malay special positions and land privileges, the Chinese and to some extent, the Indians, were granted the freedom to continue to pursue their economic interests.[8]

The PAP, on the other hand, attempted to replace this political arrangement with one that centred on the equality of all ethnic groups. The rallying call of 'Malaysian Malaysia' advocated by the PAP as well as the other Opposition parties in Malaysia, was taken as a direct challenge by UMNO and the other parties in the Alliance. It was during this period that Singapore saw some of its worst racial riots. The inability of PAP leaders and their counterparts to reconcile this issue and many others, including that of being compounded with the initial ambiguities of merger agreement, ensured the inevitably of separation.

Since then, the PAP government has based its system of governance on meritocracy and the careful management of inter-ethnic relations. No single ethnic community was to be given any privileges over others; advancement in Singapore's society came about through hard work and individual merits. The bitter experiences of racial riots during this period also explained the PAP government's social engineering and nation building policies. Ranging from ethnic quotas in housing policies to making the discussion of sensitive issues such as race and religion taboo, Singapore is perennially managing ethnic issues to prevent the repeat of events in the 1960s. This also marked the commencement and entrenchment of the 'out-of-bounds' (OB) marker culture in Singapore politics, which has persisted to this day.

The relationship between Singapore and Malaysia is extremely hard to define in its entirety. Once a mirror of each other in terms of societal configurations, the two neighbours have moved in different directions in terms of their principles of governance since 1965. Bilateral relations between Malaysia and Singapore since 1965 have had its share of ups and downs. Many key bilateral issues have been settled such as the sale of water by Malaysia to Singapore, the redevelopment of Malayan Railway (KTM) land in Singapore, the Customs, Immigration and Quarantine (CIQ) issue, and the ownership of *Pedra Branca* (or *Pulau Batu Putih* in Malaysia). Some others remain unresolved such as the withdrawal of Central Provident Fund (CPF) savings by West Malaysians upon leaving Singapore, the use of Malaysian airspace by the Republic of Singapore Air Force and proposed bridge between Singapore and Johore.[9]

Although a generation of Singaporeans and Malaysians has passed since the 1960s, some of the leading political figures from the time of merger and separation

---

[8] R. S. Milne and Diane K. Mauzy, *Malaysian Politics under Mahathir*, op. cit., p. 18.
[9] K. S. Nathan, "Malaysia-Singapore Relations: Retrospect and Prospect", *Contemporary Southeast Asia*, Vol. 24 No. 2 (August 2002).

are still active in politics. In particular, the children of some of those political leaders are currently holding power in Malaysia and Singapore. This can add to the complexities of negotiations between the two states. Today, many of the contentions between these states remain unresolved as negotiations over the years have moved in an erratic manner. Examples of Malaysian ill-feelings towards Singapore include Malaysia's former Prime Minister, Mahathir Mohammad, who stated that with the "narrow nationalism characterising Asia today, and influencing the thinking of Malaysian and Singapore leaders, the only relationship which can result is one of destructive confrontation".[10] Even younger Malaysian leaders such as Khairy Jamaluddin, the son-in-law of Malaysia's former Prime Minister, Abdullah Badawi and currently a cabinet minister in Najib Tun Razak's cabinet stated that:

> We have to look at this from the geopolitical angles because we have our own strengths, we have land, the intellect and a huge population compared to Singapore. If we take advantage of all these strengths in addition to SJER's (Southern Johor Economic Region) development, one day they would definitely depend on us … this is what we want.[11]

It is clear that some elements within Malaysia still harbour deep-seated antagonism towards Singapore even though these two states have been separated since 1965. For many Singaporeans, this is partly explained by Malaysia's inability to treat Singapore as an 'equal' and the persistence to view the Republic as an '*adik*' (younger brother) to the '*abang*' (elder brother).

Singapore's sudden exit from the Federation and its birth as an independent state posed severe challenges to Singapore. Not only did it have to worry about its security as an independent state, Singapore had to be concerned about its ability to survive in the long run. The PAP government has never ceased to reiterate that the Japanese Occupation, merger and separation, and Singapore's sudden independence have made the Republic extremely vulnerable. This has been translated into the rationale that survival is Singapore's utmost important goal, a goal that the PAP government has successfully achieved for the Republic. This is also one major factor explaining the extremely high legitimacy and support the PAP continuously received from the electorate.

It would be wrong to accept the conception that Singapore had to start from scratch in 1965. The British as a colonial master did not fail to develop Singapore's economic infrastructure and state institutions such as the civil service and the police.

---

[10] Mahathir Mohammad, *The Malay Dilemma* (Singapore: Times Book International, 1970 (2001 reprint)) p. 186.
[11] Reme Ahmad, "Khairy's Use of Race Card Raises Eyebrows", *The Straits Times*, 26 August 2006.

Singapore did have a clear head start and one should not forget Singapore's position vis-à-vis Malaysia: the island state was to be regarded as a potential 'New York' of the Federation to serve as its financial hub. In terms of military security, British forces were still present in Singapore in 1965 and only completely withdrew from Singapore's shores in 1971. However, what is most important with regard to Singapore's military security is the institution of National Service, the compulsory conscription of able-bodied male Singaporeans into the armed forces. National Service in Singapore has served its function of providing Singapore with security, and it has infused the Republic's society with a praetorian culture. Since 1967, the Singapore Armed Forces (SAF) has progressed to be amongst the region's leading armed forces. Although the SAF is not battle-tested, it has the best armaments in the region and its close cooperation with the United States and other leading armed forces in the world makes it a credible fighting force.

In conclusion, the critical junctures in Singapore's history are very important to the understanding of contemporary politics of Singapore. History is able to shed light on the evolution of Singapore's political system, inheriting and later, reforming the Westminster parliamentary system to suit the needs of modern Singapore. Moreover, history has revealed the key themes that are constantly being reiterated in the governance of Singapore. Vulnerability and survival have become, to a certain extent, the 'bogeyman' of Singapore society. The PAP government, in its effort to create a sense of nationhood, has turned to history not only to justify current policies, but also to legitimise the unbroken rule of the PAP and the continued need of the PAP leadership to guide Singapore in the future. The PAP itself has not been spared by the lessons of history. During the party's formative years in the 1950s, it experienced many attempts by pro-communist and left-leaning groups within the party to stage coups and protests against the moderates who were in power. These traumatic years have taught the PAP to fear defections from within and it has shaped the political culture of the PAP and inadvertently affected the leadership renewal of the party and Singapore as well.

Think Questions

1. How have colonial policies affected the challenges facing Singapore today?
2. How have the experience of the merger and separation shaped the politics of Singapore?
3. How did the PAP come to power?

Chapter Three

The Singapore Political System — A Hybrid Westminster Model?

> Singapore was a 'hybrid' system which combined many formal elements of democracy — multiparty electoral competition, universal suffrage, fair counting of the votes on election day, a highly developed rule of law in many sectors of society and economy outside of politics, relatively little overt coercion in daily life …[1]

Introduction

On the attainment of political sovereignty in August 1965, Singapore was faced with the task of establishing its own political system. Singapore, although a newly independent state, was not void of the political experiences it needed for developing its own political system. From the period of self-government in the 1950s and Singapore's short inclusion in the Federation of Malaysia, concepts of the elected representative, electoral processes and the mechanisms of governance have been exposed to Singapore's polity and elites.

It came as no surprise when Singapore, as a former British colony, adopted the Westminster parliamentary system. This system of government or at least its fundamentals had already been introduced to Singapore during the period of self-rule in the form of the Legislative Assembly. However, upon Singapore's expulsion from the Federation of Malaysia, contention was not centred on the choice of an institution of government but on the nature of governance. As Shee Poon Kim notes, it was at this critical juncture, based on Singapore's immediate past experience, that the political elite in Singapore was adamant on creating a multiracial polity and a modern mixed

---

[1] Larry Diamond, "Can the whole world become democratic?", www.ips.org.sg/events/PL/rep_Larry%Diamond_120906htm, accessed 15 September 2016.

economy.[2] While these aspects of governance have been addressed earlier, this chapter critically examines Singapore's model of government.

The Westminster parliamentary system is a model of government where the executive is drawn from the legislative. This model of government has its origins in the English Parliament sitting in the Palace of Westminster, which also gives the model its name. In the Westminster parliamentary system, Members of Parliament are generally elected by popular vote, and the political party with the largest number of MPs is invited by the Head of State to form the government. Typically, the Head of State is a ceremonial position and the powers of governance reside with the Head of Government, that is, the Prime Minister. This parliamentary system model has been lauded as being able to provide an 'effective' government because the executive, also commonly known as the cabinet, is drawn from the party in control of Parliament, placing it in a theoretically more advantageous position to push for bills and legislations to be passed in Parliament. Through this system, the executive is able to carry out its plans and implement its policies with greater ease, hence, producing an 'effective' government. This advantage is more obvious when contrasted to a system where there is a distinct separation between the executive and legislative. For example, in a presidential system, the chief executive, the President, may not have the support from the legislative body, and may meet obstructions and opposition on a regular basis, which may undermine the efforts of the executive to implement its desired policies.

The Westminster parliamentary system may either have a bicameral or unicameral house, and the electoral system is usually a simple plurality or first-past-the-post electoral system.[3] Although there may be theoretical merits of this system in delivering an 'effective' government, there are some negative aspects of this model of government. As James Danziger notes, this type of parliamentary system "is a fusion of executive and legislative functions and structures".[4] Often, this model of government is associated with strict party discipline and the government is in control of Parliament. This reduces the roles of Parliament as an arena of debate and a check of the executive into merely a 'talk shop' or 'lobby fodder'.[5] Rather than acting as a balance to the executive, the legislative body is held 'captive' by the executive which is mostly, if not always, made up of leaders of the dominant party in Parliament. With the enforcement of party discipline by the party whip, errant members who vote

---

[2] Shee Poon Kim, "The Evolution of the Political System" in Jon S. T. Quah, Chan Heng Chee and Seah Chee Meow (eds.) *Government and Politics of Singapore* (Singapore: Oxford University Press, 1985) pp. 3–24.
[3] Andrew Heywood, *Politics* (London, England: Macmillan, 1997) p. 31.
[4] James Danziger, *Understanding the Political World: A Comparative Introduction to Political Science*, 7th Edition (New York, NY: Addison-Wesley Longman, 2005) p. 184.
[5] Andrew Heywood, *Politics*, p. 296.

against their own party in Parliament are reprimanded and may be expelled from their party or possibly lose their parliamentary seats.

The Westminster parliamentary system is widespread in many former British colonies who, upon independence, adopted their former colonial master's model of government. Singapore is an example of such a state. In Singapore, the ceremonial Head of State is the President and the Prime Minister is the Head of Government. Singapore has a unicameral house and since independence in 1965, has held regular elections to elect members of Parliament. Although the Singapore government is modeled after that of the British, Singapore has introduced several innovations, leading many to question whether the system of government in place in Singapore can still be referred to as a Westminster parliamentary system, and what the implications of these innovations are for the government and politics of Singapore. The subsequent sections look at the Non-Constituency Member of Parliament (NCMP), Nominated Member of Parliament (NMP), Group Representative Constituencies (GRCs) and the Elected Presidency (EP) as political innovations that have impacted the nature and essence of Singapore's Westminster parliamentary system.

NCMP

The NCMP scheme was introduced in 1984 to ensure the inclusion of the Opposition in Parliament. The scheme was meant to provide a 'backdoor entry' for the Opposition into Parliament, as it allowed for up to three of the 'best losers' in the general elections to be inducted into Parliament, albeit with limited voting powers. This number was later raised to nine with the passing of the Parliamentary Elections Amendment Act in 2010. Though first received negatively by Opposition leaders who viewed the arrangement as an insult, the scheme was eventually accepted after the Opposition recognised the benefits of having a parliamentary presence.

Given that the PAP controls nearly all seats in Parliament and that NCMPs only have limited voting rights, the NCMPs' role is limited to merely being a 'voice' in parliamentary debate. Neither being able to influence PAP Members of Parliament (MPs) nor having the ability to tip the balance of arguments, the NCMP has effectively little impact on the voting patterns in Parliament. Essentially, the NCMP scheme functions as a way for the PAP to pacify the electorate as it conveys the message that if the latter wants Opposition presence in Parliament, the former is willing to provide it, therefore giving the electorate no need to vote for the Opposition and against the PAP.

This innovation to the parliamentary system was arguably done by the PAP to accommodate the need for a non-threatening Opposition in Parliament. First shocked and later, coming to terms with the electorate's choice in the 1981 by-election and the 1984 General Elections which saw the PAP's complete dominance of Parliament broken, the party has been alleged to have introduced the scheme for two main purposes. First, since it interpreted the actions of the electorate as a vote of disgruntlement rather than disapproval of the PAP, this scheme would pacify the electorate's desire for alternative voices in Parliament. Second, by admitting NCMPs into Parliament with limited voting rights, the PAP was implicitly portraying the Opposition as an impotent electoral force, and in need of the good graces of the PAP. By satisfying the wants of the electorate while holding firm grip over Parliament, the PAP was able to retain its hegemony over the government and politics of Singapore.

The NCMP scheme is clearly an innovation to the original Westminster parliamentary system. Although in some cases of Westminster parliamentary systems whereby some MPs are appointed rather than elected, the Singapore case is different as NCMPs have only limited voting rights and the rationale behind their inclusion is certainly in need of further questioning. Rather than serving as an expansion to the plurality of views in Parliament, the NCMP scheme is often viewed as an attempt by the PAP to effectively neutralise any potential threat of Opposition members being elected into Parliament as full-fledged members.

NMP

The NMP scheme was introduced in 1991 during Goh Chok Tong's tenure as Prime Minister. Outstanding members of the public could be nominated to be non-partisan MPs with limited voting powers. NMPs are to provide feedback, generate debates against MPs and contribute their individual talents and expertise in Parliament. The scheme was part of Goh's desire to develop a more consultative form of governance. Realising that there may be talented individuals in society who may shun public office due to the consequences of political life and given Singapore's limited talent pool, the scheme would allow such individuals to serve a two-year term in Parliament. Without the need to be a member of any political party or to contest elections in order to gain direct induction into parliament, it was hoped that more talented individuals would be willing to step forth and serve as NMPs. The introduction of this political innovation was taken positively as it increased the diversity of opinions in Parliament. However, since NMPs do not represent any political constituency, they too like NCMPs, have limited voting rights. Since its induction in the early 1990s, NMPs, though not directly challenging the PAP hegemony in Parliament, have in their own right proved their worth by pushing for certain bills regarding social welfare issues to be passed in Parliament.

The NMP scheme, when taken in an alternative light, is a particularly successful PAP strategy of cooptation of potential societal or oppositional elites. By bringing these talents into the political system in a 'safe' and non-threatening manner, the PAP is effectively denying oppositional forces the possibility of recruiting these talents into their ranks. Moreover, by being allowed a short two-year stint without the hassle of having to join a political party and running for office, the NMP scheme allows these outstanding members of the public who may have issues with the current government a channel to voice not only their concerns but a platform for them to actively engage the PAP government in partnership rather than in opposition.

The contentious issue of the NMP scheme is that potential NMPs are evaluated by a panel of experts who are in turn appointed by the PAP government. Critics of the system look at the NMP scheme with caution as it seems that the PAP is in control of NMP appointments. The NMP scheme is certainly a political innovation that differs from the Westminster parliamentary system. While the performance of NMPs over the years has been encouraging, NMPs are still not sufficient as a form of check and balance to the PAP in Parliament. With limited voting powers and often 'tame' debates against PAP MPs, the long-term political impact of the NMP scheme to the government and politics of Singapore remains to be seen.

GRC

The GRC scheme was first introduced in 1988 and further refined in 1991, 1997 and 2009. The rationale for the introduction of GRCs was to enhance administration based on economies of scale.[6] The GRCs, which initially consisted of three-member groups, were later expanded to four-member groups, and finally set at a maximum of six members. In the formation of GRCs, it is also stipulated that at least one member of the team must be a minority candidate, that is, at least one of the candidates must be of either Malay, Indian or Eurasian descent. This potential candidate is required to submit an application to the Elections Department to obtain a certification that confirms the applicant's ethnic minority status.

The rationale of such a policy by the PAP was to ensure sufficient ethnic minority representation in Parliament. Singapore's rigid housing quota policies have resulted in ethnic minorities losing their dominant enclaves. Given the current demography of total Chinese electoral majorities in the electoral system, the PAP government was fearful that representatives of ethnic minorities may not be able to be voted in and hence, be accused of not taking ethnic minorities' views into consideration. While this action is consistent with the PAP government's pro-multiethnic governance, the Opposition has raised its objections against GRCs. The GRC system is accused of favouring large political parties who have the necessary political machinery and funds to finance a tremendously enlarged constituency. Opposition parties which at the onset are already challenged by their limited talents, manpower and funds, find it

---

[6] Narayan Ganesan, "Singapore: Entrenching a City-State's Dominant Party System", *Southeast Asian Affairs 1998* (Singapore: Institute of Southeast Asian Studies, 1998) p. 230.

difficult to form a team to contest a GRC. Even when they do contest, the Opposition parties are fearful of losing their electoral deposit, which in the 2015 General Elections stood at S$14,500 per candidate. A forfeit of their electoral deposit would certainly create a large dent in any Opposition party's funds. Then Prime Minister Goh Chok Tong has admitted that GRCs do favour large political parties.

It is common for PAP GRC teams to be anchored by a senior politician with the rest of the team being relatively new faces. This often is perceived as new PAP candidates 'riding on the coattails' of their senior colleagues, though it is also an excellent strategy for bringing new PAP members into Parliament. The Opposition, which lacks a large pool of talent from which to draw its members, is unwilling to compete head on with senior PAP candidates. For example, key leaders of the Opposition, Chiam See Tong and Low Thia Khiang, only contested Single Member Constituencies (SMC) for a while, which, to their credit, they successfully retained. In the 2006 General Elections, however, the Opposition parties were much more vibrant as they made a laudable effort to mount a large-scale challenge against the PAP across various GRCs. This effort escalated in 2011, where all constituencies with the exception of Tanjong Pagar GRC were contested, an unprecedented feat in itself. On top of this, both Chiam and Low chose to compete in a GRC, with the Workers' Party (WP) winning in Aljunied and Chiam's Singapore People's Party losing in Bishan-Toa Payoh. The WP also won in the Aljunied GRC in the 2015 General Elections.

The GRC scheme clearly sets the Singapore model of government apart from the typical Westminster parliamentary system. Enlarged representation is a distinct political innovation that contrasts the traditional SMC which is a defining characteristic of the Westminster system. The electorate is unable to cast its vote for a particular candidate and has no choice but to accept all the candidates in a GRC team or reject the team entirely. Although accepting the merits of the GRC scheme in ensuring minority representation, such a system also reduces the relationship between the electorate and its representatives, since the relationship has evolved from individual-to-individual to that of the individual-to-team. A counter argument to this, however, is that the electorate is still able to relate directly with the individual MP as the GRC is merely an electoral mechanism, with the normal MP-to-electorate relationship largely intact and unchanged in every other sense.

EP

The role of the President of Singapore has traditionally been ceremonial. Since 1984, with the Opposition's success in breaking the PAP's complete control of Parliament, the ruling party began to seek active ways of limiting the intrusion of the Opposition and neutralising its impact on Singapore politics. Chief amongst the PAP's concerns was to safeguard its vast national reserves in case an 'irresponsible' government came into power. By 1991, the PAP government released a White Paper stating the creation of an EP, which would be tasked with guarding Singapore's financial reserves and key appointments. The EP would form part of a 'two-key' mechanism that would release the reserves: The Prime Minister as the Head of Government would hold one key, while the elected president would hold the second key to the lock. Unlike the four-year term of the appointed President, the EP's term was for six years.

However, the EP scheme was greeted with much cynicism when Ong Teng Cheong, a long time PAP Deputy Prime Minister, resigned from the PAP to contest the first presidential elections in 1993. Although Ong's road to the presidency was not without challenge, the other contender, Chua Kim Yeow, was very much a reluctant candidate, pushed into action "after some arm-twisting by PAP stalwarts Goh Keng Swee and Richard Hu".[7] In addition, the inaugural elections appeared very much as a staged event, and the general public did not receive the entire EP scheme with much enthusiasm either.

To his credit, Ong, as the newly EP, pushed for a much clearer role for the office. Ong was at odds with his former colleagues over the level of information and authority over Singapore's reserves that he should have as the EP. Not surprisingly, the PAP government in 1994 began to cull the powers of the EP. In the later years of Ong's tenure, the differences he had with the PAP government over the role, functions and independence of the EP intensified and were widely covered in the local press. These disagreements and contestations between Ong and his former colleagues further diminished the possibility of Ong seeking a second term as the EP. Ultimately, ill health was cited as the reason for Ong not seeking a second term, and the office of the EP was won uncontested by S. R. Nathan, a distinguished civil servant and former diplomat with close ties to the PAP leadership.

The EP, in essence, is an innovation of the Singapore government. However, the PAP by limiting the discretionary powers of the EP, has reduced the role of the EP and returned the role of the presidency to that of a pre-dominantly ceremonial role. Even though the EP can act robustly under certain circumstances, this is something that has never been exercised and is yet to be tested. With a set of stringent criteria in place for the selection of EP candidates, few are able to fulfill the requirements, and those who do are mostly linked in one way or another to the PAP government. Moreover, the EP is compelled to accept the advice of the Presidential Advisory Committee, a committee appointed by the PAP government, essentially a check by the executive on the EP.

Even though the EP has been in operation since 1993 and its powers have been systematically whittled away, the PAP government has continued to insist that the EP

---

[7] Diane K. Mauzy and R. S. Milne, *Singapore Politics under the People's Action Party* (London, England: Routlege, 2002) p. 153.

is a critical office for safeguarding Singapore's interests. In a forum on governance, Lee Kuan Yew reiterated the need for the EP to counter a rogue government.[8] In the same forum, Lee argued, "Even with an Elected President, if they (the Opposition) win a second time, the reserves are open, because they can then arrange for their president to be elected and the country comes to a grinding halt".[9] This statement demonstrates clearly the poor opinion that Lee Kuan Yew and the PAP have for Singapore's political Opposition. More importantly, the statement, while referring to the inability of the Opposition to install its selected candidate for the role of EP, implicitly revealed the same ability of the PAP to install the EP of its choice.

Following what was seen as a somewhat divisive presidential elections in 2011 and where some people had the impression that the EP could function as an 'alternate government', in January 2016, Prime Minister Lee proposed that there would also be the need to amend the system to allow for minorities to be elected to the post, especially if someone from a minority group had not held the post for a long time. This saw the appointment of a nine-member Constitutional Commission headed by the Chief Justice Sundaresh Menon and whose report was submitted to the Government in August 2016. In September 2016, the government published a White Paper on the EP, broadly accepting the recommendations of the Constitutional Commission. Before it became law, the White Paper was debated in Parliament in November 2016. All being equal, some of the proposed changes include: raising the qualifying criteria for presidential candidates, introducing provisions to ensure that ethnic minorities are elected to office from time to time and to enhance the role of the Council of Presidential Advisers whom the EP is obliged to consult when exercising the latter's executive powers. After three days of debates in Parliament from 6 to 9 November 2016, the Bill to amend the Constitution on the EP was passed with 77 PAP MPs supporting and six from the WP opposing. Prime Minister Lee also announced that the next presidential election, scheduled for August 2017, would be reserved for a qualified Malay candidate. This, according to him, would mean that Singapore would have again a Malay president after 46 years, the last one being Yusof bin Ishak [August 1965-November 1970].[10] Later, it was announced that the EP's election would take place in September 2017.

---

[8] Peh Shing Huei, "S'pore Must Preserve Its System of Govt: MM", *The Straits Times*, 16 September 2006.

[9] "Singapore Must Preserve Its System of Government: MM", *The Straits Times*, 16 September 2006.

[10] See "Elected Presidency: Amendments to Constitutions Passed in Parliament", *Channel News Asia*, 9 November 2016, http://www.channelnewsasia.com/news/singapore/elected-presidency-amendments-to-constitution-passed-in/3271856.html; Charissa Yong, "Parliament: 2017 Presidential Election Will Be Reserved for Malay Candidates, Says PM Lee", *The Straits Times*, 8 November 2016.

Conclusion

Examining the four political innovations to Singapore's political system, it is undeniable that the current system differs from the system that was established in 1965. These institutional changes have altered the nature of elected representatives, created degrees of differences between full-fledged MPs, NMPs and NCMPs and most importantly, differentiated the voting rights of each category. The NMP and NCMP schemes, although being new channels of representation that have increased the plurality of opinions in Parliament, only minimally impact the decision-making process in Singapore. Due to the nature of PAP's hegemony in Parliament and the constitutional constraints of NCMP and NMP voting rights, the powers of decision-making are still firmly in PAP's hands.

On the GRCs, they are a distinct contrast to the typical SMCs of a Westminster parliamentary system. The key impact of the GRCs on the political system is the increase of disproportionate representation of the electorate in Parliament. Traditionally, the first-past-the-post electoral system in Westminster parliamentary systems has been argued to produce disproportionate representation in Parliament, that is, the number of seats a political party may win in Parliament is not proportionate to the percentage of popular votes it receives. The GRC scheme further increases this disproportion, as the stakes in each enlarged constituency is no longer a single seat in parliament, but may be as high as six seats in Parliament.

At the same time, the EP appears to be moving the Singapore parliamentary system into that of a hybrid system, that is, a combination of a presidential and parliamentary system. In a full parliamentary system, the powers of the state rest in the hands of the Prime Minister and his cabinet. With the introduction of the EP, at least potentially, an alternative centre of power has been created in the Singapore system. Although the EP's powers are confined to the state's financial reserves and key appointments, the size of Singapore's reserves makes it an important and critical appointment. The PAP government has, however, been reducing the powers of the EP. This may be due to differences between the first directly elected EP, Ong and his former PAP colleagues over the role of the PAP, the EP as an independent institution, and the EP as PAP's final line of defence against a 'rogue' government. Nonetheless, due to these issues and controversies over the independence and role of the EP, marred by the apparent lack of real contestation for the post, the EP is viewed by many as yet another tool of PAP's entrenchment and control.

Are changes to the system inevitable? To some extent, change is always expected as society progresses. In the case of Singapore, the Westminster parliamentary system is certainly a part of its colonial legacy, implemented pre-dominantly by inheritance rather than as a conscious choice. The direct adoption and implementation of a system derived and evolved in the West in a newly created state which is conspicuously different from the country of the system's origin may not be completely feasible.

The system may require certain adaptations, innovations and refinements to cater to its new environment, especially the political culture of wanting greater participation and involvement in national politics. This may be true in the case of Singapore and many other former colonies who attempt to implement the system of government of their former political masters. The political elite of the state must take into consideration the constraints and limitations facing their own state and policy.

However, these changes to the Westminster parliamentary system in Singapore have to a certain degree facilitated the perpetuation of the PAP's power. From the NMP to the GRCs, these political innovations have further marginalised the Opposition. Additionally, the NCMP and NMP schemes have arguably pacified the demands of the electorate for the presence of alternative voices in the decision-making process, but with the PAP still in power. Through these schemes, the PAP appears willing to 'hear' these voices in Parliament, but because it knows that it is ultimately in control of the entire decision-making process, is not required to really 'listen'.

The GRCs have hampered the Opposition by increasing the barriers to challenging the PAP's power. The Opposition, literally 'poor' in talent and funds, is unable to gather the required resources to effectively challenge the PAP in a GRC. However, this has not prevented the Opposition from mounting a challenge, at least in one GRC. During the general elections over the years, some of the Opposition's most significant electoral contestations in GRCs have taken place against PAP GRC teams in Bedok, Cheng San and Aljunied. In 2011, Opposition parties managed to contest all but one of the constituencies and even won in one GRC. The same was true in 2015 where every GRC was contested with the WP winning in the Aljunied GRC.

The EP, a system designed to safeguard the nation's reserves and integrity of the public service, appears to be a double-edged sword for the PAP, as a non-partisan EP may actually unravel the party's complete control over Singapore's huge financial reserves. It thus cannot be denied that the current political system in Singapore is not the same as it was in August 1965 when Singapore gained its independence. The system, though still retaining elements of a Westminster parliamentary system, has evolved to such an extent that it cannot be just known as a Westminster parliamentary system but a Singapore parliamentary system for its uniqueness and at time, 'decorative' adaptations to the original system.

Think Questions

1. Why did Singapore adopt the Westminster political system?
2. What are the benefits and drawbacks of the various political innovations since 1965?
3. Does the present system still qualify as a Westminster political system?

Chapter Four

Political Parties — The Resilience of the One-Party Dominant State

It is a law of nature that all things must atrophy. The steady state does not exist in nature.[1]

Introduction

In the study of government and politics, understanding the role of political parties is extremely important. Part and parcel of any political system, political parties exist in nearly every modern state ranging from authoritarian states such as the People's Republic of China to the most liberal-democratic of states such as the United States and Great Britain. The question is, what exactly are political parties and what are their functions in and importance to the political system?

Andrew Heywood characterises a political party as a "group of people that is organised for the purpose of winning government power, by electoral or other means".[2] Similarly, James Danziger defines a political party as "an organised group that attempts to capture political power directly by placing its members in government office".[3] Political parties are different from interest groups, which merely seek to influence the government by means other than direct participation in elections. Political parties have several key functions which include, but are not limited to, candidate nomination, electoral mobilisation, issue structuring, societal representation, interest aggregation, forming and sustaining governments, and social

---

[1] See Simon Tay S. C. (ed.), *A Mandarin and the Making of Public Policy: Reflections by Ngiam Tong Dow* (Singapore: NUS Press, 2006) p. 22.
[2] Andrew Heywood, *Politics* (Basingstoke, England: Macmillan, 1997) p. 230.
[3] James N. Danziger, *Understanding the Political World: A Comparative Introduction to Political Science*, 7th edition (New York, NY: Pearson Education, 2005) pp. 501–502.

integration.[4] Political parties are important not only as the representatives of their respective social bases and cleavages, but are recognised as institutions that are integral to the operation of modern political systems, especially democracy.

Singapore's political system has been described in many ways including that of a dominant political system, an authoritarian state and even an illiberal democracy.[5] These labels of Singapore's political system can be said to stem from a single political party's dominance over Singapore since 1959. The PAP, since the late 1960s, has steadily increased its hold over Parliament. It controls nearly all seats in Parliament to this day. Singapore's party system is clearly a one-party dominant system, where there is only one party, the PAP, that is capable of winning elections to form the government. A one-party dominant system differs from that of a one-party state such that in the former, while there is only a single party with the potential to be in power, other political parties do exist in the system. In the latter, there is only one party that is legally allowed, an example being the Communist Party in the People's Republic of China. In Singapore's one-party dominant system, there is little or no possibility at all of a party other than the PAP to be in power. Opposition political parties in Singapore, though present even in Parliament, have little impact on the decision-making process and their "influence, if any, in shaping the Republic's policy agendas is manifestly miniscule".[6] Nonetheless, Opposition parties are part of the political landscape in Singapore and hence, the importance of understanding their role, relevance and future in Singapore politics.

The party system in Singapore inadvertently leads to two important questions. Firstly, what other political parties exist in Singapore besides the PAP? Secondly, given the fact that there are many political parties in Singapore, how has such a situation emerged whereby the PAP is the dominant, if not, the hegemonic political party in Singapore? The various Opposition political parties in Singapore will be examined before explaining how such a one-party dominant system emerged in Singapore and continues with little, if any, hope of change.

Currently, there are approximately 20 registered political parties in Singapore, including the PAP (Table 4.1) Opposition parties in Singapore like the Workers' Party (WP) and the Singapore People's Party (SPP) can generally be characterised as mass-based political parties. These political parties are considered mass-based as their membership is open to all and they attempt to appeal to all Singaporeans. There are also several ethno-centric political parties such as the *Pertubuhan Kebangsaan Melayu*

---

[4] Richard Gunther and Larry Diamond (eds.) *Political Parties and Democracy* (Washington D.C.: John Hopkins Press, 2001) pp. 7–8.
[5] Hussin Mutalib, *Parties and Politics: A Study of Opposition Parties and the PAP in Singapore* (Singapore, Eastern University Press, 2003) pp. 8–20.
[6] Ibid, p. 4.

Table 4.1: Functioning Political Parties in Singapore

People's Action Party (PAP)
Singapore Democratic Alliance (SDA)
National Solidarity Party (NSP)
Pertubuhan Kebangsaan Melayu Singapura (PKMS)
    (Singapore Malay National Organisation)
Singapore People's Party (SPP)
Singapore Democratic Party (SDP)
Workers' Party (WP)
Democratic Progressive Party
Parti Kesatuan Ra'ayat (United Democratic Party)
United National Front (UNF)
United People's Front
Alliance Party Singapore
Katong United Residents' Association
National Party of Singapore
People's Republican Party
Persatuan Melayu Singapura (Singapore Malay Society)
Singapore Indian Congress
Singapore First Party
Singapore National Front

Source: Author.

Singapura (PKMS) or Singapore Malay National Organisation and the Singapore Indian Congress. However, the activities of these parties are limited as Singapore is devoid of any traditional ethnic minority wards. The PAP's strict housing quota system under the administration of the Housing and Development Board (HDB) has ensured that no housing estate is dominated by any ethnic minority. If anything, in line with national population dynamics, every political ward in Singapore has been transformed, mainly through housing policies, into a Chinese majority region with no chance of any minority group emerging dominant anywhere in Singapore on the basis of race, except for the Chinese. In general, Opposition political parties organised along communal lines operate at the fringes of the political system and their membership often comprises of a limited pool of Singaporeans.

Of all the Opposition political parties, only a few have regularly contested the general elections. Only the numerically larger Opposition political parties such as the WP, the Singapore Democratic Party (SDP) and the Singapore Democratic Alliance (SDA), an Opposition coalition comprising of the National Solidarity Party (NSP), the SPP and the PKMS, have been able to field candidates for the general elections. Between the 1990s and 2011, the Opposition never managed to win more than four parliamentary seats in any general elections. Following the 2006 General Ele~˙ there were only two Opposition candidates in Parliament, namely, WP's

Khiang and SDA's Chiam See Tong. This changed dramatically in 2011, when six WP candidates won parliamentary seats in the General Elections, resulting in a threefold increase (Non-Constituency Members of Parliament, NCMPs excluded) in Opposition presence in Parliament. The WP added another seat when it won the Punggol East by-election. In the 2015 General Elections, the WP also won six parliamentary seats.

The lack of contestation by some Opposition political parties in Singapore challenges basic definitions of what makes a political party. Political parties are differentiated from interest groups and civil society by the fact that they actively aim to contest in elections in order to win public office. Although registered as a political party, some Opposition parties are only active in the immediate period before a general elections, and the furthest that they have gone during these periods is merely to issue statements on their political positions. This raises interesting questions regarding the reason for their existence as Opposition political parties in Singapore: Are these political parties symbolic organisations for political expression against the PAP? Or are they so severely incapacitated by the system that, although they are genuinely interested in contesting elections, are unable to do so as they have been systematically challenged by structural and institutional constraints?

Besides those currently registered Opposition political parties in Singapore, there are many parties that are defunct. Prominent Opposition parties such as the *Barisan Sosialis* and the Labour Front no longer exist. However, some of these political parties have not disappeared into the annals of history but rather have evolved and metamorphosed to form new parties. The *Barisan Sosialis* and the Singapore United Front, for example, merged with the WP in 1988.[7]

Even though there are many Opposition parties in Singapore, they have been unable to establish a presence in Parliament and the PAP's hegemony remains unchallenged. Why is there a situation of near-perpetual political hegemony by one party, the PAP, in the Singapore political system? To explain the primacy of one over the other, one must analyse whether this is due to the outright superiority of one party over others or a function of other factors that have perpetually condemned all other parties to a situation of nothing more than 'political decorations' in the system. In the case of Singapore, the PAP has clearly excelled over other parties both as a political party and a government in power. The Opposition at the same time is extremely weak due to both internal and external constraints. The combination of these factors explains the current dominance of the PAP in Singapore politics.

The PAP's success can be explained on a number of counts. The party is well organised and well led, and has the benefit of having been in power since 1959,

---

[7] Workers' Party of Singapore Website, "History of the Workers' Party of Singapore", http://www.wp.sg/party/history.htm.

thereby capturing the political imagination of a few generations so far. Incumbency has thus been a crucial factor. The PAP has branches in all constituencies in Singapore. The PAP, however, is not a mass-based party as history has taught it to be cautious of the vulnerabilities of being overly inclusive, especially in internal elections. It must be remembered that in the late 1950s and early 1960s, the Lee Kuan Yew-led moderates in the PAP faced severe challenges from the party's left-leaning members who nearly managed to oust the moderates from the party by means of internal elections. While PAP membership is open to all, not all members are given voting rights within the party. The PAP is an elite party, where the most important decision-making structure in the party is grounded in a cadre system. Only after a stringent selection process is one admitted into the ranks as a cadre and subsequently given voting powers within the party. The identities of the cadre members have been kept a secret, with their numbers approximating 1,000.[8]

The PAP branches merely serve as locality for party events, especially during general elections. Although they have their own organisations, PAP branches have no influence over the party's decision-making process. Branch members are usually long-time PAP members from various walks of life. However, unlike some other political parties, loyalty to the party does not guarantee promotion within party ranks. The party selects its leaders based on meritocracy and often, many of its electoral candidates are recruited directly into the party and immediately elevated to the top ranks of the party. These select few usually have no previous links to the party but due to their individual merits and potential, are promoted very quickly in the party hierarchy.[9] This system has allowed the PAP to field well-educated and high-profile candidates who have proven themselves as leaders within their own particular niches prior to joining politics. However, the majority of these newly-recruited and newly-promoted party members lack the experience of working at the grassroots level and this has been a key criticism of the PAP's style of elite recruitment. To the benefit of the PAP leadership, the long-standing party members and workers have, to a large extent, accepted this arrangement and remain staunch party supporters. As such, long-standing party members and workers usually do not aspire for top party or political positions but tend to 'service' top leaders who have been 'helicoptered' to strategic political positions by the leadership.

The PAP has also been able to provide many social welfare services. One of its most successful programmes includes the PAP's childcare and pre-school facilities. These PAP childcare and pre-school centres are conveniently located in nearly all housing estates and cater mostly to middle and lower income Singapore families. The

---

[8] Koh Buck Song, "The 1000 PAP 'cardinals' who appoint the 'Pope'", *The Straits Times*, 4 April 1998.
[9] Chan Heng Chee, "Political Parties" in Jon S. T. Quah, Chan Heng Chee and Seah Chee Meow (eds.) *Government and Politics of Singapore* (Singapore: Oxford University Press, 1985) p. 162.

ability of the party to provide such basic services has earned it the support and loyalty of most middle income Singaporeans. At the same time, these services continue to boost the presence of the PAP and help it retain its image as a party that is able to provide and care for Singaporeans. The PAP, relative to other political parties in Singapore, also has massive funds. Each PAP Member of Parliament (MP) is required to contribute $600 per month to party coffers while PAP Ministers are required to contribute $1000 per month.[10] With the PAP's clear dominance of Parliament, the party is ensured approximately $50,000 per month to fund its activities. Besides contributions from elected MPs and Ministers, the PAP also receives political donations from other groups and individuals.

Using Larry Diamond and Richard Gunther's observations of the functions of a political party, the PAP clearly excels in each and every category.[11] In candidate nomination, the PAP has been able to constantly recruit high quality individuals. Given Singapore's small population and a smaller pool of talented individuals, the ability of the PAP to recruit most, if not all, available talents means that the Opposition is deprived of enlisting these talents into its ranks. Furthermore, the PAP is extremely successful in electoral mobilisation. This is due to both the incumbency of the PAP in government, having the edge of preparing for elections and knowing precisely when elections will be held, as well as the strong presence of the PAP in all electoral constituencies, as PAP branch members are expected to support party efforts during election periods.

The PAP is also adept at structuring issues and providing not only effective leadership, but PAP leaders, in particular the old guard, are visionaries who have been able to steer Singapore in the direction of their goals. Being a secular political party, the PAP, with its calls for a multi-ethnic and meritocratic society, has to a great extent been able to represent the general populace in Singapore without much controversy. Their ability to aggregate interests, compounded with their track record in forming and sustaining the government of Singapore, are critical keys to the PAP's longevity in power. The PAP's unbroken grip over Singapore has allowed the party to structure Singapore's social integration along the lines of the party leadership's vision and expectations. This has effectively tied the fate of Singapore to the party's continued governance of the island republic. Clearly, the PAP is a well-organised political party with established norms and structures that continue to ensure the party's primacy in Singapore. With healthy party funds and success in recruiting new talents as well as generating new leaders in the party ranks, the PAP is able to provide a multitude of services and offer top quality candidates during elections. However, the success of the

---

[10] Diane K. Mauzy and R. S. Milne, *Singapore Politics under the People's Action Party* (London, England: Routledge, 2002) p. 43.
[11] Richard Gunther and Larry Diamond (eds.) *Political Parties and Democracy*, pp. 7–8.

PAP as a political party is also assisted by the fact that the PAP has been in power since 1959.

Over the years, it has become more difficult to distinguish the PAP as a political party and as the government. The PAP's excellent track record in governing Singapore gives the party an added, some say, unfair advantage over all other political parties. In short, the government of Singapore is essentially a creation of the PAP and has remained the exclusive institution of the PAP. Typical of many political parties in power, the PAP has access to machineries of state, including control over the media, and has used these to benefit the party. The longer the PAP is in power, the more it is able to formulate, create, and raise barriers against other political parties.

For instance, Singapore has been admired for its ability to make long-term plans for the challenges and needs that it might face in the future. The Scenario Planning Unit under the Prime Minister's Office is tasked with making predictions and coming up with recommended solutions and plans to take on these future challenges. The PAP leaders, as the incumbent Prime Minister and the cabinet, have access to these scenarios, and are thus able to co-opt them into their party platforms. Political innovations such as the NCMP and Nominated Member of Parliament (NMP) schemes have arguably undermined the importance of an elected Opposition in Parliament. Critics of these schemes have accused the PAP of creating them to placate the desires of the electorate to see more Opposition in Parliament. By introducing NCMPs and NMPs with limited voting rights in Parliament, the PAP hopes to prevent the electorate from casting votes for the Opposition during general elections. As former Minister Mentor Lee Kuan Yew said, the Singapore electorate may be a 'freak' at times, hence indicating the desires of the PAP as the government of the day to mold and innovate the political environment in its favour. Similarly, the Elected Presidency scheme is also a safeguard to ensure that the PAP has an 'insider' in the event that the freak Singapore electorate decides to vote the Opposition into Parliament. The Group Representation Constituencies (GRCs) also pose a great challenge to Opposition parties who by nature are relatively small with limited resources. For the Opposition to contest in a GRC, it is forced to commit huge proportions of its resources for uncertain gains. While the Opposition has proven itself capable of winning a GRC, as shown by the WP in the Aljunied GRC in 2011 and 2015, the Opposition still faces tough barriers in the form of PAP GRC teams composed of new faces and incumbent MPs, and anchored by senior politicians of ministerial rank.

The PAP government policies are also responsible for the marginalisation of the ruling party's political opponents. In the interest of protecting the fragile social fabric, certain issues have been made taboo in Singapore politics. Issues with regard to race and religion are clearly out-of-bounds and political parties are not allowed to exploit these traditional cleavages of politics for fear of igniting underlying tensions between the various ethnic communities in Singapore. Although this policy is respected, it has

tently denied the Opposition a platform to contest against the PAP. Moreover, in all ethnic self-help groups such as the Chinese Development Assistance Council (CDAC), Mendaki and Singapore Indian Development Association (SINDA), PAP ministers always serve as chairpersons or key advisers. By 'capturing' these traditional cleavages of political bases and reducing them into apolitical organisations, the PAP has effectively denied the Opposition from capitalising on ethnic issues. Paradoxically, the PAP is in a position to influence communal leaders, thereby commanding their loyalty and support.

The current situation cannot be simply explained by the PAP's excellent organisational and political tactics. Opposition political parties themselves are partly to blame for the PAP's current domination of the political system. The weak Opposition's organisational capacity, its lack of alternative ideology, and limited resources due to the PAP's overwhelming dominance in recruiting talent and amassing resources for contesting elections have worked to the Opposition's own detriment. Opposition political parties in Singapore do not have a highly developed and institutionalised organisation as that of the PAP. The Opposition parties tend to be 'parties of personality', where the entire party is centred on particular leaders.[12] Such parties are anchored around key individuals, and therefore are unable to institutionalise themselves into a strong political party because changes in leadership or the incapacitation of its leaders would render the party weak, or worse, lead to its dissolution. This particular weakness of the Opposition has been fully exploited by the PAP leadership. The PAP leaders such as Lee Kuan Yew, Goh Chok Tong and Lee Hsien Loong have in the past used the long arms of the law against their political opponents. Key Opposition leaders have been sued in court for defamation, and often, liabilities and legal costs would bankrupt the targeted Opposition leaders. Examples of Opposition leaders made bankrupt in suits by PAP leaders include J. B. Jeyaretnam and Chee Soon Juan of the WP and SDP, respectively.

Moreover, aside from the banned Malayan Communist Party, no other Opposition political party has a well-defined ideology that can be pitted against the PAP. While the PAP can be categorised as a centre-right party, most Opposition parties occupy the centre-left. However, *Operation Coldstore* and the treatment of communist ideology in the 1960s have stamped out the possibility of a clear leftist ideology coming to the fore. Additionally, such an ideological bent would be unfeasible with a large middle class and state control over the unions. Without a clear ideological platform, Opposition parties typically justify their existence as a check and balance to the PAP instead of being an alternative to the PAP. This implicitly recognises the strengths of the PAP and the inability of the Opposition to replace the PAP as the government. Opposition parties, although being channels for articulating

---

[12] Diane K. Mauzy and R. S. Milne, *Singapore Politics under the People's Action Party*, p. 146.

grievances against PAP rule, are unable to provide cohesive alternatives to PAP policies and programmes. Often enough, the Opposition is only able to call for greater transparency in governance and can ask of little more than that.

Some leading Opposition political parties are "wracked by internal dissension".[13] A case in point includes the ouster of the former senior Opposition MP, Chiam from his post in the SDP by a then relative novice, Chee. While Chiam portrayed the image of a gentle Opposition, the SDP under Chee took on more radical tactics to challenge the PAP. The SDP, for instance, accused the PAP of being involved in a cover-up of the National Kidney Foundation scandal that emerged in June 2005. To no one's surprise, the PAP took firm legal action against the entire SDP leadership including Chee. The SDP eventually fell apart in the 2006 General Elections as the leadership was split between those who were willing to apologise for the allegations and hence, cease the defamation suit, and those such as Chee who insisted on upholding their allegations, thus having to face a legal case. Such incidents, to a certain extent, demonstrate not only the self-destructive strategies of the Opposition but also reveal the inability of the Opposition to be cohesive. Granted, there is no compulsion for the Opposition to be unified, but given the context of Singapore, intra-party factionalism and rivalry have reduced the public's opinion of the viability of the Opposition as an alternative to a PAP government. No right thinking and rational Singaporean would want to hostage his/her future and well-being on an Opposition that is not able to get its act together. This has also, by default, extended and entrenched the PAP's hold on the Singapore's political system.

On the issue of Opposition leadership and recruitment, Opposition political parties have also clearly been unable to attract individuals of similar calibre as that of the PAP. While the PAP is able to co-opt and recruit top talents from the public and private sector, the majority of the Opposition candidates are often individuals from 'normal' walks of life. Opposition candidates cannot boast to be neither former top military men nor successful corporate figures. While some may argue that politicians should be representative of the electorate, in Singapore, high education and occupational success remain key criteria for evaluating an individual's potential. The Opposition has at times managed to attract leaders of some potential even though many have not performed up to expectation. Here, one only needs to take the example from the former NCMP Steve Chia of the National Solidarity Party. He was viewed as a rising star in the Opposition's ranks until a scandal involving him taking pictures of a scantily dressed maid and his penchant for taking nude pictures of himself erupted. In Singapore's largely conservative society, such scandals, if one may call them so, of public figures are not well received. Following the 2006 General Elections, Chia announced his retirement from politics after he failed to be elected into

---

[13] Ibid, p. 147.

Parliament in three general elections, which had taken a toll on his personal life. He was supposed to contest in the 2015 General Elections but withdrew in the last minute even though he contested in the 2011 general elections.

Again, using Diamond and Gunther's observations of the functions of a political party, none of the present Opposition parties in Singapore are able to fulfill those expectations. In candidate nomination, let alone in electoral contestation, only several parties have been able to field candidates, and it should be said that the qualities of the candidates are also questionable. In interest aggregation and issue structuring, the Opposition is unable to come up with alternatives to PAP policies, and their challenges are limited to calling for greater transparency in governance. In other key expectations of societal representation and social integration, the Opposition has been unable to mobilise the masses as many of the electorate, although desiring greater participation of the Opposition, are overly dependent on the PAP to provide governance and leadership in Singapore. Accepting that there is a significant proportion of voters who cast their votes against the PAP, one cannot conclude with certainty that the votes cast are a reflection of the electorate's support for the Opposition. More often than not, these tend to be protests and grievances against the PAP government and its policies, and the protest votes are aimed more at eliciting concessions from the ruling party.

In conclusion, the current one-party dominant system in Singapore has come about due to the initial success of the PAP at identifying with the electorate and its eventual total consolidation of power in the Parliament when the *Barisan Sosialis* boycotted the 1968 General Elections. Since then, the PAP has continued to better itself as an organisation and has used its privilege as the party in power to create an environment that perpetuates its hegemony. The Opposition, on the other hand, has failed to further influence Singapore politics due to its own inherent weaknesses, as well as barriers placed against them by the PAP. Thus, in answering why the PAP is dominant and hegemonic, it is a case of both the PAP being excellent at what it does best as a political party and the inability of other political parties to provide a credible challenge to the PAP and its rule. To that extent, the PAP can be expected to continue outdistancing the other political parties despite regular elections and the fact that the electorate actually has the choice of selecting amongst more than 20 functioning political parties in the system.

Think Questions

1. Does Singapore have a multi-party system?
2. How did the PAP come to dominate and maintain its dominance over the political system?
3. Are Opposition political parties relevant in Singapore?

Chapter Five

Para-Political Organisations in Singapore

> The close relationship between the unions and the party has achieved much. The PAP and NTUC are not ashamed of what we have done. Singaporeans can be proud of this. We can look in the face and eyes of Singaporeans and be proud of ourselves and the rest we leave to history.[1]

Introduction

A study of Singapore politics is in many ways a study of the PAP's political hegemony and dominance, both in terms of how it achieved and maintained it. To understand this, the role of para-political organisations must be assessed because they have arguably been central to the PAP's iron grip over power as well as part of the reason for the Opposition's inability to make lasting gains politically. Defined as mass-based institutions that function to "provide the organisational framework by which [the government] mobilises mass support" and "give opportunities for political participation [thus allowing the government to] avoid a situation of having to suppress demands for participation", para-political organisations are a key element of Singapore's political landscape.[2] It is against this backdrop that this chapter investigates four types of such organisations — the civil service, grassroots organisations, the mass media, and trade unions — to show how they have contributed to the PAP's political dominance.

---

[1] Ong Teng Cheong, the NTUC Secretary-General in 1984, cited in *The Sunday Times*, 1 August 1984.
[2] Seah Chee Meow, "Para-Political Institutions" in Jon S. T. Quah, Chan Heng Chee and Seah Chee Meow (eds.) *Government and Politics of Singapore*, revised edition (Singapore: Oxford University Press, 1987) p. 174.

Civil Service

Role of the Civil Service

The Civil Service or bureaucracy, in any state, is generally the institution which translates policies and guidelines derived from the political leadership into tangible programmes and actions, and is essentially the working backbone of the political system. The Civil Service is concerned with efficiency, implementation, coordination, planning and optimising the policy process, while political leaders are mainly concerned with the effectiveness, ideology, changes and optimising the outcomes that can benefit and legitimise them politically. The ideal Civil Service is meant to be neutral, to be an instrument of the community to run the state effectively and be free from corruption, and not be subject to the influences of political jockeying by leaders.[3] However, the reality is that the Civil Service, due to its close relationship and interdependency with the political leadership and government structure, finds it difficult to maintain a truly neutral position. It generally takes on either: (a) a subservient role, (b) a representative role, or (c) a combination of the two.

When a Civil Service is seen to be subservient, it means that civil servants are appointed to perform tasks at the service of those holding political power and responsibility, regardless of whether it is for the king, president or parliament. The Civil Service's administration exists primarily to satisfy the needs of higher authorities more efficiently, carry out their goals, and not alter or challenge the authorities' objectives and actions.[4] In this form, it is seen to be the duty of the civil servant to obey the orders of his/her superiors to the extent that even if there are objections, the civil servant is still obliged to carry out his/her duties. One of the main critiques of the subservient Civil Service is that civil servants may blindly carry out orders irrespective of their nature and act irresponsibly and unconscientiously. This, however, assumes that civil servants are passive recipients of directives from their political leaders. Civil servants, by giving form to the policies to be implemented, may also bring to bear upon these policies their expertise, and are intimately involved in ascribing and arranging what they believe to be the priorities of the state. Their extensive involvement in the policy-formulating and implementation stages gives them a substantial collective power against the political leadership.

A representative Civil Service is supposedly more impartial and democratic. Measures are implemented to ensure that the administrative system remains neutral

---

[3] Seah Chee Meow, "The Civil Service" in Jon S. T. Quah, Chan Heng Chee and Seah Chee Meow (eds.) *Government and Politics of Singapore*, revised edition (Singapore: Oxford University Press, 1987) p. 92.
[4] Michiel S. de Vries, "Democracy and the Neutrality of Public Bureaucracy" in Haile K. Asmerom and Elisa P. Reis (eds.) *Democratization and Bureaucratic Neutrality* (Great Britain: Macmillan Press, 1996) p. 84.

as a whole and that it would listen to a multitude of interest groups as opposed to only listening to the political leadership.[5] This form of Civil Service is characterised by the provision of checks and balances within the system to ensure accountability and a more consultative process to take into consideration a wide range of views and opinions. The representative form of Civil Service also allows for public participation, which is factored into decision-making. However, the consultative process means that policies can sometimes take years to be approved and implemented, which can make this form of Civil Service cumbersome, time-consuming and inefficient. The Singapore Civil Service is largely a combination of the subservient and representative form, the result of colonial legacies of public administration and nation building constraints.

Origins of the Singapore Civil Service

The Civil Service in Singapore was first organised by the British colonial power to further British commercial and political interests in the region. In terms of composition, important posts were held by civil servants recruited and trained in Great Britain, while local officers carried out supportive and subordinate roles. This created a chasm within the Civil Service structure as it created difficulties for talented locals to join the bureaucracy even if they had sufficient qualifications. While concessions relating to the recruitment of local talents and the opportunities afforded to them were eventually made, this failed to address the discontentment on the ground.

The Japanese Occupation had an important effect on the Civil Service in Singapore. For the first time, local officers were assigned positions of significant responsibility as their British superiors or counterparts were either abroad or held as prisoners of war. Being able to cope with these responsibilities gave local civil servants confidence in their abilities, which accelerated the pace and increased the desire for political independence with the re-establishment of British political rule after August 1945. While a policy of 'localisation' was eventually adopted to promote local civil servants to positions of importance, their numbers were few, and with British bureaucrats leaving because they felt marginalised by this new policy, the Civil Service's efficiency and effectiveness were compromised.

The PAP and the Civil Service

The PAP's relationship with the Civil Service can be characterised as one preoccupied with political loyalty and competence. At the time of the PAP's assumption of political office in June 1959, the Civil Service was seen as a liability in the course of the

---

[5] Ibid, p. 89.

state's development,[6] given that local civil servants were ineffective, and had loyalties to parties other than the PAP government. As these factors hindered the implementation of government policies, the PAP government began 'politicising' the Civil Service,[7] a process which involved the PAP exercising control over the bureaucratic or administrative apparatuses in order to establish stability and legitimacy, sustain social penetration and promote economic development.[8]

In order to ensure the loyalty of the Civil Service to Singapore and the PAP's cause, civil servants were given the major duty of establishing the authority of the government and facilitating the delivery of goods and services required by the people. Various initiatives to change civil servants' mindsets were also undertaken as the PAP government felt that such a measure was necessary for its agendas and policies to be successfully implemented. As such, the Political Study Centre was established in 1959, offering courses and seminars for senior civil servants with the aim of reorienting their attitudes. Other reorientation measures included voluntary weekend participation in mass civic projects by government employees; recruitment of Chinese-educated graduates to reduce the pre-dominance of English-educated graduates in the public service; tougher disciplinary measures against civil servants found guilty of misbehaviour; and selective retention of competent senior officials due for retirement, together with premature retirement of incompetent senior officials.[9] By the mid 1960s onwards, the public service was much more responsive to the needs of the political leadership.

The issue of loyalty to the government remains pertinent today and can be seen in the way civil servants are rewarded and compensated quite generously to ensure employee satisfaction. Generally, the PAP government has sought to continually make conditions of employment and career advancement in the Civil Service as competitive, if not, better than those offered by the private sector. Other than the attractions of serving the 'public' and the enormous challenges of power and discretion, monetary rewards for all divisions have been improved, especially during the last few years. Other forms of compensation such as fringe benefits, ample scope for retraining and the availability of local and overseas scholarships, have made the Civil Service a

---

[6] Jon S. T. Quah, "Singapore Meritocratic City-State" in John Funston (ed.) *Government and Politics in Southeast Asia* (Singapore: Institute of Southeast Asian Studies, 2002) p. 303.
[7] Chan Heng Chee, "Politics in an Administrative State: Where has the Politics Gone?" in Seah Chee Meow (ed.) *Trends in Singapore* (Singapore: National University Press, 1975) p. 34.
[8] Ho Khai Leong, *The Politics of Policy-Making in Singapore* (Singapore: Oxford University Press, 2000) p. 143.
[9] Jon S. T. Quah, "The Public Bureaucracy in Singapore, 1959–1984", in You Poh Seng and Lim Chong Yah (eds.) *Singapore: Twenty-Five Years of Development* (Singapore: Nan Yang Xing Zhou Lianhe Zaobao, 1984) p. 291.

worthwhile place for lifelong employment.[10] To increase staff morale and show recognition of their work efforts, the government also gives financial assistance to ministries for staff welfare and related recreational events. These funds can be used for social events, training programmes or even as financial help for officers who are in serious need of monetary assistance.

The Civil Service being the administrative backbone of the government means that it plays a vital role in effectively carrying out government policies and programmes. As such, the government has continued to stress the importance of the public sector and civil service with Lee Kuan Yew once stating that it was desirable and necessary to retain at least a third of the best 'brains' in this sector.[11] Recruitment and promotion in the Civil Service are based on merit. To be eligible for appointment, a candidate must satisfy criteria pertaining to citizenship, age, education, experience, medical fitness and character.[12] In particular, academic qualifications play a key role in assessing the suitability of candidates. The quality of Singapore civil servants can also be seen in the way the Civil Service functions as a recruiting pool for the PAP, with 'high flying' civil servants regularly being invited to switch over to government positions and politics, as Members of Parliament (MPs) and Ministers in the government.

To ensure the resilience and strengthening of its political legitimacy, and for greater efficiency and public trust in the Civil Service and in turn the government, the PAP leadership saw it necessary to maintain a clean and upright Civil Service, free from abuse and corruption. As such, fighting corruption in the Civil Service has been a cornerstone of the PAP's approach to mold the public service. Upon assuming office in 1959, the PAP government strengthened existing anti-corruption laws and increased the severity of penalty for corruption offences. The powers of the Corrupt Practices Investigation Bureau (CPIB), established in 1952, were strengthened as it became directly responsible to the Prime Minister, enabling it to perform its duties more effectively, as it now had the authority and power of the Prime Minister behind it. The CPIB has been to date widely known as a success.[13] Not only has it help set the moral tone of the government, it has also helped create a corruption 'free' and

---

[10] Seah Chee Meow, "The Civil Service", p. 111.

[11] See National Day Speech by Prime Minister Lee Kuan Yew to local constituency leaders in August 1979. The importance of top administrators was reiterated by the Prime Minister in his address to university dons in May 1980 when he argued that they were more crucial and indispensable to the country's development.

[12] David C. E. Chew, "Economic Restructuring and Flexible Civil Service Pay in Singapore" in Christopher Colclough (ed.) *Public-Sector Pay and Adjustment: Lessons from Five Countries* (London: Routledge, 1997) p. 26.

[13] Patrick Meagher, "Anti-Corruption Agencies: Rhetoric versus Reality", *The Journal of Policy Reform*, Vol. 8 No. 1, p. 73.

clean administration. Its credibility is further strengthened by its investigation scope to include Ministers, MPs and even senior directors in government agencies and companies. However, it should be noted that the CPIB's image has compromised the transparency in which it operates as it still remains relatively secretive and there are no strong guidelines to make the CPIB accountable or open to the public. Still, the anti-corruption movement in Singapore is commendable and the Singapore model has also at times been seen as a role model for other countries in developing their Civil Service.

Grassroots Organisations

Role of Grassroots Organisations in Singapore

Grassroots organisations are primarily voluntary bodies that aim to implement government policies, canvass the ground and tune in to popular sentiments, organise activities or campaigns, and coordinate the mobilisation of citizens in times of crisis or emergency. These organisations are made up of ordinary citizens who are concerned with and motivated to take action about various social, political and economic issues. One would assume that as the number and presence of grassroots organisations grow, there would be more collective actions, dialogues and interactions between society and the leadership, and hence, rising democratisation in the state. This is based on the assumption that as community networks increase and bonds are formed, these would facilitate the development of shared values, attitudes, collective memories and more importantly, trust.[14] This, however, is not always the case as grassroots organisations are seldom politically neutral and can be leveraged by the political leadership to pursue specific agendas. In Singapore, grassroots organisations are closely linked with the government. Many of them have been created by government initiatives and are used to promote and spread the government's policies and values.

The major grassroots organisations in Singapore are as follows: Community Centres, Community Centres' Management Committees, Citizens' Consultative Committees, Residents' Committees, Neighbourhood Committees, Community Development Councils, Youth Executive Committees, Community Sports Clubs, Community Emergency and Engagement Committees, Women Executive Committees, Senior Citizens' Executive Committees, Indian Activities Executive Committees and Malay Activities Executive Committees. These bodies are administered by the People's Association, that is directly controlled by a government's minister.

---

[14] Kenneth Paul Andrew Sze-Sian Tan, "Democracy and the Grassroots Sector in Singapore", *Space & Polity*, Vol. 7 No. 1, p. 3.

People's Association

During the 1950s and early 1960s, Singapore went through a difficult and turbulent period of racial riots, rampant strikes and economic uncertainty. With so many racial groups and little interaction between them, Singapore was a relatively backward and divided society with closely-knit communal groups pulling in different directions. The PAP government realised that Singapore needed to overcome these basic problems to ensure its long-term political, economic and social survival. As such, the People's Association (PA) was formed on 1 July 1960 to help foster racial harmony and social cohesion. This was to be the bedrock of nation building.[15] The PA was also to coordinate activities among various local groups to enhance unity and understanding. Given its status as the body to which the other grassroots organisations report, it is arguably the most important organisation in the grassroots structure. In essence, the main areas of concern and interest to the PA are community action, promoting racial harmony as well as lifestyle and skills upgrading.

Racial harmony is a key concern for the PA. With its diverse ethnic make-up, the Singapore government is aware of the need to maintain racial harmony and mutual respect between the various ethnic and religious groups in Singapore. Therefore, the PA, together with its grassroots organisations, is charged with the responsibility of organising programmes to promote and enhance understanding, mutual respect, support and interaction between citizens of different backgrounds. Some of the initiatives and programmes developed include the Inter-Racial and Religious Confidence Circles (IRCCs), which consist of important leaders from different sectors of society and ethnic backgrounds. The IRCCs create a platform for discussing issues of concern to each ethnic community and help establish a bond that is fundamental in bringing different ethnic groups together, particularly in times of crisis.

One other key role of the PA is the coordination of other grassroots organisations. After the PAP became the government and formed the PA, the role of community centres became that of political mobilisation, communication and support. This was because in 1961, the PAP government faced challenges of economic instability, trade union strikes and intra-party strife, which made it even more conscious of the importance of the PA and the community centres. Having lost skilled organisers and party members to the pro-communist *Barisan Sosialis*, the PAP government felt extremely vulnerable, especially in rural constituencies where it did not have strong support or interaction with the masses. It was vital for the government to capture and ensure loyalty from these residents quickly in order to consolidate its political power and legitimacy. As such, community centres were constructed in rural areas to expand the PAP's reach and serve as a feedback unit from the masses to the government to allow

---

[15] People's Association website, www.pa.gov.sg/1153988278915/1153988278958.html, accessed 17 November 2006.

the latter to assess its level of support. On a secondary level, community centres also functioned to counter communist propaganda and act as a communication bridge or platform between the government and the citizens.

Today, community centres, some of which are now called Community Clubs to reflect their recreational focus and to attract the youth, continue to be a vital channel of political communication between the public and the political leadership. They also help promote racial harmony and social cohesion through various cultural, educational, recreational, sports, social and other community activities organised for residents.[16] Their importance in helping the government reach out to the public is evident from how they are utilised as polling centres during elections or as venues for mass public speaking events. With greater autonomy from the PA to run their own programmes or even specialise in certain areas, community centres are now more than equipped to cater to the needs and wants of Singapore citizens, indirectly garnering support, approval and legitimacy for the ruling government.

Significance of the Grassroots Organisations in Singapore

While grassroots organisations in Singapore consist primarily of volunteer members and organisers, their link to the PAP government is undeniable. Most of the time, the formation of new grassroots groups or committees is at the initiative of the PAP government. Although the reasons for this may be simply altruistic and truly for the benefit of the Singaporean society, the formation of grassroots organisations under the wing of the PAP government has also helped it maintain its political dominance and extend the party's ideological hegemony. Grassroots organisations allow this to happen by securing mass public and political support through the programmes and activities they organise. By offering a wide range of services and activities that satisfy citizens, grassroots organisations such as community centres and the various area/issue specific committees are able to indirectly project the PAP government's effectiveness and help mobilise political support and acknowledgement of the legitimacy of the ruling government. These organisations and associations also help inculcate the political ideas and values of the ruling government to the public through their various campaigns and programmes. They also give the PAP a permanent presence in the various constituencies while simultaneously providing visibility to PAP MPs and party workers.

Another significance of grassroots organisations is that by working closely with citizens at the ground, they are able to pick up real-time social and political trends more quickly. They also serve as feedback units who bring public expectations, complaints

---

[16] People's Association website, www.pa.gov.sg/1148093110402/1148970724032.html, accessed 20 November 2006.

and views about various issues and policies to the attention of the government. This allows the government to be sensitive about the sentiments of the public and leads citizens to perceive and believe that their views are being heard. In the past, especially at the height of the PAP's struggle with the Left, grassroots organisations also provided surveillance on residents and watched for any potential subversive or politically hostile acts. As such, they performed the role of 'eyes and ears', on the one hand, while winning the battle of 'hearts and minds', on the other.

Lastly, by ensuring that members of all ethnic and social groups are equally represented in grassroots organisations and by initiating ethnic self-help groups/associations, the government has been able to co-opt even traditional leaders who are usually more respected in their respective communities. This helps to perform two roles. First, these leaders allow the PAP to harness their mass mobilising skills against political opposition, and second, it is also a means of checking and preventing these leaders from becoming powerful, independent and alternative sources of political opposition.[17] Having traditional and ethnic leaders feel as though they are part of the government also allows them to be responsible for helping to maintain racial harmony, particularly during times of crisis.

For a small nation-state like Singapore, surprisingly, there are a large number of grassroots and para-political organisations. Although most are formed for altruistic purposes and as spaces of socio political interaction, their close association with the ruling PAP government can create doubts about their actual relevance and aims. For one, it is obvious that by initiating the formation of so many grassroots organisations under its wing, the ruling party seeks to expand its influence and control over the masses in Singapore and keep in check the growth and rise of any form of political opposition including the Opposition parties. However, the proliferation of grassroots organisations can aid the growth of democracy in a nation by providing platforms for citizens to speak out. For these organisations to remain relevant and credible in the long run, they and the ruling government in Singapore may need to re-examine their relationship and working order to pursue matters that are truly of concern to Singaporeans and the nation, and not give the impression that grassroots organisations are merely appendages and lifelines of the government. Also, the entire populace must be served by such organisations. Presently, the Community Centres are mainly located in large population centres such as in Housing and Development Board heartlands with most private residential estates devoid of their services. This can create a dangerous political divide in the coming years between the public and private housing estates. At the same time, the true effectiveness of these grassroots organisations needs to be reassessed in view of the massive resources that are injected into them at the taxpayers' expense. In the final analysis, politically, the grassroots organisations have

---

[17] Kenneth Paul Andrew Sze-Sian Tan, "Democracy and the Grassroots Sector in Singapore", p. 7.

become an important element of the Singapore's political landscape and their role must be taken into account to explain the power dynamics at work in the Republic at any one time.

Mass Media

The Mass Media in Singapore

Political socialisation in any society requires certain institutions or agents that propagate and cultivate the political attitudes, opinions and expectations of the individual. Amongst the more widely known agents of political socialisation such as the family, education, religion and government, the mass media has also made its impact as a powerful institution that is capable of shaping opinions and discourses. The mass media, as is argued by Andrew Heywood, comprises "societal institutions that are concerned with the production and distribution of all forms of knowledge, information and entertainment".[18] The element of 'mass' in the concept of mass media characterises the media's large and diverse audience as well as the general sophistication of the circulation of information in huge quantities often in the shortest period of time. Mass media ranges from the print media of daily broadsheets, commonly known as newspapers, and magazines to the broadcast media of radio and television. While the different medium of the transfer of information, either through reading via the print media or listening via the broadcast media, may target or bear influence on different strata of society, in general, all media operate within a model of political influence closely related to the system of governance and societal expectations.

The mass media is an important tool in governance due to its ability to reach a wide audience. Those that are in control of the media therefore are able to communicate and direct public attention to their choice of issues. The mass media is inadvertently a dual-edge sword in governance when appropriated for positive measures, *pro bono publico*, for the good of the public, it can help improve governance and move society towards a mature political citizenry that cultivates responsible political attitudes. When used inappropriately, such as in the employment of dictatorial regimes, its usefulness to governance is merely to serve as the dictatorship's propagandist machine. Not only is the exchange of ideas curtailed, the mass media becomes a tool of hegemonic dominance to capture and sustain control over societies. The mass media's powerful potential in advocating good governance as well as its duality in the ability to divide and dominate society, grants the mass media a deserving spot in any serious study of politics, government and governance.

---

[18] Andrew Heywood, *Politics* (London: Macmillan, 1997) p. 188.

Presently, the mass media in Singapore does not wield strong influence in the political socialisation of Singaporeans due to the various forms of control over domestic, foreign, and cyber media that the PAP government has exercised. Mainly through legal apparatuses, the government has bound the media by restrictive laws that limit its ability to act as 'invigilator', 'adversary', and 'inquisitor' of the administration. Upon coming to power in 1959, the PAP was quick to control the media by enacting a series of laws and structural changes such as the requirement of annual permits from the government to the establishment of a government ministry to oversee the media. The government's displeasure towards critical and investigative journalism was evidenced in how during the 1960s and 1970s, journalists were detained under the Internal Security Act during *Operation Coldstore*, and several English publications like the *Eastern Sun* and the *Singapore Herald* were banned by the PAP government on grounds of being infiltrated by the Left. By 1974, the Newspaper and Printing Presses Act (NPPA) was amended to allow the government to own newspapers, the result being that press organisations were forced into becoming public organisations so that their operations became transparent and easier to be regulated by the state. Since 1984, the government-controlled Singapore Press Holdings (SPH) has owned all major domestic press organisations and given its complete monopoly of the domestic press. Tight reins are kept on the media entity with its top management being individuals close to the ruling party and appointed by the government.

Similarly, the international media in Singapore has not been free of government control either. Since the 1970s, the PAP government has had several disputes with international publishing houses which have circulations in Singapore. The Singapore government is somewhat allergic towards a liberal media and frowns upon foreign publications which it deems to be intruding into the political space of Singapore. At first, the government strategy was to exert pressure on foreign editors and journalists to limit their critical and investigative journalism on Singapore politics. In the 1980s, this strategy changed from merely exerting pressure to the use of legal and financial penalties against errant foreign publications. The PAP government was displeased with the foreign media's coverage of the domestic political opposition, in particular, after the PAP's suffered a dent in electoral support in the 1984 General Elections. In 1986, the NPPA was further amended to enable the government to have control over the local circulation of newspapers published outside of Singapore. Under this amendment, foreign publications that were considered to be engaged and interfering in the domestic politics of Singapore, a judgment that was left to the full discretion of the then Minister of Culture, would have their circulation restricted. Under the new amendment to the NPPA, *Time* was the first foreign publication to come under fire from the Singapore government. An article on long-time Singapore Opposition leader J. B. Jeyaretnam titled 'Silencing the Dissenters' published in *Time* in October 1986 drew anger from the PAP government. When *Time* refused to print a letter by

James Fu, the Press Secretary to the then Prime Minister Lee, in response to the article, the government slashed *Time*'s circulation which was then at 18,000 copies per week to 9,000 copies by the end of October 1986 and by January 1987, *Time*'s circulation in Singapore was reduced to 2,000 copies per week.[19]

The PAP and the Mass Media

The PAP's position on the conduct of media and the resultant legislations, limitations and harsh reprisals against the mass media (especially the owners and managers) in general can be traced to the PAP's leadership and its perception of the functions and role opened to media in Singapore. In a speech to the International Press Institute in 1971, Lee explained the PAP's caution towards the media, especially when it could be easily manipulated to harm Singapore's stability and development:

> My colleagues and I have the responsibility to neutralise their intentions. In such a situation, freedom of the press, freedom of the news media, must be subordinated to the overriding needs of the integrity of Singapore, and to the primary purpose of an elected government. The government has taken, and will from time to time have to take, firm measures to ensure that, despite divisive forces of different cultural values and lifestyles, there is enough unity of purpose to carry the people of Singapore forward to higher standards of life, without which the mass media cannot thrive.[20]

It is clear that Lee viewed the media as an important tool of governance. Given its ease of being manipulated and the impact it has on society, the media must be harnessed for good governance, which in this case, means the PAP's worldview of governance must be supported, not opposed. As was argued by Lee , "the mass media can help to present Singapore's problems simply and clearly, and then explain how if they support certain programmes and policies, these problems can be solved. More important, we want the mass media to reinforce, not undermine, the cultural values and social attitudes being inculcated in our schools and universities".[21]

It can be concluded that Lee did not view the media as being an important platform for the free exchange of views, but instead argued that the media play second fiddle to the government and cautioned the mass media on the firm measures that the

---

[19] Garry Rodan, *Transparency and Authoritarian Rule in Southeast Asia: Singapore and Malaysia* (London: Routledge Curzon, 2004) p. 28.

[20] Speech by Lee Kuan Yew to the International Press Institute, 9 June 1971. The full text can be found in Han, Fook Kwang, Warren Fernandez and Sumiko Tan (eds.), *Lee Kuan Yew and His Ideas*, pp. 425–430.

[21] Cited in Eddie C. Y. Kuo and Peter S. J. Chen, *Communication Policy and Planning in Singapore* (London: Kegan Paul International in association with East-West Centre Communication Institute, Honolulu, 1983) p. 43.

PAP was willing to take against them if they stepped out of line. Hence, Lee once argued, "one value which does not fit Singapore is the theory that the press is the Fourth Estate. And in Singapore's experience, because of our volatile racial and religious mix, the American concept of the 'marketplace of ideas', instead of producing harmonious enlightenment has, from time to time, led to riots and bloodshed".[22] The PAP has also identified the primary motivation of the media as being profit-seeking and hence, the incentive for the media's submission would be the huge consumer market that would be opened to it if it plays by the 'rules'.

The PAP's tight control over the mass media is interesting because it stands at odds against its desire to transform Singapore into an international media hub. Despite economic liberalisation and the desire to join the forces of globalisation, Singapore is still reluctant to allow market forces to dictate the mass media scene. The draconian measures that have regulated the mass media in Singapore has earned it the wrath of international journalist associations such as *Reporters Without Borders* who have consistently ranked Singapore's media at the bottom end of their worldwide Press Freedom Index. In the 2016 Press Freedom Index, Singapore earned 154th place out of 180 countries ranked, a 14-place drop since its 2005 ranking. Former Chief Minister, David Marshall, had also been a critic of the Singapore media scene, arguing in 1994 that "journalists (in Singapore) were pathetic and were only concerned with their own survival". He described the Singapore media as a 'running dog' of the government. He blamed the government for the 'suffocation of dissent' and the 'stranglehold on the press'. It was in this context that he argued that "the mass media is a poor prostitute of the Government".[23] Marshall's criticism of the press called into question the role of journalists in Singapore and whether they had the freedom to report as professionals and personal integrity. The issue of the media's biased reporting in favour of the government was taken up by none other than the long-serving editor of *The Straits Times*, Leslie Fong. According to him:

> Where the issue in question is one over which the government has taken a determined stand, there is no doubt whose view will prevail. Should any journalist feel that he cannot accept such an outcome, then resignation is the only honourable course open to him. This is just one of the harsh realities which the press here faces.[24]

---

[22] Cited in Achal Mehra (ed.), *Press Systems in ASEAN States* (Singapore: Asian Mass Communication Research and Information Centre, 1989) p. 120.

[23] 'David Marshall: Praise as Well as Criticise Govt', *The Straits Times*, 18 January 1994; Chee Soon Juan, *Dare to Change: An Alternative Vision for Singapore* (Singapore: The Singapore Democratic Party, 1994) p. 109.

[24] See Cherian George, 'Freedom from the Press: Why the Media Are the Way They Are', see cherian.blogspot.com/, 25 October 2001.

In conclusion, the traditional mass media in Singapore, both the domestic and international media, do not enjoy the privilege and right to play the role as the 'fourth estate' of the state. The media's role according to the PAP is limited to supporting government policies aimed at creating a stable and growth-oriented society. The validity of the PAP's tough stance on the need to regulate the media stems from Singapore's turbulent history and the persistence of ethnic and religious conflicts in Singapore and its immediate neighbourhood. With the world constantly evolving and the corridors of cyberspace widening, the traditional regulatory powers of the state have been somewhat clipped and the government's measures, though still highly effective, may face new challenges from the onslaught of new media and citizen journalism. Clearly, the new and social media have brought new challenges in the way the Singapore government manages and controls the media, which may not be that amenable to control as has been the traditional printed media.

Trade Unions

The role of trade unions in Singapore may seem contradictory and out of place given that the political system is similar to that of an illiberal democracy. However, trade unions have an important role in the progress of Singapore's economy, and through revamps and constant improvements, remain relevant as an integral part of the Singaporean economy and society. A trade union is an association of wage earners who band together for collective bargaining to improve their wages and working conditions through negotiations with their employers and, at times, with the government. In Singapore, trade unions are legal entities but they are strictly governed by the Trade Unions Act, and registration is compulsory. The government also retains the power to de-register a trade union if the latter is found to be conducting activities other than those stated in its constitution. The largest trade union in Singapore is actually a body of various trade unions. The National Trades Union Congress (NTUC) is a national body with more than 60 registered trade unions and a membership of more than 900,000. Although there are a few independent trade unions in Singapore, they are not significant, and thus the role of coordinating organised labour falls on the NTUC.

There is a close relationship between the government and the NTUC due to both historical origins as well as functional purposes. There have been a number of union leaders who are simultaneously PAP members, and this dual membership has led to active union involvement in Singapore politics and vice versa. This participation by the government also allows it to retain some form of control or supervision over the activities of the trade unions and to prevent any possibility of social and labour unrest. The system of tripartism characterises the relationship between government and trade unions in Singapore, and it has proven to be effective. It is a three-way relationship between the government, employers' organisations and trade unions, devised and promoted to improve the channels and effectiveness of consultations between parties, and to raise national productivity. The current state of trade unionism in Singapore is largely a function of its historical past, especially in the 1950s and 1960s.

Origins and Development of Trade Unions in Singapore

When the Japanese surrendered to the Allies on 15 August 1945, the British reoccupied Malaya and established the British Military Administration a month later. Although the people of Malaya had expected growth and stability with the return of the British, they were disappointed at the slow progress of economic reforms and the authoritarian manner in which the British governed them. More unsettling was the presence of widespread corruption, unemployment, food shortage and inflation, which left the people disillusioned with the British administration. As a result, the widespread dissent prompted the Malayan Communist Party (MCP), which had spearheaded and organised labour movements during the Japanese Occupation, to try and form a Malayan Peoples' Republic controlled by the MCP with the long-term target of workers' solidarity and awareness. Efforts at local democratic government by the Communists were curtailed by the British who refused to cede power, which led to the first post-war strike on 21 October 1945, with 7,000 dock workers at Tanjong Pagar walking out on their jobs to protest against low wages and the shipping of arms to Java.[25] This sparked a series of labour strikes and demands from, amongst others, the Singapore Transport Company and the Singapore General Labour Union (SGLU), asking for better wages, social insurance and working conditions improvement across the board.

In an effort to regulate union activity and promote pro-British unions, the Trade Union Ordinance was made operative in May 1946, and all trade unions were asked to register by 23 August 1946. However, the initial response from the unions was not very positive.[26] The SGLU did register in 1947, but under the name of Singapore Federation of Trade Unions (SFTU). Additionally, the Trade Union Ordinance guaranteed at least three years of employment for all union affiliates in the industry in which the union functioned, which addressed the workers' worry of employment security and thus reduced the possibility of trade unions being exploited by other parties for political purposes. Regardless, strikes continued from 1945 to 1948, resulting in widespread acts of violence. Ultimately, this culminated in a State of Emergency

---

[25] Charles Gamba, *The Origins of Trade Unionism in Malaya* (Singapore: Eastern Universities Press Ltd., 1962) p. 62.

[26] Lim-Ng Been Eng, *Chronology of Trade Union Development in Singapore, 1940–1984* (Singapore: NTUC, 1985) p. 2.

being declared in June 1948, with both the MCP and the SFTU being declared illegal, forcing Communist trade unionists into hiding and losing them much of their popular support.

The State of Emergency and the inability of the trade unions to satisfy workers' needs made many disillusioned with the unions. At the same time, new legislations by the British administration made it increasingly difficult for trade unions to function without restraint. The workers realised that resorting to violence and militancy would not be the best way to secure their employment and welfare, and they began to look at alternative methods of airing their concerns. Although the trade union movement lost momentum in the late 1940s, the British administration believed in the necessity of forming a political and responsible trade union. The Singapore Trades Union Congress (STUC) was thus set up in 1951 with full support of the British, but this was not very successful due to limited representation.[27]

PAP and the National Trades Union Congress: Beginnings of a Political Union

After the PAP formed the government in 1959, the issue of merger with Malaya led to a split within the PAP, resulting in two separate groups consisting of the Left and the PAP moderates. As a consequence, the STUC also split into two camps: the Singapore Association of Trade Unions (SATU) under the Left with leaders such as Lim Chin Siong controlling it, and the NTUC led by PAP members such as Devan Nair.[28] When the PAP sealed its victory with a strong margin at the 1963 Legislative Assembly elections, it heralded the beginning of a new trade unions body in Singapore, with the rise of the NTUC alongside the PAP. Between 1961 and 1965, the PAP and the NTUC won the support of the people, and from then on, the NTUC has represented almost all trade unions in Singapore.

Independence and the New Labour Movement

Singapore's separation from Malaysia and its new-found independence in 1965 forced the PAP to adopt a new industrial policy based on exports promotion. With Singapore being a new, small, independent nation with limited resources and the impending pullout of British troops (first scheduled for in 1968 but later postponed to 1971), the PAP and the NTUC were faced with the intense challenge of ensuring Singapore's

---

[27] Pang Eng Fong and Tan Chwee Huat, "Trade Unions and Industrial Relations" in Peter Chen (ed.) *Singapore Development Policies and Trends* (Singapore: Oxford University Press, 1983) pp. 53–91.

[28] Devan Nair, "Organised Labour in Singapore — Past, Present and Future", *Productivity*, October-November 1973.

survival economically, militarily and politically. To deal with the problem of unemployment, the government focused on an export-oriented policy and created a new emphasis on attracting foreign investments. To achieve this, the PAP and the NTUC aimed to make production costs attractive and create a smooth operational environment for foreign investments. As such, two labour legislations were introduced in 1968 that reduced production costs, and gave employers greater independence and discretion, thus facilitating a more efficient work system, which would be seen as an advantage to employers.

While these pro-employer legislations diluted the NTUC's powers, the NTUC supported them as they realised their importance of attracting foreign investments to stimulate full employment in Singapore. This compelled the NTUC to look at other areas to safeguard workers' interests and welfare. The NTUC expanded its role to become a nation building institution, starting with a trade union seminar in November 1969 on 'Modernisation of the Labour Movement' aimed at restructuring and revamping the trade union organisation to help it stay relevant in the modern economy. Under this scheme, trade unions were now concerned and involved with the overall planning and development of Singapore's economy, particularly in the areas of productivity and economic growth. Workers' cooperatives were also set up to improve the social and economic well-being of its workers by providing affordable services and necessities.

PAP–NTUC–Employers' Associations: Tripartitism in Singapore

While Singapore proved quite successful at attracting foreign investments, this led to a labour shortage by the early 1970s. Still, the PAP government was mindful not to allow this excess demand of labour to dictate an unrestrained rise in wages in case it caused a backlash in economic and industrial growth. Thus, rather than allowing wages to rise substantially, the government made efforts to increase the labour supply, by expanding the workforce base to attract more female workers and by admitting foreign workers into certain designated industries. These measures were, however, insufficient to address the shortage of labour, and growing fears that the shortage of workers might lead to a wage explosion and affect the competitiveness of Singapore's economy. To address this problem, the National Wages Council (NWC) was set up in February 1972, which aimed to allow wages to rise in a systematic manner, in line with productivity growth so as not to compromise Singapore's competitiveness. The NWC was founded on a principle of greater representation and participation from all parties involved in the areas of labour and wage determination, and thus has a tripartite structure, consisting of representatives from organised labour unions or organisations, employers' associations as well as the government.

Conclusion

The functions of para-political organisations as laid out over the course of this chapter can be summed up as follows: (i) helping to secure mass political support for the PAP (to the detriment of the Opposition); (ii) co-opting traditional leaders in the business, racial, and religious spheres; (iii) co-opting women and youth; (iv) surveillance and control; (v) as a mouthpiece for government policies and principles; (vi) as a feedback channel; (vii) for manpower, logistical, organisation, and informational support; (viii) allowing PAP MPs to serve as local-constituency administrators; and (ix) as a pool for recruiting potential political leaders. Most important of all, the para-political organisations provide a useful two-way bridge between the government and the governed, partly explaining the longevity of PAP's rule in Singapore as it has the advantage of access and control of organisations that have sunk deep roots into society as a whole for more than 50 years.

Given the many functions that para-political organisations have, it is clear that the PAP's control over such organisations has been crucial to its dominance of Singapore politics. Additionally, it is important to note that while using para-political organisations for political advantage, the same organisations function to the Opposition's disadvantage. Unable to use para-political organisations in the same way as the PAP, the Opposition has been deprived of the organisation, communication, and mobilisation resources that para-political organisations offer, inflicting a huge blow, given how deeply such organisations penetrate into a Singaporean's daily life.

Think Questions

1. What political role do para-political organisations perform in Singapore?
2. Are para-political organisations a liability for the government?
3. Are the manner para-political organisations operate in Singapore likely to change in the coming years?

Chapter Six

Nation Building and National Identity

> We are a nation in the making. Will we make it? ... If you believe it's a reality, then I think you're making a mistake. It's an aspiration, it's something we must make into reality probably in another 20, 30, 40, 50 years.[1]

Introduction

Nation building is of great importance to a small state like Singapore. Its short history has been coloured by episodes of racial tensions and social unrest. These were brought about by the struggles against Communism, communalists and labour unrests as well as economic recession. To ensure national harmony, it has been vital to build a nation and promote a modicum of a national identity amongst its diverse people so that the society remains united in times of crisis. As Singapore is not an ethnically homogenous state, the government has adopted a multi-pronged approach through a concept of 'Singaporean Singapore'. This is to ensure that through national policies of social equality and mobility based on meritocracy, a sense of nationalism and national belonging can be imbued in its people, enrooting the people to the state. The government has experimented with various approaches to construct the 'imagined community' called a Singapore Nation.

Multiculturalism

Multiculturalism and multiracialism are key pillars of the Singaporean society and have been adopted as the basic philosophy governing its management. This philosophy is one of the fundamental rules of engagement in the Republic. In Singapore, the principle of multiculturalism revolves around the idea of giving equal status to all

---

[1] Lee Kuan Yew, "Singapore 'Not Yet a Nation': MM Lee", 21 January 2011. See http://sgforums.com/forums/3317/topics/420968.

ethnic and racial groups regardless of race, creed or size. Each race is separate but equal. The need to maintain racial harmony among the various races and cultures is crucial for peace and development. This is because Singapore's society is fundamentally diverse and pluralistic, resembling a 'salad bowl', where many different cultures despite being tossed together, still retain their individual identities, while contributing to one distinctive main culture.[2] The *'Singapore Rojak'*, be it Chinese, Indian or Malay, is a useful metaphor that conveys the essence of what drives Singapore's politics and essentially, what characterises its political culture.

The policy of multiculturalism continues to be emphasised by the government to ensure stable intra-societal relations. Through various policies and deliberations, it aims to cultivate a sense of national identity. This is to ensure that regardless of race or religion, Singaporeans will be rooted to the country with a strong sense of loyalty. This has become all the more challenging as the forces of globalisation have exposed Singaporeans to a vast array of competing cultures, values and lifestyles, many of which have diluted the sense of belonging to Singapore and what it stands for.

Singapore is composed of four primary races: Chinese (74.3%), Malays (13.3%), Indians (9.1%), and other Ethnicities (3.3%). Within these major racial groups, there are further differences based on dialects and languages. All these contribute to make Singapore's society extremely diverse but with distinct fault lines. To promote racial harmony and integration within society while allowing each race or ethnic group to retain and promote its unique characteristics and values, a two-pronged policy is pursued by the government. This entails the promotion of self-help and leadership by the communities, on the one hand, and policies that emphasise meritocracy and equality for all races, on the other.

Malays

The Malays in Singapore have been pro-active in forming organisations to further the community's interest. Presently, there are about 200 Malay/Muslim organisations involved in a range of issues from education, job opportunities, cultural preservation and interaction with other racial communities. At the forefront of these organisations is Mendaki which was established in 1981, with the primary goal of providing education and scholarship recognition to local Malays. The *Yayasan Mendaki*, an off-shoot of Mendaki, was subsequently formed to focus on education and social development of the Malay community.[3]

---

[2] John Clammer, *Race and State in Independent Singapore, 1965–1990: The Cultural Politics of Pluralism in a Multiethnic Society* (Ashgate, 1998) pp. 71–87.
[3] Mendaki website, http://www.mendaki.org.sg/index.jsp, accessed 20 October 2006.

Mendaki has been prominent in leading the Malay community by developing programmes like the 'Community Intranet' to impart and teach knowledge and skills to better prepare its community for challenges in the 21st century. It also collaborates with other Malay organisations in Singapore such as *Jamiyah Singapura* or Singapore Muslim Missionary Society, *Majelis Ugama Islam Singapura* (MUIS) or the Islamic Religious Council of Singapore, *Persatuan Ulama dan Guru-Guru Agama Islam Singapura* (PERGAS) or Singapore Islamic Scholars and Religious Teachers Association, the *Muhammadiyah* Association of Singapore and PERDAUS, a Muslim voluntary organisation, to address issues like social welfare and personal career development, and actively sources for opportunities to work with governmental institutions like the Singapore International Foundation, the National Youth Council and the People's Association to promote the community's interests. There are other active organisations within the community that were formed by individuals and groups to promote different aims and interests. The Association of Muslim Professionals (AMP), for example, consists largely of educated professionals, business leaders and executives to provide a bigger voice for the Malay community in the society with an emphasis on building network support for families.[4]

Chinese

The Chinese community is the largest racial group in Singapore. It is a diverse and complex community, consisting of different dialect groups like the Hokkiens, Teochews, Cantonese, Hakkas and Hainanese, all of whom speak different languages. The Chinese in Singapore have always had a tradition of entrepreneurship and self-reliance, and today, they dominate almost every aspects of society. The Chinese dominance has, however, not created tensions with other ethnic groups and a high degree of inter-racial harmony exists in the Republic.

The Chinese also have strong institutions and community groups that seek to promote their interests and goals. Amongst the most important is the Singapore Chinese Chamber of Commerce (SCCC), officially established in 1906, which is the largest business organisation in Singapore. It remains a key institution to promote economic, cultural and community activities to meet business needs as well as contributing to the preservation of Chinese cultural values and traditions in Singapore. The SCCC has strong ties with relevant economic groups in China and constantly develops business and language workshops to allow the local Chinese business community to better grasp and enter the vast international Chinese market.

---

[4] Association of Malay Professionals (AMP) website, http://www.amp.org.sg/wd/web/cms/main.asp?voteErr=&vtype=&topic=Intro&aid=ART00031-2004&pn=1, accessed 20 October 2006.

The various dialect groups have their own clan associations by which they preserve and pass on their distinct dialect cultures, while maintaining an overall Singaporean Chinese identity. These clans are firstly concerned with the welfare of their own dialect groups, and often come up with education bursaries, scholarships, private welfare assistance and career advice workshops to ensure that their communities' interests are being looked after. This is not to say that each clan is exclusive and not concerned about the greater good of the larger Chinese community in Singapore. These clans and associations often work together to promote Chinese interests. The Chinese Development Assistance Council (CDAC) is a joint project between the Singapore Federation of Chinese Clans Association (SFCCA) and the SCCC, and this reaches out to all Chinese, regardless of dialect group and clan association, to provide assistance towards educational opportunities, like tuition and study loans as well as skills training.[5]

Indians

The Indians are the third largest racial community in Singapore. Just like the Chinese, they are extremely diverse in terms of language, culture and religion. This is perhaps a result of different origins and even historical legacy, when the southern Indians, most of whom were Tamils, first arrived in Singapore during the British colonialism. Besides Tamils, there are also other Indians from other parts of India such as West Bengal, Gujarat and Punjab. The differences in regions have led to different Indian languages being spoken by the Indian community in Singapore, although Tamil is one of the four official languages in Singapore (together with Mandarin, English and Malay). Religion also plays an important role in Indian culture, and here too, religious variation is prominent, with affiliations ranging from Buddhism, Hinduism, Islam, Christianity and Sikhism.

The Indian community has also formed societies and self-help groups to address educational and socio-economic issues facing the Indian community in Singapore. One of its greatest successes has been in the field of education, where the overall academic performance is improving and the number of Indian students being admitted to universities is also consistently increasing. These achievements have largely been credited to the efforts and initiatives of the Singapore Indian Development Association (SINDA), which was formed in 1991 to strengthen the Indian community in Singapore through a self-help approach.[6] It also acts as a core to bring together Indians of different backgrounds and regions to find common ground, unite and co-exist harmoniously even though different Indian groups have also their own self-help groups.

---

[5] Chinese Development Assistance Council website, http://www.cdac.org.sg/eng/about_us/about_us.htm, accessed 21 October 2006.

[6] Singapore Indian Development Association website, http://www.sinda.org.sg/about.htm, accessed 21 October 2006.

Eurasians

Eurasians do not belong to a particular race, but rather a community made up of other different Asian and Caucasian races. The Eurasian community, while significantly smaller than the other major racial groups, has strong roots and history in Singapore. They used to be not as prominent as compared to the other racial groups in taking part in community projects, but they are a united community and the Eurasian Association has also stepped up efforts to cooperate and jointly organise social events and development programmes with other self-help groups and associations such as CDAC, Mendaki and AMP.[7]

Guarded Assimilation

The very fact that Singapore is a mixed pot of racial identities and ethnic beliefs means there is a very real threat that Singapore could be divided by ethnic, racial and religious fault lines. The greater danger, however, is to the formation of a strong national identity, which is vital for a small nation like Singapore for unity and long-term survival. The formation of a national identity hinges importantly, among other factors, on how the various races reconcile the relationship between ethnicity and nation. It is perhaps unrealistic to assimilate the different racial and religious groups into one new national identity, as it might provoke serious resentment from the various communities should the government try to do so. As such, the government treads a careful line in 'intervening' or getting involved in the various racial communities' issues, preferring to adopt a coordinator and/or mediator role to ensure racial harmony in society, while leaving each community to develop and function almost independently. One of the ways in which the government guides or ensures stability and cordiality between the different races is through its policy of meritocracy and equal opportunity.

Meritocracy and Equal Opportunity

Meritocracy is a key underlying principle of government policies and directives in Singapore. It is in essence a system of social justice which rewards individuals according to their achievements and efforts. Meritocracy and the concept of equal opportunity are vital for a nation as diverse and multicultural as Singapore. Such a system of rewards, benefits and opportunities based on one's efforts and achievements, regardless of race or religion, is crucial in maintaining social stability and harmony among

---

[7] Alexius A. Periara, "No Longer 'Other': The Emergence of the Eurasian Community in Singapore" in Lian Kwee Fee (ed.) *Race, Ethnicity and the State in Malaysia and Singapore* (London: Brill, 1996) pp. 5–32.

the various ethnic and racial groups as it minimises any accusations that one is being treated unfairly or marginalised due to their ethnic, cultural or religious affiliations. Another advantage of meritocracy is that it can minimise corruption and charges of nepotism, since one rises through the ranks, not by personal connections and nepotism but based on one's ability and how much one contributes.

Such a system is also useful in motivating Singapore citizens to be hardworking, efficient and self-reliant since advancement and survival are dependent on how well one progresses and succeeds. While the government ensures that all citizens have the same opportunities to realise their full potential, it does not guarantee that they will all finish at the same place together. This spurs individuals to maximise their potential and this policy of meritocracy can be credited for being partially responsible for Singapore's growth and accelerated progress.

There is, however, a flipside to the idea and principle of meritocracy that can create discontentment and unhappiness amongst some groups in society. This has to do with the prevailing definition and view of what meritocracy is, that is, one that is too steeply couched in academic and economic terms. This definition places priority on the academically bright and can marginalise those that are not academically inclined. The Singapore government has identified this problem and has sought to broaden the narrow definition of meritocracy and success to allow lesser achievers in the academic and material fields to attain success in their respective fields, whereby success should be broadly defined in terms of excellence which is specific to the job.

There have also been suggestions and reforms proposed to consider non-academic measures such as leadership qualities, community spirit and social skills to be included in the list of criteria in selecting scholars and people for key appointments in the government to combat the notion that the Singapore public sector is an elitist and exclusive group. This would set an example for the private sector to follow and create a healthier environment whereby the community will recognise individual excellence that is multi-dimensional and encourage individuals to pursue areas such as sports and the arts. This improvement for broader inclusion will allow citizens to feel more assured of their individual well-being and not feel left out by certain governmental policies. This will lead to greater involvement and participation in society and contribute to a united front for progress and success of the nation.

Education

The historical, social, political and economic imperatives of Singapore to a large extent shape the emphasis and objectives of education in Singapore.[8] The political

---

[8] Sng Bee Bee, "A Critical Discourse Analysis of the Mission Statement of Education in Singapore", *AARE 2001 Conference*, Nanyang Technological University, Singapore, 2–6 December 2001.

consciousness of Singapore is very much determined by threats to social and racial stability of the country as experienced through the threat of Communism, ethnic tensions, the process of merger and separation, and ultimately, independence. This gave rise to a sense of crisis and insecurity that marked the nation's birth and led to an overriding concern on the government's part to maintain racial harmony in the state.

The government is therefore constantly examining possible threats to this ethnic harmony, and this has led to the formation of one of two important objectives in education, that of shaping an identity in the people, an identity that is marked by a cultural distinctiveness, as well as nationalistic values. The government would like the people to preserve their cultural values, and at the same time, put the community before the individual. The second and equally important objective is that of economic reconstruction, which is seen as a way of solving the political problems that resulted from a poor economy.

Education is viewed pragmatically in Singapore. The investment in education must have certain payoffs in the economy and society. Education allows a workforce to be trained and have its skills upgraded for economic continuity, growth and social stability. During the 1960s and 1970s, the focus was on vocational education to meet the needs of a newly industrial economy. This focus became inadequate as global markets opened up and competition began to increase. With the growth of information based industries, Singaporeans needed to specialise in terms of work skills and capabilities, and hence, the re-direction to focus on sciences, mathematics, information technology and more recently, the bio-sciences, to better equip students and citizens to compete in an increasingly tough international market marked by rapid industrial changes and directions. Meritocracy acts as the basis of the education system in Singapore, where there is a heavy emphasis on assessment and grades to allow people from all classes of society, the opportunity to climb up the social and professional ladder.

Language as the key medium of education also plays a significant role in identity and nation building. The 'Speak Mandarin' Campaign was first mooted in 1979 to promote cohesion and unity among the many Chinese dialect groups in Singapore. This was extended to the school curriculum with the introduction of Higher Chinese to promote and teach advanced Chinese language skills to those assessed to be qualified and capable. This, however, was further expanded to allow other racial ethnic groups to pursue further studies of their Mother Tongues like Malay and Tamil to prevent allegations that the Chinese were being prioritised and the others marginalised. English remains the common language of communication as it is shared and used by other racial groups. This simultaneous presence of a common language and the freedom to pursue and promote each race's Mother Tongue allows for the fostering of a common identity, while maintaining individual cultural and language distinctions.

National Education

The other purpose of education is to mould students "into good citizens, conscious of their responsibilities to family, society and country". Early on, the government implemented policies for inculcating values in schools and the economic imperative of education. With a large population of Chinese, it seemed that Confucianism provided a suitable ideological framework for education in Singapore with its emphasis on social discipline. This led to the introduction of religious studies in schools which in 1990 was abandoned when it was found to lead to divisions in religion and ethnic identity. This was replaced by the study of core values of the nation, known as 'Shared Values'. These values consist of placing the nation before the community and self; seeing the family as a basic unit of society; giving of community support and regard for the individual; consensus, instead of conflict, as a way of making decisions; and racial and religious harmony.

National Education took on a renewed emphasis and direction after the then Prime Minister Goh Chok Tong announced at a Teachers' Day Rally in 1996 a major initiative to strengthen National Education in the Singapore education system.[9] A National Education Committee (NEC) comprising of representatives from the Ministry of Education, Ministry of Defence and other agencies with the interest and resources to facilitate the National Education effort in schools was set up. The Committee commissioned a total of 13 teams to look into strategies and measures for the implementation of the National Education programme in schools and tertiary institutions.

The approach taken by the NEC is a two-pronged strategy, targeted both students and educators at all levels in the cultivation and promotion of national instincts. The two aims are to develop an awareness of facts, circumstances and opportunities facing Singapore, so that they will be able to make decisions for their future with conviction and realism; and second, to develop a sense of emotional belonging and commitment to the community and nation so that they will stay and fight when the odds are against them.

National Education is not taught as a subject in school, but rather, it is infused into the curriculum through subjects like Social Studies, History, Civics and Morals, and Geography to impart knowledge and shed relevance of certain national issues. Students are taught the significance of historical events, Singapore's vulnerabilities, the diverse multiracial society, and the importance of staying united and harmonious. The values of multiculturalism are built into the education curriculum to ensure that the right social values, as deemed by the government, are inculcated into the students

---

[9] Prime Minister Goh Chok Tong Speech, http://www.moe.gov.sg/corporate/contactonline/pre-2005/rally/speech.html#National%20Education, accessed on 15 October 2016.

from the start. This teaches students to put community and nation before oneself, and contributes to the forging of a common national identity within the minds of the students.

Another core initiative of National Education is the organisation of designated activities in schools to foster camaraderie and bonding among pupils of different races and academic abilities and to develop a sense of belonging to the community. The NEC came up with certain community programmes that schools were expected to get involved in. This includes commemorating important historical events such as Total Defence Day, International Friendship Day and Racial Harmony Day. This is in the hope that these will help foster a sense of commitment and responsibility to the nation and society.

Housing

Housing is an effective way by which the ruling elites gain support and loyalty of the electorate to both the party and government.[10] The government believes in the importance of adequate housing for the masses and that whenever possible, it should be the duty of the government to provide affordable housing for the population. The rationale behind this is simple. Having one's own home, however, modest, would give him/her a high level of satisfaction and a stake in the nation, as well as help foster feelings of being committed and loyal to Singapore. To this day, this subject is still given significant priority, especially during elections where citizens express concerns or satisfaction at the government's housing policy.

Housing is a source of security and of great importance to most Singaporeans. While most Singaporeans are living in relatively comfortable housing, this was not always the case, especially during the early days of limited self-government under British rule. Back then, the majority of the population was living in dilapidated pre-war housing in the central city areas while many others lived in shanty huts in congested squatter areas. There was no adequate building industry or sufficient financial resources until the PAP government established the Housing and Development Board (HDB) on 1 February 1960 with the initial aim of redeveloping the slums and building proper public housing for Singaporeans at low and affordable prices.

To facilitate and ease the financial burden when it came to home ownership, HDB came up with a number of schemes and policies to assist Singaporeans. The first of these schemes was the Home Ownership for the People Scheme in 1964 which made it legal for eligible Singaporeans to own property as a form of financial security and to allow them to possess an asset in their country. Subsequently in 1968, the government

---

[10] Michael Hill and Lian Kwen Fee, *The Politics of Nation Building and Citizenship in Singapore* (United Kingdom: Routledge Publishing, 1995) pp. 113–139.

allowed property buyers to repay their loans using their Central Provident Fund (CPF) accounts. This increased the attraction of the scheme since using their CPF savings meant that their daily income would not be affected. To further increase the draw of the scheme, the government broadened the target audience and extended the CPF Housing Grant Scheme in 1994 to allow first-time citizens to buy resale HDB flats, and then in 1998 to first-time citizen families and singles to buy executive condominiums.

The government's success in providing housing for its people is clearly reflected in the statistics. Today, HDB estates are scattered throughout Singapore and approximately 80% of the population resides in public housing. Contrary to perceptions of public housing, HDB flats in Singapore are modern and comfortable, some with security systems, and most recently, HDB flats with condominium facilities have been offered to the public.

Stable housing in the form of HDB flats for most Singaporeans has contributed much to the well-being and comfort of Singaporeans. It is remarkable that Singapore is one of the very few countries in the world to have successfully introduced and implemented a large-scale public housing programme with private ownership of individual units, and where building houses can actually serve nation building objectives.[11] The HDB directly contributes to the attainment of these by adding on nation building dimensions to its building and provision of homes.

Central Provident Fund

The CPF is the chief means of providing a form of social security to Singaporeans, and just like the HDB, is a national institution that helps the stake-in-the-land idea, that Singaporeans should have a sense of belonging in the country where their economic welfare and money are. The CPF is also a legacy of the British rule, whereby it was a British tradition for companies, and not the government, to look after their employees' welfare. Singapore chose to continue with this scheme after independence as it realised the benefits of a savings plan for individuals and society.

The CPF is a social security savings scheme, with the ultimate aim of ensuring that individuals have sufficient funds and savings for retirement. It entails compulsory contributions from employers as well as employees in both the public and private sectors, and throughout the years, contributions by employers and employees have varied between 10–25% of an employee's salary. In 2016, the employer-employee contribution rate ranges between 12.5–37%. This rate is likely to rise as Singapore faces stiffer competition from the region and beyond. Primarily to enhance Singapore's competitive edge, the government is likely to opt for a more flexible arrangement of contribution to deal with higher costs while ensuring that its social benefits remain

---

[11] Raj Vasil, *A Citizen's Guide to Government and Politics in Singapore* (Singapore: Talisman Publishing Pte Ltd, 2004) pp. 128–129.

intact. The CPF board has over the years accumulated large funds which have been available in part for use in national development projects. It acts as a constant source of investment funds for the expansion and growth of the Singapore economy.

The government holds all contributions through the CPF board until retirement but makes CPF relevant and viable to all Singaporeans largely because it makes CPF earnings tax exempt and guarantees payments of CPF savings. The CPF has also evolved to meet the changing needs of society. In fact, the CPF caters to numerous schemes other than Home Ownership such as Family Protection, Asset Enhancement, Healthcare and Education to allow citizens to further utilise their CPF savings for better financial planning. Similarly, the CPF also provides financial protection through insurance schemes. This form of financial security and planning allows citizens to be assured that their economic welfare is being looked after, and thus fosters a greater sense of commitment and loyalty to the government and nation.

National Service

The National Service (NS) Amendment Act was introduced and passed in 1967 in view of the security vulnerabilities that Singapore faced after independence. With the withdrawal of the British troops after independence, the Singapore Armed Forces (SAF) consisted merely of two infantry battalions, two naval ships and no air force. The Ministry of Interior and Defence was set up in 1965 to address the issue of security, and concluded that with a small population that needed to channel its limited resources into economic development, Singapore would have to rely on a citizens' armed force to defend its borders.

As such, the government implemented compulsory military service for all male Singapore citizens in March 1967. Male Singaporean citizens and permanent residents are required to register for National Service upon reaching the age of 16½ and are called up for enlistment at 18, although this can be deferred until the completion of tertiary education, or even commenced at the minimum legal age if so chosen by the individual. To further expand the size of the citizens' defence and to foster a sense of commitment to the nation by foreigners who work and live in Singapore, children born to foreigners after they have taken up permanent residency in Singapore are required to serve National Service. However, foreigners who are employed locally or have become permanent residents themselves are not required to serve National Service. To ensure continuity in the defence system and that battle skills are kept up to mark, upon completion of National Service, national servicemen proceed to serve as operationally ready national servicemen (NSmen). NSmen are liable to be called up for a maximum of 40 days of National Service every year until the age of 50 years (for officers) and of 40 years (for others).

The rationale for National Service is two-fold. Besides the constraints of a small population where an army comprising of just regulars would be inadequate to defend the country, National Service is thought to be extremely useful for nation building and to foster racial harmony among the many ethnic groups in Singapore. National Service applies to all male citizens across all ethnic groups and by making them go through similar experiences, it helps foster greater cohesiveness and understanding across the different ethnic groups and most importantly, inculcate an overriding sense of loyalty to Singapore and the commitment to defend it. To ensure that no one tries to evade National Service and to portray equal treatment to everyone, the government has made it an offence to evade National Service. Anyone attempting to do so shall be liable on conviction, for imprisonment of a term not exceeding three years, or a maximum fine of S$5,000, or both.

National Ideology

When Singapore gained independence in 1965, the PAP government adopted cultural democracy as the founding principle of the new state. It was believed that Singapore was to remain a multiracial, multicultural, multilingual and multi-religious nation in order to successfully manage its diversity. The government realised that it was difficult to devise a common Singaporean identity and culture because all the racial communities had distinct identities, languages and cultures. As different ethnic values could not be shed just to form a homogenous national identity, the government utilised a strategy to accommodate the unique characteristics of every ethnic group by building on the strengths of ethnic diversity in order to maintain social and national stability.

During the late 1980s, however, the government became concerned about the apparent decline in traditional values with the rise of Western values and beliefs amongst Singaporean youths. Senior leaders of the PAP, especially Lee Kuan Yew, argued vehemently that the 'corruption' of Western values would eventually lead to national disunity and hinder social cohesion and economic progress. The government thus advocated the principle of 'Asian Values' which promoted and praised the value of communitarian commitments, that is, putting community or nation before self, and obeying and trusting the government as it would surely put the interests of the community first before anything else.

This new concept of national 'ideology' backfired as it struck a chord of distaste and suspicion amongst the other minorities. 'Asian Values' resembled Confucian ethics too much and the other ethnic groups were concerned that this might just be an attempt to strengthen the Chinese and sinicise Singapore. Other ethnic groups felt that they were left out of the debate on this new ideology and that it did not include or consider the heritages and values of the minorities. This unease was all the more prominent due to the cumulative effect of other government initiatives such as the 'Speak Mandarin Campaign' which started in 1979.

To allay the fears and concerns of minority groups, the government began to revise its approach towards 'Asian Values' in the 1990s. In moving forward with the idea of a national ideology that would appeal and sit well with all ethnic groups, the government took efforts to ensure that its initiatives were not perceived to be exclusively Chinese-oriented and thus engaged in consultative discussions with leaders of various ethnic groups and organisations. The notion of 'Shared Values' was revitalised having first been mooted by then Deputy Prime Minister Goh in 1988.[12] The government's 'White Paper on Shared Values' issued in January 1996, sought to emphasise Singapore's multiracialism and multiculturalism, and maintained that it was necessary to have a national ideology to bring together Singapore's many communities.

Official Languages and a National Language

The decision behind Singapore's official language was a continuation of the government's strategy of multiracialism and multiculturalism. The PAP saw greater benefits and conveniences to accept diversity rather than forcing a homogenous identity for nation building. Hence, four languages — Malay, Mandarin, Tamil and English — were designated as official languages. Malay was made the national language of Singapore due to the historical significance and presence of the Malay community as well as due to Singapore's location in the heart of the Malay World.

However, from a practical standpoint, it was necessary to have one common language for ease of communication and as a medium of instruction for all races. English thus took on this role, allowing access to modern communications and the international market. English was also deemed to be politically neutral since it belonged neither to the indigenous Malays nor to immigrant Chinese and Indians, and as such, could serve as an acceptable medium language that allowed all Singaporeans to communicate and compete at the same level.

National Symbols

The National Anthem, Flag and Pledge of a nation serve as symbols of unity and national identity. When Singapore achieved limited self-government in 1959, the PAP introduced a new National Anthem — *Majulah Singapura* — which was written by composer Zubir Said, and in the national language of Malay. A new national flag — red and white, consisting of a crescent moon and five stars — was also created. These five stars represent democracy, peace, progress, justice and equality while

---

[12] Singapore National Library Board website, http://infopedia.nlb.gov.sg/articles/SIP_542_2004-12-18.html, accessed 24 October 2006.

red represents universal brotherhood and equality, and white represents purity and virtue. The Singapore Pledge and National Anthem emphasise that racial differences can be overcome and that ethnic stability and harmony should be the basis for a Singaporean society.

The government has made great efforts to ensure that nation building is a continued process that involves all layers and segments of society. Rather than trying to assimilate different ethnicities and cultures into a forced homogenous identity, the government has chosen practical and feasible approaches to foster a common sense of belonging and identity to Singapore apart from individual cultures and values. Through a combination of policy directives and restrained intervention in ethnic affairs, the PAP government has thus far been very successful in ensuring a stable and harmonious society in Singapore.

Is Singapore a Nation?

Singapore leaders have repeatedly stressed that nation building and the construction of a national identity remain a 'work-in-progress'. By all counts, Singapore is a 'nation-in-being' and this can be largely attributed to the various successful strategies that have been implemented since 1965. Despite being a new and highly pluralistic state, ethnic peace and harmony are highly cherished goals of the populace. Being well-aware of the domestic conflicts elsewhere in the region, including in Singapore's past, Singaporeans have developed a strong commitment to social, ethnic and religious peace. This commitment is fed by their common experiences in school, National Service, public housing, and work place. While the challenges of globalisation and rising ethnic and religious assertiveness have led to increasing consciousness and even ethno-nationalism, these have not been allowed to threaten domestic cohesion and peace. At the same time, due to the growing political maturity of Singaporeans, the emphasis on ethnic self-help groups has not widened the racial divide in the Republic. This is because, through a strategy of strengthening the 'elements' to solidify the 'whole', the sense of nationhood has been effectively and continuously promoted. Even though Singapore is still not a nation, its sense of nationhood has been strengthened and is growing day-by-day.

Think Questions

1. Is Singapore a nation?
2. Are racial and religious identities compatible with nation building in Singapore?
3. Are there policies in Singapore that are counter-productive to the nation building process?

Chapter Seven

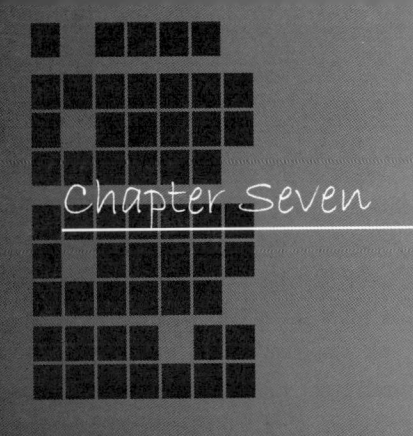

Political Leadership and the Challenge of Renewal

The younger leaders will have different personalities, characters and perhaps, even different motivations. They have grown up in a different age. Their cast of mind will be different. Their political style will be different. Their attitudes to life, their value judgements, their motivations, are not the same. What is more, the generation they will have to lead will be even more different … To smoothen the passage … there will be gradual changes in the political style. A younger generation of men has to discover their political 'feel' and to be accepted as leaders in their own right, to prove themselves and their policies. They will have to win respect and command confidence in their own way and in their own time.[1]

Introduction

In Singapore politics, terms such as 'political renewal', 'new blood', 'new faces', 'rejuvenation' and even 'political succession' are widely used. It is a short hand to describe replacement of personnel in key political positions. Essentially, there are three types of 'political renewals' in Singapore. First, at the highest constitutional level, there is the 'selection' and 'election' of the President. Since independence and to date (2017), Singapore has had seven presidents, namely, Yusof bin Ishak, Benjamin Sheares, Devan Nair, Wee Kim Wee, Ong Teng Cheong, S. R. Nathan and Tony Tan. Second, there is the critical renewal of the highest political executive, namely, the Prime Minister. Since 1965, Singapore has had three prime ministers, Lee Kuan Yew, Goh Chok Tong and Lee Hsien Loong. At the third and final level is the renewal at the Member of Parliament (MP) level. This is the main focus of the 'politics of new blood' where the successful ones become ministers and eventually, the *crème de la crème*, the Prime Minister. The public and political elites in Singapore, and many

---

[1] Lee Kuan Yew, "What of the Past Is Relevant to the Future?", *People's Action Party, 1954–1979*, (Singapore: Central Executive Committee, PAP, 1979) pp. 42–43.

external observers have credited Singapore's success to its political leadership and this makes understanding this issue vitally critical in unraveling the essence of politics and governance in Singapore.

As evident from the quote at the start of this chapter and keeping in view how the late first Prime Minister of Singapore, Lee Kuan Yew defined leadership, the importance of political leadership and political renewal in Singapore will be analysed. A number of sub-themes will be examined including the theoretical concepts of leadership and authority, the framework to better understand the different types of leaders and their sources of authority, the nature of leadership in the pre-World War II years, the issue and importance of political renewal, and the implications of political leadership 'system' on Singapore politics.

Concept of Leadership

Leadership can be understood either as a pattern of behaviour or as a personal quality. As a pattern of behaviour, leadership is the influence exerted by an individual or group over a larger body to organise or direct its efforts towards the achievement of desired goals. As a personal attribute, leadership refers to the character traits that enable the leader to exert influence over others.[2] In order for an individual or group to be seen as 'leaders' in society, they must be able to exercise some form of authority over the people that are 'being led' by them. 'Authority', is seen as 'legitimate power' whereby power is the ability to influence the behaviour of others. Therefore, authority is regarded as a right to influence the behaviour of others based on an acknowledged duty to obey rather than any form of coercion or manipulation.[3]

The legitimacy of this authority can be derived from three different sources as identified by Max Weber; namely traditional authority, charismatic authority and legal-rational authority.[4] Traditional authority is based on long-established customs and traditions that are often sanctioned by history because of the acceptance by past generations. A common example of traditional authority is found amongst tribes and small groups in the form of patriarchalism which involves the domination of the father within the family structure or a 'master's control over his servants', and gerontocracy, which is the 'rule of the aged'.[5] A second form of authority is charismatic authority which is based on the power of individual's personality, that is, on his or her 'charisma'. Owing nothing to a person's status, social position or office, charismatic

---
[2] Andrew Heywood, *Politics* (New York: Palgrave Macmillan, 2002) p. 348.
[3] Ibid. p. 5.
[4] Hans Gerth and C. Wright Mills (eds.), *From Max Weber: Essays in Sociology* (New York: Oxford University Press, 1946) pp. 295–301.
[5] Andrew Heywood, *Politics*, p. 211.

authority operates entirely through the capacity of a leader to make a direct and personal appeal to followers as a kind of hero or saint. Past leaders such as Napoleon Bonaparte, Adolf Hitler and Benito Mussolini are examples of leaders who managed to derive authority through personal appeal.[6]

The third form of authority — legal-rational authority — links authority to a clearly and legally defined set of rules. The power of a President, Prime Minister or government official is determined by formal, constitutional rules, which constrain or limit what an office holder is able to do.[7] Thus, power is derived through the office an individual holds and is independent from personal characteristics or traditional customs and beliefs. The theoretical knowledge of the different sources of authority is critical to our understanding of the nature of the leadership present in Singapore as well as its evolution from a society founded on traditionally accepted notions of leadership to one where leadership becomes highly political and increasingly linked to charismatic and legal-rational authority.

Concept of Leadership in Singapore: Changes and Evolution

Singapore's society evolved following several historical landmarks and this in turn led to a change in the population's definition of 'leaders' and 'leadership'. Before 1942 and the onset of the Second World War, Singapore was regarded as an economically lucrative trading base for the British. The nature of society was mainly based on immigration from countries such as China, India and the surrounding Malay World. The societal emphasis was on the economic well-being of the individual. The public perceived prominent businessmen such as Lee Kong Chian and Tan Kah Kee as natural leaders of society. Moreover, due to the immigrant nature of the population, there was an increased importance in clan associations. Often, these businessmen tended to hold leadership post in such associations, further cementing their position as leaders of society.

An example of such a leader was Tan Kah Kee. He was not only a successful businessman and leader of the Hokkien community in Singapore but was also widely respected for his contributions to education and philanthropy. Thus, during the pre-Second World War period, leadership was seen in a rather tribunal and communal sense with a significant lack of political motivation. Furthermore, due to the migrant nature of Singapore's population, there was no real sense of belonging to the country. Instead, political affiliation was directed back towards the motherland of the immigrants. This was reflected in the help rendered by the Chinese business community towards China's war against Japan during the 1930s. Thus, there was a lack of

---

[6] Ibid, p. 212.
[7] Ibid, pp. 212–213.

political motivation and leadership towards Singapore. However, important external events were to change this.

The Second World War, which saw the defeat of the British colonial power and the subsequent Japanese Occupation, was an event that awoken the political consciousness of the population. Realising that dependence on an external power for domestic security was highly undesirable, the end of the Second World War led to a growth of nationalistic feelings that demanded some form of local autonomy in governing of the state. This led to the emergence of political leaders such as David Marshall and Lim Yew Hock as well as the formation of political parties such as the Singapore Labour Party. There was a significant shift in the nature of leadership from a communal to a more political form based on political objectives and motivation.

The post-Second World War era saw the emergence of the PAP in 1954. This was led by Lee Kuan Yew who was seen as a new breed of Singapore politician from the English-educated middle-class background, emerging in part, due to the failure of the colonial regime in 1942. Within its midst were several Chinese-educated leaders such as Lim Chin Siong and Fong Swee Suan. The ideological differences between the radicals led by Lim Chin Siong and the moderates led by Lee Kuan Yew gave rise to factionalism within the party since its inception. The internal struggle within the party came to an end with the radicals splitting from the PAP to form the *Barisan Sosialis* (BS) on 26 July 1961.[8] The power struggle between these two groups of political leaders was to shape the character and future of Singapore politics and government. This also defined the nature of political leadership and greatly affected the way Singapore evolved since the early 1960s to the present period.

Power Struggle between the PAP and the Communists: The Turning Point in Singapore Politics

The key turning point in Singapore politics was the failure of the Communists to win the referendum on merger with Malaysia in September 1962. This was followed by the defeat of the Communists and the Left in the September 1963 General Elections. The BS only won 13 out of 51 seats, garnering 33% of the total votes.[9] The Communist failure was compounded by the BS's boycott of the 1968 General Elections which ended up marginalising it from Singapore politics permanently. The PAP was returned unopposed in 51 constituencies and won the remaining seven with over 80% of the

---

[8] Jon S. T. Quah, Chan Heng Chee and Seah Chee Meow (eds.), *Government and Politics of Singapore* (Singapore: Oxford University Press, 1985) p. 4.
[9] Lee Kuan Yew, *From Third World to First: The Singapore Story* (Singapore: Times Editions, 1998) pp. 131–132.

valid votes cast.[10] This was the beginning of a one-party dominant political system in Singapore which saw no Opposition member being elected into parliament until J. B. Jeyaretnam of the Workers' Party (WP) managed to "break the PAP's spell of unprecedented total support in a by-election in 1981".[11] As Raj Vasil observes:

> It was this comfortable position and the growing age of its first generation leaders that made Prime Minister Lee Kuan Yew reflect on the future and prepare for leadership renewal and succession with a special urgency and thoroughness.[12]

As a consequence, the dominance of the PAP in Singapore politics created a "climate [that] could only fertilise PAP seedlings. In such a situation, the PAP had to ensure that it absorbed all potential leaders within its fold".[13] Lee Kuan Yew's outlook towards good governance, which focused on individual leadership and capabilities rather than the political system per se, was consolidated by the struggle against the Communists in the 1960s. His personal preference on this issue was reflected in his earlier address to the Legislative Assembly on 27 April 1957. He expressed his reservations about the democratic system and placed premium on the leader instead:

> If a people have lost faith completely in their democratic institutions, because they cannot find men of calibre to run them, then, however, good that system, it perishes. Ultimately, it is the men who run the system who make it come to life.[14]

The rise of individuals such as Lim Chin Siong provided strong leadership towards the Communist cause as well as a viable and alternative source of leadership to the PAP. However, the strength of the Communists declined seriously after *Operation Coldstore*, a security operation in 1963 where activists such as Lim Chin Siong, the leader of the open united Communist front in the 1950s and 1960s, were detained. This effectively "creamed off the leadership of the radical Left and subsequently, the BS lost its unity, direction and any sign of clear objective".[15]

The next phase of the Communist struggle was led by Dr Lee Siew Choh. However, his political strategy of abandoning constitutional politics and 'taking the battle to the streets' not only lost public support but also literally split and destroyed

---

[10] Ibid, p. 133.
[11] Ibid, p. 146.
[12] Raj Vasil, *Governing Singapore: Democracy and National Development* (Singapore: Allen & Unwin, 2000) p. 119.
[13] Ibid.
[14] Lee Kuan Yew in an address to the Legislative Assembly on 27 April 1957.
[15] Bilveer Singh, *Quest for Political Power: Communist Subversion and Militancy in Singapore* (Singapore: Marshall Cavendish, 2015) p. 139.

the BS. This episode consolidated the attitude of the PAP towards leadership. The PAP realised that good leadership was the key to political power and control. The moment an unsuitable leader steps in, whatever initial advantages and strengths developed by past leaders, may instantly disintegrate. Hence, the PAP's past experience of power struggles with the Communists and its subsequent dominance in the political arena greatly shaped and consolidated the first generation leaders' perception on the importance of leadership as well as leadership renewal.

What Is Political Succession in Singapore?

Since the 1968 General Elections, when the PAP was returned unopposed in 51 constituencies and won the remaining the seven with over 80% of the valid votes, there was a shift in the emphasis on political succession. The 1968 elections marked a new beginning in Singapore politics whereby there emerged a one-party dominant system. Due to the hegemonic nature of the PAP rule, coupled with the lack of credible Opposition, the PAP was able to 'dictate' the process by which political succession was to take place. From a position of political supremacy, the focus was on internal party renewal and how the first generation of leaders was to go about grooming their successors to have a similar mindset and values as them.

Significantly, in 1967, Lee Kuan Yew talked about the need for a systematic process in the renewal of political leadership to remove any unpredictability and uncertainty towards the capabilities of a new generation of leaders in continuing the legacy of the past:

> So we are confronted, now, with this problem of succession ... unless we want long periods of anarchy and chaos, we must create a self-continuing — not a self-perpetuating — power structure ... The problem of all countries in Asia is how to establish some system which will bring forth an unending stream of people with character ... if we leave these things to chance, then surely, we are taking chances with our own people's lives and destiny.[16]

The need for an efficient, systematic process and the importance of recruiting the 'right' candidate for the job was the guiding principle underpinning political succession in Singapore and in particular, within the PAP.

Then Prime Minister Lee Kuan Yew abandoned the traditional passive approach of depending on political activists to join them. Instead, he adopted a proactive strategy of active recruitment of capable personnel from different sectors of society. The

---

[16] Speech by Lee Kuan Yew, Singapore's Prime Minister at the East Asia Christian Conference held in Singapore on 10 April 1967.

rationale for this was that while the first generation of leaders was literally 'thrown up' by traumatic events such as the Second World War, the Japanese Occupation and the Communist insurgency, the lack of such powerful impetuses from the 1960s onwards meant that it would be difficult to imagine another group of leaders emerging with similar strengths, character and values.

Political succession then becomes a highly deliberate and planned process of active recruitment and subsequent evaluation of one's capabilities and character. This is often done through "systematic talent scouting, testing good men, and re-testing on the job for steadiness, for strength, character, for coolness under fire, for dedication to a cause to the people of Singapore".[17] In fact, the process of political succession within the PAP has become institutionalised whereby "an orderly and planned self-renewal process is being built into our political system".[18] This has in turn benefited Singapore as it created a sense of predictability and continuity through transitional periods.

The next step in this process after individuals have been selected by the PAP will be for them to participate in elections in order to get elected into Parliament. Moreover, the introduction of the Group Representation Constituency (GRC) in the 1988 elections can be seen as an innovation that helps in the introduction of 'new blood' into the political system. Previously, through the single-member constituencies, the individual's personality and charisma played an important role in influencing the electorate. New candidates faced a tougher challenge in establishing themselves against more seasoned Opposition candidates. However, with the GRCs, the system allows new candidates to get elected through party affiliation. The GRCs allow for the new candidates to 'bandwagon' on the credibility established by the more experienced MPs and Ministers as well as the credibility built up by the PAP.

The PAP's policy of political renewal has been evident in every general elections since 1968. In the 1968 General Elections, 18 out of the 58 candidates were 'new faces'.[19] During the 1980 elections, Lee Kuan Yew demonstrated his commitment towards self-renewal by leaving 'old guards' such as Toh Chin Chye out of the cabinet amid internal disagreements. The path towards an institutionalised process of self-renewal had been firmly drawn out.

The 2006 General Elections continued a similar trend where 24 new PAP MPs were elected, together with one new Non-Constituency Member of Parliament (NCMP). This meant that nearly one-third of the MPs in the 2006 Parliament were

---

[17] Speech by Senior Minister Lee Kuan Yew at a PAP rally in Hougang on 26 December 1996.
[18] Speech by S. R. Nathan at the swearing-in ceremony of Prime Minister Lee Hsien Loong and his cabinet at the Istana on 12 August 2004.
[19] Lee Kuan Yew, *From Third World to First*, p. 738.

new.[20] The same phenomenon continued in the 2011 and 2015 General Elections. Prime Minister Lee Hsien Loong further emphasised the long-term view held by the government regarding political succession at a dinner for retired MPs:

> Each time we call a general election, one key consideration is the lineup of candidates — whether we have enough candidates, what new faces to field, which serving MPs to retire. It is a long process which starts very early. In fact, immediately after every general election, the party is already hunting for potential candidates to field the next time … My concern is not so much this election, but the next one.[21]

Thus, an institutionalised process of political renewal has been effectively embedded into the Singapore's political system since 1968 and has been implemented robustly and judiciously ever since. Not only does it emphasise the need for continuity and stability during transitional periods, it also reflects the commitment on the part of the Singapore government to keep up with the changes within society in terms of needs and expectations. As Diane K. Mauzy puts it, "political succession is a supreme expression of the PAP's belief in elitism, meritocracy, and planning".[22] This is perhaps an accurate summary of a process of political succession whereby meticulous planning is carried out to pick the elite from various sectors of society and through a stringent process of selection, candidates are earmarked for future leadership positions.

Political Succession: Its Importance in Singapore's Context

Competent political leadership is essential in the efficient governing of a state. This is even more so when the state is relatively new and confronted with manifold challenges, especially vulnerabilities. Singapore is divided by sharp ethnic and religious cleavages, is resourceless and faces ever sharper competition from resource- and manpower-endowed countries in the region and beyond. These were just some of the problems facing the PAP government after gaining independence in 1965. Singapore's success today has been largely attributed to the leadership of the PAP government. One single decisive factor identified that aided Singapore's development is "the ability of its ministers and the high quality of the civil servants who supported them".[23]

---

[20] Speech by Prime Minister Lee Hsien Loong at the swearing-in ceremony on 30 May 2006.
[21] Speech by Prime Minister Lee Hsien Loong for retired MPs on 22 July 2006 at Parliament House, Singapore.
[22] Diane K. Mauzy, "Leadership Succession in Singapore: The Best Laid Plans", *Asian Survey*, Vol. 33 No. 12 (December 1993) p. 1173.
[23] Lee Kuan Yew, *From Third World to First*, p. 736.

Effective political leadership and renewal have had a positive multiplier effect on the all-round development in the city-state. First, Singapore's success was due to the strong and effective leadership exercised by past leaders such as Lee Kuan Yew and his comrade-in-arms such as Goh Keng Swee, Toh and S. Rajaratnam. Hence, for Singapore's success to be sustained there must be future leaders that are capable of taking over the mettle from the past leaders. Lee Kuan Yew, during a seminar on Communism and Democracy in 1971, talked about how Singapore's fate depended on just 300 men. Reflecting on the relatively small pool of talent that he was able to tap into, he emphasised the contributions of this small group of leaders in helping in the development of Singapore:

> Without a stable political situation and a rational and realistic political leadership, there can be no economic development.[24]

This experience has been deeply etched in the PAP's mindset, which among others, believes that many of the younger generations, who have not gone through the struggles of nation building, tend to take Singapore's progress and prosperity for granted.

The emphasis placed on the political leadership as a significant factor for the nation's success is clear and few can deny the causal link between the two. One of the PAP's strengths in general elections have been its past record in 'delivering the goods' promised to the people during election campaigns. This is apparent in the economic sector where Singapore's economy continues to grow at 'tigerish rates' as well as in the public service sector where Singaporeans enjoy standards that compare favourably to those anywhere else in Southeast Asia and even in most of the developed world.[25] As such, many have identified the leadership of Singapore to be the main driver behind Singapore's success. It will thus be important for the current leadership to ensure efficient and effective political succession to keep this success story going.

Also, due to the nature of Singapore, with its unique set of constraints, its prosperity is "a result of a continuing act of will".[26] As Lee Kuan Yew put it,

> Few people really understand how and why Singapore is and has to be different. We are not a natural country. If we simply follow the formula of other countries, we will

---

[24] Speech by Lee Kuan Yew at a seminar on Communism and Democracy on 28 April 1971, in Han Fook Kwang, Warren Fernandez and Sumiko Tan (eds.), *Lee Kuan Yew: The Man and His Ideas* (Singapore: Singapore Press Holdings [and] Times Editions, 1998) pp. 313–315.

[25] 'Ten in a Row for the Men in White", from *The Economist* print edition 11 May 2006. Downloaded from www.economist.com/world/asia/displaystory.cfm?story_id=6919244.

[26] Speech made by Senior Minister Lee Kuan Yew at the PAP rally at the UOB Plaza on 30 December 1996.

fail. To get where we are we had to assemble an exceptional team in the political leadership and in the Civil Service.[27]

The lack of natural resources, hinterland, an educated population and problems such as housing shortages were urgent issues faced by the government and required active intervention. This needed capable and far-sighted leaders to come up with plans and measures to cope with a unique set of problems and constraints. It took proactive and interventionist-oriented efforts by the political leadership to turn this unfavourable context around and mould Singapore into what it is today. Again, this reflects the point that political leadership is at the core of Singapore's success and this needs to be continued to ensure similar competence in dealing with a new set of problems and constraints in the future.

Moreover, taking into consideration the 'mixed' nature of Singapore's population, comprising of a Chinese majority and minority groups such as Malays, Indians and Eurasians, it will be difficult for these various groups to see politics in the same light.[28] Therefore, the focal point will be on a strong leadership that will be able to reconcile these different viewpoints and shape a common goal that is essential to nation building and the development of a national identity. While these racial problems do not seem as relevant now as they were during the 1950s and 1960s, the fault lines are still present and a strong political leadership is necessary for maintaining the cohesiveness of society.

Second, the reality in Singapore is such that politics has been dominated by the PAP in a one-party dominant system since 1959. This effectively means that political renewal of Singapore is dependent on the political renewal within the PAP. Effective political renewal and rejuvenation are the only ways for the party to sustain itself and maintain its relevance and hegemony. Political continuity, however, is a double-edged sword. While it allows for political stability within the country, there is also a high likelihood of the dominant party becoming complacent due to the lack of Opposition. This is evident from the fate of similar political parties in Japan, India and Indonesia. Hence, while political stability can be a boost to the country, it will still be dependent on the political leadership to make use of this advantage for national interest and not private gains of individuals or the party.

An article in the *Economist* contends that the reason the PAP has managed to maintain its form while other dominant parties have become corrupt is in part due to "its obsession with seeking new talent, and the ruthlessness in turfing out established figures to keep its line-up of ministers and MPs fresh".[29] Given the political

---

[27] Ibid.
[28] Speech by Lee Kuan Yew at a seminar on Communism and Democracy on 28 April 1971.
[29] "Ten in a Row for the Men in White".

context of Singapore where the Opposition and civil society are relatively weak, it will be crucial for political renewal within the PAP to prevent it from falling into the many pitfalls of having a one-party dominant system.

In the PAP context, the formation of the party occurred during a completely different generation. Hence, the third point on the importance of political succession and renewal lies in coping with the changing demands of the population. Looking at the three prime ministers of Singapore to date, we see three distinctive approaches towards governing the state, especially in terms of the relationship between the government and the citizens. This in turn reflects the different needs and demands that society has imposed on the government.

In this light, the 1984 General Elections are often regarded as a watershed in Singapore politics. This saw a 12.9% drop in the percentage of votes obtained by the PAP as well as two Opposition MPs being voted into Parliament. This result signalled a shift in the attitudes of the electorate who was less willing to accept the style of government practised under Lee Kuan Yew that has often been described as "overly-protective, paternalistic, authoritarian and even arrogant".[30]

In contrast, Goh Chok Tong's style of government has been described by then President S. R. Nathan as being "more consultative and participatory".[31] Due to the changing demographics of the population such as a general increase in the educational level, it was necessary for the second generation leaders, led by Goh Chok Tong, to adopt an approach that was more suited to the demands of the population. This idea of political renewal being in tune with generational transition was brought up by Prime Minister Lee Hsien Loong during his swearing-in speech on 12 August 2004:

> This political transition is not just a change of Prime Ministers, or of a Cabinet. It is a generational change for Singapore, a shift to the post-independence generation in a post-Cold War world.[32]

Hence, due to the changing nature of the electorate, it is essential for the government in power to reflect the current needs of society and consequently address them. This can only be done if the political leadership is renewed in line with these generational transitions to keep the elite in touch with the grassroots, and thus allow them to frame policies to better suit the changing demands of the population.

---

[30] Carolyn Choo, *Singapore: The PAP and the Problem of Political Succession* (Singapore: Asiapac Books and Educational Aids, 1985) p. 224.
[31] Speech by S. R. Nathan at the swearing-in ceremony of Prime Minister Lee Hsien Loong and his cabinet at the Istana on 12 August 2004.
[32] Speech by Prime Minister Lee Hsien Loong at swearing-in ceremony at the Istana on 12 August 2004.

Implications: Difficulties and Challenges

Given how important an effective and efficient process of political succession is to the survival and development of the country, it is noteworthy that the process is not as smooth as the leaders want it to be. One of the main problems with the process of political renewal is the dilemma of balancing continuity and renewal. This was framed by Prime Minister Lee Hsien Loong as follows:

> If the turnover rate is too fast, we lose good people unnecessarily, and the team will not gel. But if the turnover is too slow, the organisation will become too settled, promising people at the next rung will stagnate, and eventually we will also lose good talent.[33]

The solution to this dilemma as suggested by Prime Minister Lee Hsien Loong would be to persevere with the policy of leadership renewal, while concurrently judging the pace of it to make sure that successors are ready at every level.

However, the question still remains: How is this judgment going to be made? Will it be a reaction to another general election shock? Or is there an internal system within the PAP and the administrative apparatus to determine when it is time for renewal to take place? Logically, one will only realise that the pace of renewal is too fast when the new leaders are seen to be incompetent and ill-prepared to take office. Will the realisation come too late for the situation to be salvaged, given the nature and pace of global economic, social and political developments? Therein lays a potential pitfall in the PAP's policy of political renewal that has to be dealt with caution and circumspection. While rejuvenating the government through an injection of 'new blood' may lead to positive dynamics within the political system, there is also the probability that new leaders who have yet to develop their full potential are being forced into situations whereby their capabilities and experience are insufficient to deal with crises, leading to a breakdown in the current system.

In terms of challenges, there is also the potential for internal strife, especially in relation to the 'old guards' who may feel that they have been unfairly treated by this process of political renewal. An example of this will be Dr Toh's response after being left out of the new cabinet in the aftermath of the 1980 elections. As the first Prime Minister, the late Lee Kuan Yew recollected:

> He stayed on in Parliament for another two terms, sniping at me and the PAP, never enough to be accused of disloyalty, but enough to be a mild embarrassment.[34]

---

[33] Speech by Prime Minister Lee Hsien Loong at the 2005 Administrative Service Dinner on 24 March 2005.
[34] Lee Kuan Yew, *From Third World to First*, pp. 742–743.

Such a situation will inevitably affect the morale of the political party and raise the possibility of factionalism within the party. To avoid such a situation, it will be critical for political elites to have a uniform mindset towards the importance of political succession and the pace at which it has to be carried out in order to benefit the PAP and Singapore in general.

Another problem faced by political leaders is the recurring difficulty of recruiting capable people due to the unattractive nature of politics. The nature of politics is such that success has implications for one's privacy, time and income, which makes political office unattractive. Thus, there is clearly no real incentive present to lure capable professionals from their high-paying private sector jobs to join the political arena. Therefore, the focus of recruitment is not only dependent on the capabilities of the individual but also on one's character and values. There is a need for there to be "a habit of putting their country's interest above their own".[35] Only with a genuine desire to help the country can the disincentives of political office be overcome.

This in turn leads us to another problem — how do we judge one's character? The PAP uses psychological tests designed to define their character profile, intelligence, personal backgrounds and values.[36] While superficially this deals with the ambiguities of one's character and values, several loopholes are still present in this process. First, there is a possibility where a candidate can 'fake good'. Second, under a crisis situation, will the result still hold true? Thus, while the various tests and stringent selection process may effectively eliminate those who are obviously unsuitable, it is only in time that we can find out whether a leader is indeed capable in time of crises.

The above mentioned difficulties are compounded by a geographical constraint which is the country's small population, translating into an even smaller pool of talent. Taking into consideration the PAP's intensive recruitment and co-option of potential leaders from different sectors of society, this brings up the question on whether there will be a dearth of leadership that lies outside of the PAP's production line. While the PAP's system has thus far been successful, an over-reliance on it puts Singapore in a very vulnerable position where the system does not allow for alternative pockets of leadership to develop outside the jurisdiction of the PAP. The lack of alternative sources of leadership means that a failure in the PAP's system will in effect mean the failure of the nation-state.

Another problem of political succession in the Singapore's context is the challenge faced by the new generation of leaders in establishing their credibility in view of the legacy left behind by Lee Kuan Yew and the first generation leaders. The success of the first generation leaders has posed a problem for future leaders in such that they

---

[35] Speech by Lee Kuan Yew at a seminar on Communism and Democracy on 28 April 1971.
[36] Lee Kuan Yew, *From Third World to First*, p. 740.

will not only have to maintain the high standards of national development achieved in the past but also improve on these standards. As Goh Chok Tong noted:

> They started from a very low base. They brought about the colossal, physical transformation of Singapore. The people appreciated the quantum improvement of their lives. Now, thanks to their achievements, we start from a very high base. They achieved 8 to 10 per cent economic growth every year for many years. We will find it difficult to sustain that. Also, because they started from a low base, they were able to generate a high level of satisfaction.[37]

Moreover, due to the difference in the nature of society brought about by the economic affluence of the country, the public perception of good governance has shifted significantly. While generations in the past may have been satisfied with a roof over their heads and a decent-paying job, the demands of the population have evolved over the years. Thus, while the legacy left behind by the past leaders is one of success and achievement, this has in turn caused a problem for future leaders by setting a high benchmark for them to emulate. Failure to continue this trend of development may be seen as a failure on the part of the incumbent government and also in the system of political succession. While this is the result of the immense success achieved in the past, it also means that new leaders will have to jump faster and higher to achieve success and credibility. While 'fitting into the shoes' of greats such as Lee Kuan Yew and even Goh Chok Tong and Lee Hsien Loong might not be easy, still, to be a credible leader, there would be a need to do and even more important, create new niches so that legacies can be left behind for others to emulate and benchmark.

Current Debates

A significant difference between the leaders of today and the leaders of the past is that the current batch of leaders are elites, hand-picked and groomed by the PAP and literally 'helicoptered' into the political arena through elections, 'bandwagoning' on the credibility of the party, in contrast to past leaders who had to win over the support of the people through their personal appeal and capabilities. The sense of elitism within the government has caused concern over the lack of grassroots connections, which in turn may lead to a sense of apathy and even alienation of the ordinary citizen towards the political workings of the country. In political science lexicon, unlike the past 'mobilisers', presently, the 'technocrats' hold sway and how effective they will be remains to be seen.

---

[37] Interview, Singapore, September 1987 quoted in Raj Vasil, *Governing Singapore*, pp. 123–124.

However, does this really matter? Is there a need for there to be a close relationship between the nation's leadership and the population that it governs? Or has the relationship between the 'leaders' and the 'led' evolved to such an extent that it is more impersonal and pragmatic, where as long as the 'leaders' deliver economic prosperity to the population, there is no need for there to be any close interaction? Given the increasing trend of the government engaging the youth in discussion forums, it does seem that the government acknowledges the need to develop a closer rapport with the population, in particular, the younger generation. There is a definite need to 'get connected' with the younger and more discerning electorate. Perhaps, with the basic needs provided by the economic success of Singapore, the younger generation sees a greater need to be more directly involved in policy-making and the direction of governmental initiatives. In other words, in the past, the people felt that they owed their success and happiness to the leaders in power and were contended to a reasonable standard of living. Presently, however, the people are beginning to feel that it is within their power to vote and decide on the fate of the government. In short, it is the government that has to listen and pay heed to the views and wishes of the electorate. In other words, the increasingly matured electorate has learnt how to use its voting power to 'bargain' with the government in power.

Another issue that could have a significant impact on the leadership of Singapore will be the issue of bond breakers who obtain government scholarships going on to terminate their bonds. Does this reflect a weakness in the political leadership, whereby it is unable to keep the 'best brains' within the public sector? While it certainly illustrates the difficulties faced by the government in picking the right people with the right attitudes and character of the job, an underlying concern would be the reasons why government scholarships have become unattractive. While in the past, government scholarships were seen as prestigious awards, now it seems to have become more of a necessity for those who are in need of financial assistance for further education. Bringing this argument further, judging by the significant number of bond breakers, government scholarships are regarded as 'stepping stones' for individuals to invite more lucrative job offers from the private sector and even multinational corporations. One thing is for sure, the image and prestige of a government post have decreased in value and this will be a cause for concern for the leadership, especially in view of the need for capable leaders to govern the country.

There is also the issue of high salaries given to ranking public officers and ministers. On 21 October 1994, a 'White Paper on Competitive Salaries for Competent and Honest Government' was presented to Parliament which saw the institutionalisation of a system of salary adjustments for ministers and high-ranking civil servants. This was done by benchmarking their salaries to the average salaries of the top-four earners in six private sector professions. This measure reduced the financial disincentives involved in giving up lucrative jobs in the private sector for public office. While this was seen as a way to attract and retain capable individuals within the public service, several issues have been raised regarding this. First, the disincentives for public office are more than just financial losses. Perhaps more important is the nature of politics itself. Thus, while this move may solve one aspect of the undesirable nature of public office, other underlying problems have yet to be addressed. Therefore, it is still difficult for the government to attract the best talents for public office.

Measures of this nature may also have a negative resonance with the public in general, especially the lower income groups. This was reflected in Michael Lim's speech in Parliament on the proposed salary revision on 29 June 2000:

> There is still a significant minority of households in Singapore who are low income families. Many of these will find these million dollar salaries, especially for the high office holders, very mind-boggling numbers which they cannot quite fathom and understand … the absolute amounts that the Ministers and top civil servants will get in their remuneration package are so large compared to the average household that it will be very difficult for them to accept these numbers.[38]

Thus, while it may be necessary to offer high salaries to ranking civil servants and ministers in order to ensure a high standard of leadership in Singapore, it is also crucial for the government to take into consideration the negative impact it may have on the morale of those who do not benefit from such a scheme. The challenge for the government will be not only to justify the high salaries but also to find a balance between the benefits of having high salaries and the negative impact they may have on the population. At the same time, politics must not be seen as a means of enriching oneself with 'money' rather than the 'call' determining one's entry into national politics.

Beyond the Third Generation — Who Will Be Singapore's Fourth Prime Minister?

After the smooth and peaceful transition from the second generation of leaders led by Goh Chok Tong, to the third generation of leaders led by Lee Hsien Loong in 2004, the question now is — what happens after Lee Hsien Loong's term as Prime Minister? Looking back at the previous political successions, few will argue against the pivotal role played by Lee Kuan Yew in the planning of the future generations of leaders. In a way, the line of succession up to the third generation of leaders was clear during Lee Kuan Yew's term as Prime Minister. Many saw Goh Chok Tong as an 'ephemeral

---

[38] As quoted in Jon S. T. Quah, "Paying for the 'Best and Brightest': Rewards for High Public Office in Singapore" (Singapore: Dept. of Political Science, National University of Singapore, 2001) p. 34.

leader' before eventually handing over the reigns of Prime Minister to Lee Kuan Yew's son, Lee Hsien Loong.[39] It seemed that even Goh Chok Tong knew at the start that Lee Hsien Loong would eventually be his successor. In 1990, he said that Lee Hsien Loong's time will come: "But that time is not yet. I think this decade does not belong to B. G. Lee. I think the next century will belong to him".[40]

This clear line of succession can be credited not only to the system of political succession put in place by Lee Kuan Yew, but perhaps more importantly due to the foresight and strength in leadership of Lee Kuan Yew himself. As Mauzy argues, "elements of personalisation of rule must necessarily exist after 31 years of strong leadership by a single Prime Minister".[41] A danger of a highly personalised nature of rule will be the possibility that the individual becomes more important than his office. Although the institutionalised system of political succession seems to have solved the problem of the over-reliance on the role of a strong leader at the core of this process, one may argue that Singapore's successful transitions so far from the first generation to the third generation have been drawn out by the first generation leader. However, the system in place has yet to be really tested in the absence of Lee Kuan Yew, which will be the first test for the political system as far as political succession is concerned since the passing of Singapore's founding Prime Minister in March 2015.

Following the September 2015 General Elections, Prime Minister Lee Hsien Loong noted that as far as political succession was concerned, "the clock is ticking, we have no time to lose".[42] At a campaign rally on 8 September 2015, Prime Minister Lee Hsien Loong named seven individuals as possible successors: Heng Swee Keat, Lawrence Wong, Chan Chun Sing, Tan Chuan-Jin, Ng Chee Meng, Ong Ye Kung and Chee Hong Tat. This would mean that compared to the past, especially the transfer of power from Lee Kuan Yew to Goh Chok Tong and Goh Chok Tong to Lee Hsien Loong, the next transfer would be on a 'shorter runway', with the successor not having the time to connect with the ground or build support from within the party, both elements which are crucial for anyone to be the Prime Minister.

During Prime Minister Lee Hsien Loong's visit to Hangzhou for the G20 Summit in September 2016, when asked on the question of succession and what he was looking for in his successor, the Prime Minister replied:

> We know what the qualities and the qualifications are. The question is who will best fulfil them and will he or she be able to work out together with the team and with

---

[39] Diane K. Mauzy, "Leadership Succession in Singapore", p. 1165.

[40] *Times International, December 3, 1990* as cited in Diane K. Mauzy, "Leadership Succession in Singapore", p. 1165.

[41] Ibid.

[42] Tham Yuen-C and Charissa Yong, "Shaping Singapore's 4th-Gen Leadership", *The Sunday Times Insight*, 4 October 2015.

Singaporeans. We are looking for somebody who has that judgement and that experience, and the leadership ability. Both to understand problems, analyse them, and also connect with Singaporeans and explain to people, and mobilise people to work together, to achieve our national goals. So at the same time, you are a mobiliser and a communicator. But at the same time, you also have to be a doer, an analyst, an implementer, and a team builder. It takes time, but I have a promising team of younger Ministers and I am quite sure from amongst them, one leader will emerge.[43]

Home Affairs and Law Minister K. Shanmugam stated in January 2017 that the future Prime Minister of Singapore would need certain qualities, including courage, steel, be able to lead and connect with the people, and get the buy-in from Singaporeans to set out the nation's path, with the next generation of ministers choosing their leaders.[44]

Clearly, there are criteria for who will be Singapore's fourth Prime Minister and who from the 'Magnificent Seven' or a 'dark horse' will secure it remains to be seen.

'The Other Renewal' — The Rejuvenation of the Opposition Parties

While it was *de rigueur* in the past to talk of 'political renewal' and 'political succession' as something unique to the PAP, this is no longer so. As Singapore politics matures and more importantly, as Opposition parties have increasingly become an essential part of the national political architecture, the leadership change taking place in these political parties is equally noteworthy. In the last two general elections, namely, in 2011 and 2015, there has been a buzz on the political scene and Opposition parties are a fact of life, though not in terms of their effectiveness. Of all the Opposition parties, the one that stands out in terms of political rejuvenation is the WP, the only party other than the PAP to have a presence in Parliament after the 2015 General Elections.

The WP's leadership has openly talked about the importance of political renewal and of the need for younger leaders to move forward to take up the cudgels of leadership. Even though the top leadership of the WP is still relatively young, the emergence of 'second liners' in the party shows the importance of political renewal for the party. This is most clearly evident from the WP's Youth Wing. Currently, the key Youth leaders are: Daniel Goh (42), Tan Kong Soon (39), He Ting Ru (32), Cheryl Loh (31), Bernard Chen (30) and Ron Tan (30). In terms of the young future leaders in the WP's Central Executive Committee, the following are worth noting: Pritam

---

[43] See transcript of Prime Minister Lee Hsien Loong's interview with Caijing. Available at http://www.pmo.gov.sg/mediacentre/transcript-pm-lee-hsien-loongs-.

[44] Seow Bei Yi, "Shanmugam on qualities of next PM", *The Straits Times*, 22 January 2017.

Singh (40) who is also a second-term MP, Chairman of the Aljunied-Hougang Town Council and the Assistant Secretary-General of the party, Png Eng Huat (54), also a second-term MP, Foo Seck Guan (39), Dennis Tan (45), Leon Perera (45), Gerald Giam (38), former NCMP, and Lee Li Lian (38), a former MP. Nevertheless, the WP is generally a young political party with its two top leaders, Low Thia Khiang who is 59 years old and Sylvia Lim, the party's Chairman, who is only 51.

Hence, while it is important to monitor and analyse the trends and nature of political renewal in the PAP, one must not ignore the preparation of 'new faces' in the Opposition parties, especially the WP. In general, all the Opposition parties are similarly mindful of political renewal even though the one to watch will be the changes in the WP.

Think Questions

1. Why is political leadership important to the core of Singapore's existence and success?
2. Why is political renewal in the PAP important for Singapore?
3. What will be the key challenges faced by the third and subsequent generations of political leaders in Singapore?

Chapter Eight

Rise of Civil Society Politics and Democratisation

In Singapore today, politics is all or nothing, which is not a good thing. A model we should work towards is the French model of the elite administration ... That is the sort of Singapore elite we want, political but not totally partisan; and at the end of the day, when the crunch comes, will stand side by side and fight for Singapore. But it doesn't not mean that all of us must belong to the PAP.[1]

Introduction

Civil society and democratisation are two interrelated concepts which have emerged as issues of contention and negotiation between the state and society in Singapore's public and social space. This was poignantly evident in the domestic context of Singapore's leadership renewal from Prime Minister Goh Chok Tong (1990–2004) to Prime Minister Lee Hsien Loong (2004–) today. This chapter explores the evolving roles and contesting meanings which the concept of civil society has taken on in the context of Singapore's political and socio-economic development. This will be analysed through the juxtaposition of the PAP government's articulation of the roles of both the government and civil society against that of pressures and initiatives for 'civil' spaces from the ground and fringes of Singapore society. Focus will be placed on the emergence of a nascent civil society in the Republic. This should be appreciated against the backdrop of Singapore's rapid globalisation in the post-Cold War period. The importance of civil society and democratisation will be analysed alongside the ascendancy of younger PAP leaders on the political scene since the 1990s.

---

[1] Simon Tay S. C. (ed.), *A Mandarin and the Making of Public Policy: Reflections by Ngiam Tong Dow* (Singapore: NUS Press, 2006) pp. 24–25.

In particular, under Goh's pronouncement of a more participatory and consultative style of government, which was reiterated by Prime Minister Lee Hsien Loong.[2]

What Is Civil Society?

Any attempt to understand the theoretical meaning of civil society has to be traced to the broader 'public/private distinction' between the 'state' and 'autonomous institutions and/or organisations operating independently from the state within society respectively'.[3] First, the 'institutions of the state' such as the 'government apparatus' including 'the courts, the army and the social security system, responsible for the collective organisation of community life and funded at the public's expense, out of taxation, are meant for the broader public's interest'. Civil society, however, is "more commonly distinguished from the state and used to describe 'private' institutions, independent from government and organised by individuals in pursuit of their own interests".[4] This includes institutions such as the family and kinship groups, private businesses, trade unions, clubs and community groups set up and funded by individual citizens.[5]

A second aspect is the notion that civil society lies in "the attitudinal changes in individuals (which) are especially important when they create new levels of interaction at the group or societal level".[6] Attitudes purported to be "centrally associated with the existence of civil society" include:

> ... tolerance of difference in opinions and behaviours, willingness to cooperate with others, propensity to negotiate in order to approach consensus and to avoid violence in the resolution of difference and a sense of shared identity with others.[7]

In addition, James Danziger has argued that while the presence of a civil society is not a necessary condition for the development of society; the 'values of civility' are

---

[2] Speech by Prime Minister Goh Chok Tong at the National Day Rally on 17 August 2003, at the University Cultural Centre, National University of Singapore, Singapore Government Press Release, www.gov.sg/nd/ND03.htm, accessed on 7 December 2006. See Political Succession: "... I have also put in place a more consultative style of government, and opened up more political and civic space for Singaporeans ... Singaporeans ... must have an emotional stake ...This comes with active participation in the development of their community".
[3] Andrew Heywood, *Politics*, 2nd edition (Great Britain: Palgrave, 2002) p. 8.
[4] Ibid, p. 8.
[5] Ibid, p. 8.
[6] James N. Danziger, "Change and Political Development", in *Understanding the Political World: A Comparative Introduction to Political Science*, 7th edition (Irvine: University of California, 2005) p. 253.
[7] Ibid, p. 253.

nevertheless "crucial for sustaining effective community and democracy".[8] In sum, civil society comprises of autonomous organisations organised at the societal level; which engages the state in negotiations, and can be in cooperation with the state in working towards the desired societal goal.

Relating to Singapore's contemporary socio-political scene, can we then argue that the development of a 'civic' rather than 'civil' society in Singapore essentially promotes 'values of civility' which leads to a similar outcome in terms of the development of communitarian ethos within Singapore society? Will the presence of a strong civil society lead to democratic development? What are the differences between 'civic' and 'civil' society in terms of their impact on a society's process of democratisation? What can be inferred from the processes of democratisation occurring within this city-state?

What Is Democratisation?

What is meant by democratisation in the context of Singapore politics? How is the emergence of civil society related to the process of democratisation? Is this trend already existent or likely to occur under subsequent governments? Fundamentally, democratisation is rooted in the conceptual workings of liberal democracy, "a particular model which is broadly accepted worldwide". Liberal democracy is defined as:

> ... a form of democratic rule that balances the principle of limited government against the ideal of popular consent. Its 'liberal features' are reflected in a network of internal and external checks on government that are designed to guarantee liberty and afford citizens' protection against the state. Its 'democratic' character is based on a system of regular and competitive elections, conducted on the basis of universal suffrage and political equality.[9]

It is crucial to note that within liberal democracy lies a "clear distinction between the state and civil society, maintained through the existence of autonomous groups and interests".[10]

Democratisation thus refers to "the advancement of liberal democratic reform, implying in particular, the granting of basic freedoms and the widening of popular participation and electoral choice".[11] It "involves three processes which overlap at

---

[8] Ibid, p. 253. Danziger quotes from the analysis of Larry Diamond, Marc Plattner, Yun-han Chu, and Mung-mao Tien, (eds.), *Consolidating the Third Wave Democracies* (Baltimore: Johns Hopkins University Press, 1997).
[9] Andrew Heywood, "Government, Systems and Regimes", p. 30.
[10] Andrew Heywood, "Democracy", p. 77.
[11] Ibid, p. 81.

times, including: the breakdown of the old regime; 'democratic transition'; and 'democratic consolidation'".[12] Hence, the presence of civil society serves as an important reflection of the direction and extent of the processes of democratic transition and consolidation; in particular, "specific political, economic and social conditions conducive to further democratisation".[13]

The Emergence of Civil Society in Democratising Singapore

Of salience in describing recent socio-political developments in tandem with Singapore's embrace of economic globalisation, are two conceptions of civil society: First, the promotion of a minimal state and the attendant function of civil society akin to a 'vehicle' which "takes up roles abandoned by the state".[14] Second, the development and space accorded to civil society as a measure of the extent and nature of democratisation occurring within the polity.[15] Will the emergence of civil society within Singapore pave the way for increasing and rapid democratisation? What kind of democracy is Singapore today? What would it be like in the foreseeable future? A broad assessment of the emergence and evolving nature and orientation of civil society within Singapore's national trajectory highlights two distinct phases that run alongside Singapore's state and nation building project under the PAP leadership. The transition of Singapore from 'Third to First World', from Lee Kuan Yew's authoritarian leadership to an era of consensual politics under Goh marked a significant shift in the country's 'civil society landscape', and since then, under Lee Hsien Loong.[16]

The PAP's first generation leaders identified the "balance between democracy and governance" as 'essential' for a 'political system' that would ensure the survival of the new state.[17] This led to the significant curtailment of the socio-political space accorded to civil society and other forms of political organisations beyond the ambit of the government.[18] The 'paramount' imperatives driving the PAP government's preservation of state security and promotion of prosperity and social stability were

---

[12] Ibid, p. 81.
[13] James N. Danziger, "Glossary", p. 497.
[14] Simon S. C. Tay, "The Future of Civil Society: What Next?" in Derek da Cunha (ed.) *Singapore in the New Millenium: Challenges Facing the City-State* (Singapore, Institute of Southeast Asian Studies, 2002) p. 72.
[15] Ibid, p. 72.
[16] Kenneth Paul Tan, Lecture on "The Rise of Civil Society and the Challenge of Democratization", Government and Politics of Singapore, The National University of Singapore.
[17] Raj Vasil, "Creating a Democracy That Works", in *Governing Singapore: Democracy and National Development* (Australia: Allen & Unwin, 2000) pp. 49–52.
[18] Ibid, pp. 49–52.

recurrently used to counter pressures for democratisation in the evolving dynamics of the state-society interaction and emergent civil society activity.[19]

Imperatives of state survival and national development thus explained the establishment of a strong government and the assertion of tight state control over civil society under Prime Minister Lee Kuan Yew's leadership from 1965 to 1984. As Raj Vasil aptly observed, "Lee Kuan Yew and his PAP colleagues had little interest in the worth of democratic norms, institutions and processes".[20] Rather, they saw greater importance in establishing "a democracy that set limits to the political rights and freedoms of the people and their political and other organisations allowed the state virtually unrestricted right to action, regulation and control".[21]

These imperatives stood at the crux of the government's justification for its "control over all instruments and centres of power, which prevented the growth of political pluralism".[22] A stark imbalance in the state-society dynamics is evident in how while "no limits were set on state action, intervention and regulation"; "anything that stood in the way of these legitimately formed a part of the domain of state activity and regulation".[23] More importantly, the establishment of a strong government-driven 'working democracy' was premised upon the belief that for "a people who were mostly illiterate, backward and poor"; 'adequate social and economic development' was necessary for the inculcation of a 'politically more sophisticated and discerning mass electorate in Singapore'.[24] They would then "be able to distinguish between the long-term interests of their country and the short-term benefit of existing Singaporeans and thus make Singapore less difficult to govern".[25]

This belief was further compounded by the PAP Old Guard's perceived failures of other 'new Asian states' establishment of 'institutions and processes of Western-style liberal democracies' without 'requisite social, economic and educational foundations' in which "their more open, pluralistic and competitive political systems had only intensified ethnic contradictions and conflict in their excessively divided societies".[26] A resultant consequence of these driving imperatives and operating beliefs of the first generation leadership were measures undertaken in the state building project to ensure that "only the government was seen as representing the Singapore nation and that its perceptions of the national interest alone prevailed".[27] This

---

[19] Ibid, p. 50.
[20] Ibid, p. 50.
[21] Ibid, p. 50.
[22] Ibid, p. 51.
[23] Ibid, p. 51.
[24] Ibid, p. 48.
[25] Ibid, p. 48.
[26] Ibid, p. 49.
[27] Ibid, p. 52.

entailed the incorporation of civil society in the form of "the trade unions and the organisations of different ethnic segments at the time of independence … to ensure that (they) operated only under the full control and surveillance of the government".[28]

Moreover, in view of the trade unions and Chinese community leaders' responses to the colonial environment and perceived threats to the Chinese community's interests respectively, the PAP leaders in the independence period saw the urgency of modifying the activist orientation of these organisations and their activities. For, against the broader geopolitical threat of Communism, they held the potential to unravel this dominant Chinese, multi-ethnic state's social stability.[29] Evidently, the need to co-opt these tendencies was further intensified by the trade unions "view of the government as their adversary in addition to their employers, to be dealt largely through political action, confrontation and the strength of their numbers".[30]

In response to the activist orientation of the trade unions, the government introduced 'a new strategy of development' under which "unions had to function within the framework of those industrial relations that were in harmony with the state's objectives and imperatives".[31] Underlying this strategy of the state's co-option of trade unions was the rationale that "economic growth and industrial development could not be achieved without all in society paying a high price with respect to political rights and freedoms, (thus) the unionists had to forgo some of their traditional union rights".[32] Therefore, the first semblances of an activist civil society in post-independence Singapore was effectively curtailed and co-opted right from the outset of the PAP's state building project. This more specifically resulted in the introduction of a 'totally new framework of industrial relations' which then led to the profound reduction in the nature and scope of trade union activities within Singapore.[33]

The original active interests undertaken by trade unions in 'the recruitment of staff, promotion, internal transfer, retrenchment, dismissal or reinstatement and the assignment or allocation of duties or specific tasks to an employee' were henceforth "strictly management functions, not to be interfered with by the employees or their unions".[34] Interestingly, the co-option of the trade unions in a tripartite relationship between the government, management and labour that culminated in the 'PAP-NTUC symbiotic relationship' was not achieved simply through the assertion of coercive instruments of the state but also involved some degree of negotiation between the state and the union movement.

---

[28] Ibid, p. 52.
[29] Ibid, p. 52.
[30] Ibid, p. 52.
[31] Ibid, p. 63.
[32] Ibid, p. 63.
[33] Ibid, pp. 64–67.
[34] Ibid, p. 66.

More importantly, the negotiation between the state and the union movement saw the gradual and effective de-politicisation of the union movement with C. V. Devan Nair's assumption of leadership of the National Trades Union Congress (NTUC), which was the central organisation of the unions. Devan Nair was both "a leading trade unionist and a senior leader of the PAP".[35] One can thus argue that the 'emasculation' of civil society with the de-politicisation of the union movement was established right at the outset of the newly independent state's national development project through the state's co-option and direct control of civil society activities.[36] This was effectively established through the NTUC's control "over the trade union movement" which not least, "served as a bulwark against the industrial chaos of the 1950s and 1960s and contributed significantly to the attainment of national order and social stability".[37]

The pursuit of the state imperatives of survival, stability and development was argued to be necessarily conducted through the consolidation of the state's control at the expense and place of civil society activity for the sake of Singapore's state building priorities. This was further compounded through the state's institutionalisation of "the symbiotic relationship between the government and the NTUC" in June 1980 borne out of the fear that:

> it might be more difficult to sustain and enhance a relationship that had developed because of the close ties between Lee Kuan Yew and C. V. Devan Nair after the second generation PAP leaders had taken over the government because they lacked any close contact with unionist leaders.[38]

Indeed, the institutionalisation of such state control over civil society contributed to the conducive environment for the public attainment of economic progress and national stability. Nevertheless, it resulted in the persistent curtailment and control over the operating space and 'voice' of civil society. This environment of an 'emasculated' civil society was to become increasingly incongruous with the emergence of a post-independence generation that formed a more educated, discerning and vocal populace. This has emerged as a point of contention since the late 1980s, particularly the 1990s and up to the present.

---

[35] Ibid, p. 67.
[36] Ibid, p. 68. Raj Vasil purports that the union movement has since been "closely identified with the government and functions under its overall control and supervision".
[37] Ibid. p. 68.
[38] Ibid, p. 67.

The Resurrection of Civil Society since 1984

On a political level, a startling wake-up call to the PAP government's attitudes and perception of its legitimacy and ruling mandate among its electorate was sounded during the 1984 General Elections. Specifically, "there was a big swing of 12.6 per cent of votes against the PAP, which managed to secure only 62.9 per cent if compared to 75.5 per cent in 1980".[39] More important was the impact and signal from "a significant portion of the voters (who purportedly) wanted a change in both the style of government and the substance of government policies".[40] Upon closer analysis, the electoral swing accruing from socio-economic changes and attendant national issues emerging in Singapore society was to gain salience in the succeeding decades and was an issue the second and third generation leaders had to contend with increasingly.

A trend emerged among the electorate "to withhold some support in order to influence the PAP to undertake some and desist from undertaking other policies which (the electorate) approved or disapproved accordingly".[41] This was accompanied by the growing realisation amongst the electorate of "the usefulness of an Opposition in Parliament as a check on, as well as, in ensuring greater government accountability" in the 1990s.[42] The second generation leaders increasingly had to determine the nascent re-emergence of civil society within Singapore in an age of rapid economic globalisation. The shift to a more consensual and participatory style of government was confidently articulated by Goh in his 2003 National Day Rally Speech that "he has put in place a more consultative style of government, and opened up (greater) political and civic space for Singaporeans … (for their) active participation in the development of their community".[43] For him, this was an achievement and reiteration of an earlier promise made more than a decade back in 1990 to "practice a more constructive, participatory-style democracy".[44]

---

[39] Hussin Mutalib, "Workers' Party" in *Parties and Politics: A Study of Opposition Parties and the PAP in Singapore* (Singapore: Marshall Cavendish Academic, 2004) p. 140.
[40] Ibid, p. 140.
[41] Bilveer Singh, "The Election Results", *Whither PAP's Dominance: An Analysis of Singapore's 1991 General Elections* (Malaysia: Pelanduk Publications, 1992) p. 95.
[42] Ibid, p. 95.
[43] Speech by Prime Minister Goh Chok Tong at the National Day Rally on 17 August 2003 at the University Cultural Centre, National University of Singapore, Singapore Government Press Release, www.gov.sg/nd/ND03.htm, accessed on 7 December 2006.
[44] Simon S. C. Tay, "The Future of Civil Society: What Next?", in Ooi Giok Ling and Brian J. Shaw (eds.) *Beyond The Port City: Development and Identity in 21st Century Singapore*, pp. 69–107 (Singapore: Prentice Hall, 2004) pp. 75–76. The author cites *The Straits Times* articles: "Govt to Disclose Info Used in Formulating Policies"; "Let Me Know Which Rules Stifle"; "PM: Let's Make This the Finest Nation", 30 April 1991.

It is useful to discern the differences in the meanings of the concepts of the 'civic' and 'civil'. 'Civic' refers to that "pertaining to a city or a citizen".[45] 'Civic culture' is defined as "a culture that blends popular participation with effective government; supposedly, the basis for stable democratic rule".[46] Consequently, civic society refers to the conduct of "individual duties beyond the self, comprising of shared values and norms of a communitarian nature that preaches harmonious cooperation with the state and ultimately works in tandem with the national agenda established by the government".[47]

On the other hand, 'civil' pertains to the community, the ordinary life of the individual, relating to private relations amongst citizens, a private realm outside of state intervention or control.[48] Civil society refers to the individual autonomous space that is associated with the pursuit and preservation of individual rights and self-determination as well as pluralism from a liberal perspective and thus may hold an antagonistic or confrontational relationship with the state.[49]

It can be argued that the younger PAP leaders' 'exhortation for a participatory civic society' was an ostensible response to respective global and national pressures towards democratisation in the post-Cold War period and the development and maturity of Singapore society domestically. Their interpretation of a 'civic' rather than 'civil' society presented Singaporeans with a participatory space that was closely aligned with the government's national agenda and objectives. This was also to neutralise the emergence of unsolicited initiatives from the fringes or bottom.[50] This was clearly articulated by the second generation PAP leaders, arguing, "if the creation of a strong state was a major task of the last lap, the creation of a strong civic society must be a major task of the next lap".[51]

The concept of civic society from the government's perspective was first articulated by George Yeo in 1991, when he linked 'civic society' to the formation of a 'Singapore Soul', located "just below the level of the state, at the level of civic life".[52]

---

[45] A. M. Macdonald (ed.), *Chambers Twentieth Century Dictionary* (Edinburgh: W&R Chambers Ltd, 1972) p. 238.

[46] Andrew Heywood, *Politics*, p. 420.

[47] Kenneth Paul Tan, Lecture on "The Rise of Civil Society and the Challenge of Democratization".

[48] Macdonald, *Chambers Twentieth Century Dictionary*, p. 238.

[49] Kenneth Paul Tan, Lecture on "The Rise of Civil Society and the Challenge of Democratization".

[50] Terence Lee, "The Politics of Civil Society in Singapore", in *Asian Studies Review*, Vol. 26, No. 1, March 2002 (Australia: Blackwell Publishing Ltd, 2002) p. 97.

[51] Speech by BG (RES) George Yong-Boon Yeo, Acting Minister for Information and the Arts and Senior Minister of State for Foreign Affairs at the NUSS Society Inaugural Lecture 1991 at the World Trade Centre Auditorium on Thursday, 20 June 1991 at 8.00 pm, Singapore Government Press Release, p. 4, http://stars.nhb.gov.sg/stars/public/, accessed on 6 December 2006.

[52] Ibid.

For despite having a 'strong state' and a 'strong family', "civic society which is the stratum of social life between the state and the family is still weak. Without a strong civic society, the Singapore soul would be incomplete".[53] This notion of civic society has also highlighted the importance of having 'more space to grow':

> ... the state must withdraw a little and provide more space for local initiative. If the state is overpowering and intrudes into every sphere of community life, the result will be disastrous. All of us are then reduced to guests in a hotel ... The problem now is that under a banyan tree very little else can grow. When state institutions are too pervasive, civic institutions cannot thrive. Therefore, it is necessary to prune the banyan tree so that other plants can also grow.[54]

It is important not to confuse this notion of civic society with 'civil' society. This is because the merging of the private and public realms which are kept distinct in the concept of civil society has generated ambiguity concerning citizens' interpretation and use of this space. The ambiguity of the boundaries of the civic space located between the 'state' and the 'family' was one that disallowed frivolous or unrestrained participation by individuals. This was clearly reminded by BG Yeo in the same speech that:

> ... we cannot do without the banyan tree. Singapore will always need a strong centre to react quickly in a changing competitive environment. We need some pluralism but not too much because too much will also destroy us. In other words, we prune judiciously.[55]

Indeed, the younger PAP leaders' promotion of civic participation between the private and public space was more clearly delineated as an "apolitical space staked out with shifting Out-of-Bounds (OB) markers in the 1994 Catherine Lim Affair".[56] In this case, the "well-known Singaporean novelist, Catherine Lim who had contributed a commentary on 'One Government, Two Styles' in the *The Sunday Times*, purported that the then 'PM Goh's promise of a more open, consultative and consensual leadership style had been abandoned in favour of the authoritarian style of his predecessors'".[57] Of salience were the vociferous responses from Prime Minister Goh himself, who "reprimanded Lim for 'going beyond the pale' in undermining his

---

[53] Ibid, p. 4.
[54] Ibid, pp. 8–9.
[55] Ibid, p. 11.
[56] Kenneth Paul Tan, Lecture on "The Rise of Civil Society and the Challenge of Democratization".
[57] Terence Lee, "The Politics of Civil Society in Singapore", p. 109.

authority, an action deemed unacceptable and disrespectful in the Confucianist 'Asian context'".[58]

More significantly, Prime Minister Goh's speech act clearly "set in place the out-of-bounds markers, so that everyone knew the limits of openness and consultation" particularly in the 'public'/political realm.[59] It was emphasised that the parameters of political debate meant that any 'comment' on national policy would be taken seriously by the ruling government who would then take on the commentator as a political opponent, for:

> If a person wants to set the agenda for Singapore by commenting regularly on politics, that person should do this in the political arena. Because if you are outside the political arena and influence opinion, and if people believe that your policies are right, when we know they are wrong, you are not there to account for the policy.[60]

Hence, one may infer from this episode that in practice, the delineation of 'civic space' from the 'political space' was conducted through the ruling leaders' invocation of OB markers to "limit political engagement, civic action and participation, and anything else remotely linked to politics".[61] Such response from the PAP government (as subsequent examples will demonstrate) has been poignantly described as "a curious combination of political forms and practices adopted in accommodating greater socio-cultural plurality, on the one hand, while using both suppressive and auto-regulatory structures to limit its growth and development, on the other".[62]

'Civic' Society and the Operation of 'Gestural Politics'[63]

There is immense significance in the development of civic society in the Singaporean context under the broader scheme of the ruling government's exercise of 'gestural politics'. This is particularly so, in terms of the implications on the development of Singapore society and the increasing pressures for democratisation. 'Gestural politics' refers to the "employment of auto-regulation, a disciplinary tactic to ensure a panoptical, and thus automatic, functioning of power and control".[64] This was aptly highlighted by Terence Lee:

---

[58] Ibid, p. 109. The author cites Chua Beng Huat, "The Relative Autonomies of State and Civil Society in Singapore" in Gillian Koh and Ooi Giok Ling (eds.) *State-Society Relations in Singapore* (Singapore: Oxford University Press, 2000) pp. 62–76.
[59] Kenneth Paul Tan, Lecture on "The Rise of Civil Society and the Challenge of Democratization".
[60] Terence Lee, "The Politics of Civil Society in Singapore", p. 109.
[61] Terence Lee, "The Politics of Civil Society in Singapore", p. 110.
[62] Ibid, p. 110.
[63] Ibid, p. 110.
[64] Ibid, p. 110.

The Singaporean idea of civil society is an excellent example of 'gestural politics': on the one hand, citizens are encouraged to harness the positive energies of the Singapore 21 vision, especially with regard to becoming active citizens; on the other, stern warnings are issued at regular intervals to remind people of the existence of OB-markers and other state-defined conditions.[65]

A classic case in point demonstrating the government's display of gestural politics is to be found in the actual and metaphorical silence of the Speakers' Corner located in Hong Lim Park. Opened on 1 September 2000, Singapore's Speakers' Corner was "loosely modelled after London's Hyde Park", a popular emblem of 'free speech'.[66] While the professed decision in allowing Singapore's first-ever free speech venue was to "help develop civil society" by making active citizenship 'more visible', the rules and regulations speakers have to undergo appear more a hindrance to the 'free' articulation of opinions and viewpoints relating to issues on the minds of citizens. This is evident in the requirement placed on speakers to register preferably up to a month in advance at an adjacent police post and to demonstrate proof of their Singaporean citizenship, with the reminder that "all existing Singapore laws, along with the cryptic 'OB markers' that bar discussion of racial, religious and sensitive political issues, apply unconditionally".[67] In all objectivity, one has to acknowledge that the provisions preventing the discussion of 'racial, religious and sensitive political issues' is a justifiable one for the preservation of this multi-ethnic and multi-religious state's racial harmony and social stability. At the same time, while Singaporeans are encouraged to participate in the national debate, with the government's perception that "we are now able to discuss openly sensitive issues to do with race, language and religion", perhaps, the ambiguity lies in the context and manner in which questions are raised in Singapore, namely, whether they fall within the ambit of 'civic' or 'civil' space.[68]

However, upon closer analysis, while signals sent by the ruling government demonstrate a greater desire on the part of the government to actively involve its citizens, it is apparent that such discussion will continue to be dominated and led through official channels such as the Feedback Unit or through opinion pieces submitted to *The Straits Times*, a government-controlled newspaper. The Feedback Unit, established by the then Prime Minister Goh was set up as a public consultation mechanism

---

[65] Ibid, p. 110. The author applies Michel Foucalt's theoretical concept in describing the application and use of gestural politics in Singapore's development of civic society.
[66] Ibid, p. 110.
[67] Ibid, p. 110.
[68] Speech by Deputy Prime Minister Lee Hsien Loong at the Singapore 21 Forum organised by Ang Mo Kio-Cheng San Community Development Council on 16 January 2000 at the Grassroots' Club. See Singapore Government Press Release at http://stars.nhb.gov.sg/stars/public/.

intended to promote greater consultation and open government (and vice versa) on policy matters and issues of national concern. From this, it can be inferred that any understanding of the 'civic society' is one promoted by the government and which hinges fundamentally on a collaborative relationship between the citizenry and the PAP government. Interestingly, the Feedback Unit upon reaching its 21st anniversary in October 2006 has re-positioned itself under the new name — REACH (Reaching Everyone for Active Citizenry @ Home), premised upon its progress "from being a bureau for public complaints to becoming a key driver in promoting a culture of public consultation in the government".[69]

In line with REACH's repositioning is the attempt to match up with the trends of the Knowledge-Based Economy (KBE) as well as to tap onto the availability of forms of new media, which has led to its decision to officially launch blogs on its website in the first half of 2007.[70] Underlying the increased professionalism displayed on the part of these official avenues catered for civic participation, is the PAP government's "greater finesse and subtlety" in employing the "twin strategies of co-optation and auto-regulation" within the civil society landscape.[71] Thus, it is arguable that such increasing sophistication displayed by the government's co-optation of public consultative mechanisms is likely to ensure the continuation and extension of the ruling government's control over these civic spaces in this KBE. Furthermore, one should note that "greater consultation in itself has not led and does not necessarily lead to social and political structural changes. On the contrary, it can contribute to further penetration of the state into the social body via a capillary mode of governance".[72]

Having analysed the contemporary extension of government control and management of civic spaces through official state-backed channels of feedback and consultative processes, it is equally important to explore the potential for the development of 'civil' spaces from the ground and fringes of Singapore society. More critically, it has been argued that despite the apparent achievements in engaging cross-sections of the public, there are "insufficient, if not ineffective avenues provided for the participation of critical individuals who choose not to affiliate with any of the mechanisms of

---

[69] Ibid, p. 108.
[70] Channel News Asia, "Feedback Unit to Officially Launch Blogs in First Half of 2007", 6 December 2006, http://www.channelnewsasia.com/stories/singaporelocalnews/print/245630/1/.html, accessed on 11 December 2006.
[71] Terence Lee, "The Politics of Civil Society in Singapore", p. 112.
[72] Chua Beng Huat, "Constrained NGOs and Arrested Democratisation in Singapore" in Robert P. Weller (ed.) *Civil Life, Globalisation and Political Change in Asia: Organising between Family and State* (New York: Routledge, 2005) p. 71.

the ruling party and government".[73] The onset of the internet age in the mid-1990s saw the cyberspace as one of the 'cracks in the system' that escaped government regulation.[74] This seemed the case especially with the establishment of the Singapore Internet Community (Sintercom) by a Singaporean PhD student at Stanford University in 1994, "at a time when the internet seemed tailor-made for the civic sector" which "straddles the pre- and post-regulation periods in Singapore".[75]

Sintercom had been born out of the desire to start the Singapore Electronic Forum (SEF) for the articulation of "the voice of the ordinary citizens, who respond to the current affairs of their time from a different perspective" from that of "official mass media like *The Straits Times*".[76] By 1995, with the increase in internet users, the website "found its niche as a space for open, public discussion of current affairs and national issues".[77] Nevertheless, of significance is the impact of the closure of Sintercom in August 2001, which was 'publicly' conveyed by its founder that "he was too tired to go on".[78] More specifically, the 'exhaustion' expressed by the founder was perceived as a "reference to the difficulty in liaising with the Singapore Broadcasting Authority (SBA) over the vetting and ruling of site materials and having been asked to register Sintercom with the authority as a political site".[79]

Does the closure of the Sintercom signify a 'lost cause' for the emergence of a nascent civil society in Singapore? Chua Beng Huat highlights the 'collateral damage' for 'individuals in civil society' in having the 'official policy' which seeks to ensure that "certain politically incendiary (materials) don't get on the Net".[80] With regard to the emerging spaces for nascent civil society activity in an age of globalisation, the SBA's explanation of necessary regulations to "maintain harmony and protect national security"; thus the "demand that designated political sites be registered" and the "encouragement of industry self-regulation" certainly highlight the realm of the political to be out of the boundaries of civic participation.[81] Consequently one might

---

[73] Chua Beng Huat, "Liberalization without Democratisation: Singapore in the Next Decade" in Francis Loh Kok Wah and Joakim Ojendal (eds.) *Southeast Asian Responses to Globalisation: Restructuring Governance and Deepening Democracy*, pp. 57–82 (Singapore: Institute of Southeast Asian Studies, 2005) p. 74.
[74] Chua Beng Huat, "Constrained NGOs and Arrested Democratization in Singapore", p. 180.
[75] Cherian George, "Sintercom: Harnessing of Virtual Community" in *Contentious Journalism and the Internet: Towards Democratic Discourse in Malaysia and Singapore*, pp. 99–119 (Singapore: Singapore University Press, 2006) p. 99.
[76] Ibid, p. 101.
[77] Ibid, p. 102.
[78] Chua Beng Huat, "Constrained NGOs and Arrested Democratization in Singapore", p. 178.
[79] Ibid, pp. 178–179.
[80] Ibid, p. 179. The author cites *The Straits Times*, 27 April 2002.
[81] Ibid, pp. 179–182.

argue that the de-politicisation of the citizenry albeit active, has been achieved from the examples illustrated thus far of the state's propensity to "penalise those who step out of bounds", "… either by strong public rebuke from the government or by being taken to court for defamation or other civil violations".[82]

The de-politicisation of the 'civic society' as opposed to the 'civil society' is further compounded by the stark juxtaposition of Sintercom in comparison to the relative success in the development of the more activist Association of Women for Action and Research (AWARE) in particular, since 1985. On one level, the contrasts between Sintercom and AWARE bring out the stark distinction between civil society organisations (CSOs) from political organisations within the local landscape.[83] Second and equally important is the point that where civil society activity falls within the OB markers and official channels are used, negotiations with the state have led to successes in the preservation of socio-political interests within Singapore society. This is best evident in AWARE's cautious pursuit of politically correct agenda that apparently fall within established OB markers. A good example would be its adoption of politically cautious language by "calling itself a 'women's', rather than a feminist organisation", which "may be a strategic choice to gain public discursive space and 'legitimacy' for its agenda of reforms, such as forcing the government to come to deal with family violence, particularly against the women".[84] More significantly, AWARE has demonstrated a success in "exploiting the changes in the parliamentary structure to achieve formal representation in Parliament".[85] This is evident in its "successful nomination of a 'women's' candidate as a Nominated Member of Parliament (NMP) in each Parliament", since the ruling government's introduction of the 'strategy' in order to "alleviate public pressure for Opposition voices in the single-party dominated Parliament".[86]

This effectively highlights that all is not lost for the future of civil society, more specifically alongside and in tandem with state policies and the established boundaries of civil/civic activity that is strictly separated from the political realm. The de-politicised emergence of a nascent civil and non-political society is further compounded by the successes of the Nature Society of Singapore (NSS), a "vocal and visible CSO whose core activity is green environment conservatism".[87] Its successes are best demonstrated in the "government's decision to gazette in January 2002, an area of bird sanctuary that the NSS had struggled for years to obtain which had been targeted for

---

[82] Ibid, p. 179.
[83] Chua Beng Huat, "Liberalization without Democratization: Singapore in the Next Decade", p. 62.
[84] Ibid, p. 61.
[85] Ibid, p. 61.
[86] Ibid, p. 62.
[87] Ibid, p. 62.

reclamation".[88] This is in addition to the "protection of a mud flat on *Chek Jawa* from reclamation on the account of its rich biodiversity".[89] From the successes of AWARE and NSS in negotiating with the government on policy issues that matter through official channels, there is a need to rethink the perception of an 'adversarial' state-society dynamics with regard to the civil society landscape in Singapore.[90]

Negotiation of Socio-Political Space between the State and Society — Implications for Democratisation

The notion of the collaboration between civil society and the ruling government, in areas where "civil society can complement state structures at different levels and in ways that promote developmental goals", in particular, has been highlighted under the possibility of 'state-society energies'.[91] The imperative from the trends of the globalising city-state has seen the recognition by Yeo that:

> What we are now seeing is a new mutually reinforcing relationship between the state and society. While the Singapore state supports the growth of civic organisations, the state has not got total control over them. In fact, the state increasingly relies on them to do the things which government has not got total control over them.[92]

It is important to note that this applies particularly with regard to the achievement of two goals — first, the "reinforcement of the reputation of the Singapore label" and second, the "expansion of and extension of the Singapore network into the region and beyond" which falls under the broader purview of the national-identity building and consolidation project.[93] In addition, the establishment of a 'Singapore label' is hoped to enforce greater national pride and sensibilities, thereby compounding the civic roots amongst the emergent cosmopolitan class of Singaporeans. A good example is the setting up of civic organisations such as the Singapore International

---

[88] Ibid, p. 65.
[89] Ibid, p. 65.
[90] Gillian Koh and Ooi Giok Ling (eds.), *State-Society Relations in Singapore* (Singapore: Oxford University Press, 2000) p. 1.
[91] Ibid, p. 1.
[92] Speech by BG George Yeo, Minister for Information and the Arts and Second Minister for Trade and Industry at IPS Conference on "Civil Society: Harnessing State-Society Synergies" on 6 May 1998 at 9 a.m at Orchard Hotel, http://stars.nhb.gov.sg/stars/public/, accessed on 10 December 2006.
[93] Ibid.

Foundation (SIF) which is based abroad to "facilitate and support the Cosmopolitan Singaporean" overseas.[94]

In sum, the civil society landscape in Singapore is immensely shaped after the notion of a civic society which is "bounded to the Singapore idea".[95] It is one which "involves both the heart and the mind", and "aspects like good governance, civic responsibility, honesty, strong families, hard work, a spirit of voluntarism, and the use of many languages and a deep respect for racial and religious diversity".[96] While it allows for some extent of negotiation and collaboration with valid arguments by non-overtly political CSOs, the OB markers, though shifting, have established a clear demarcation disallowing the pressures from the bottom or fringes with an overtly activist or political orientation on grounds of preserving this multi-ethnic state's racial and religious harmony and social stability.

Relating to the issue of domestic and international pressures for democratisation from the ground, it has been demonstrated and reinforced since Lee Kuan Yew's leadership till that under Lee Hsien Long today that the preservation of national security stands foremost at the necessary expense of the space and voice for civil society activities that are deemed to threaten the socio-political stability of this nation. This was clearly articulated by Wong Kan Seng, the then Home Affairs Minister:

> Excess emphases on democracy and press freedom to the detriment of good governance and stability have led to chaos and loss of confidence ... Good governance is necessary for the realisation of all rights ... Democracy, human rights and press freedom do not exist in a vacuum. By themselves, these concepts do not guarantee development and progress.[97]

Even more significant was the Singapore government's decision at the Annual Meetings of the International Monetary Fund (IMF) and World Bank (WB) hosted in September 2006 to "ban five of the 27 individuals on their official blacklist from entry into Singapore" as well as its press statement on 15 September 2006 that "it will not allow 22 of 27 officially blacklisted individuals to enter the country".[98] This was in addition to 'the official and unofficial blacklists' which the International People's

---

[94] See Brenda S. A. Yeoh, "Cosmopolitanism and Its Exclusions in Singapore", *Urban Studies*, Vol. 41 No.12, pp. 2431–2445, November 2004, p. 2436.
[95] Ibid.
[96] Ibid.
[97] See "Singapore, World Bank and IMF Attempt to Save Face; International Peoples Forum Says 'too Little, too Late'", Statement of the IPF Convenors' Committee, International People's Forum vs the IMF-World Bank, in response to Singapore 2006 Organising Committee's Sep 15 statement, 16 September 2006, Batam, Indonesia.
[98] Ibid.

Forum perceived as "the (Singapore) government's intention to curb the exercise of democracy and free speech within its territory (which) extends beyond those on its official blacklist".[99]

In the context of the Global War on Terror' and the activism of international CSOs and anti-globalisers, the Singapore government's press release emphasised its sovereign right to control the entry by foreigners into the country. This has been rationalised on the grounds of 'the current security environment' and the need to exercise caution:

> ... especially when a high profile event like the IMF/WB meetings is (sic) held here. The meetings will attract the attention of many, not least those who may want to use the ready platform and presence of the international media to stage events that will pose a security threat to Singapore, and compromise the level of security arrangements we have put in place.[100]

Therefore, in the context of the post-September 11 world and the 'Global War on Terror', there is a possibility that while Singapore which has gone past its initial phases of state-building in its early independence may in the near future face a greater curtailment of civil society space and activity. This is especially so in face of the increased securitisation of this global city among the ranks of its developed capitalist and largely Western counterparts in a region of separatist and religious fundamentalist activities.

Singapore's ban on the activists and CSOs at the IMF/WB meetings led Paul Wolfowitz, the WB President to describe Singapore as 'authoritarian'. On 15 September 2006, he argued:

> Enormous damage has been done ... A lot of that damage has been to Singapore and it's self-inflicted. I would certainly argue that at the stage of success they've reached, they'd be much better for themselves if they took a more visionary approach to the process.[101]

In a different national and global setting, one can clearly discern the importance of the preservation of state security is paramount in the minds of the government, in

---

[99] Ibid.
[100] Police News Release: Police's Statement on IMF/WB Joint Statement, Public Affairs Department, Singapore Police Force, Friday, 8 September 2006 at 6 p.m, http://www2.mha.gov.sg/mha/upload/mid27/type8/cat28/2079_313_SPF%20Statement%20on%20IMFWB%20joint%20statement.pdf, accessed on 12 December 2006 from the Ministry of Home Affairs website.
[101] BBC News, 15 September 2006. See http://news.bbc.co.uk/2/hi/asia-pacific/5348134.stm; also see Reuters, "Singapore's activist ban 'authoritarian': Wolfowitz", 15 September 2006.

spite of the leadership changes which have seen greater relaxation and negotiation of 'civic' and 'civil' society spaces. Last but not least, the evolution and negotiation of the civil society landscape in Singapore have witnessed some extent of liberalisation effected by the ruling government's "ongoing and selective opening of participatory spaces to civil society activities and organisation" as well as initiatives and pressures from civil society activities from the ground and fringes of Singapore society.

However, it has been saliently observed that in view of the state's "strict definition of 'politics' as the purview of political parties and an unyielding emphasis on the primacy of economic development", the liberalising trends within Singapore is bounded by the 'hegemonic position' of the dominant one-party political system and thus may not lead to the democratisation of the polity. Of immense importance in unravelling the paradoxical placement of an illiberal democratic system within the global economy which has embraced rapid economic globalisation is the observation that:

> ... contrary to the assumption of the causal linkage between the rise of the middle class and general political democratisation, Singapore shows a middle-class whose 'good life' is dependent on government economic policies has very little interests in disrupting the political structure and stability that are delivering that good life, even when this stability is maintained by repressive measures.[102]

Therefore, for the critical mass of 'middle-class Singaporeans', it is apparent that the material and socio-economic development of a 'good life' is privileged over abstract notions of freedom and liberal rights and a Western style of democracy which is highly unlikely to take root with the dominance of the ruling PAP government. For Singapore in the 21st century, good governance under a strong, reliable corrupt-free government appears the way to go, contented with a nascent civil and civic consciousness that is closely aligned to the national agenda of the government.

Conclusion

In summary, this study has demonstrated that economic development, affluence among a critical mass of Singaporeans and the relaxation of Lee Kuan Yew's authoritarian style of government have paved the way for the nascent emergence of 'civil' and 'civic' spaces. These activities are likely to thrive with the support and collaboration of the state. Nevertheless, these will only blossom in future as most Singaporeans remain contended with the pursuit of a 'good life' and in a landscape of racial and religious harmony and social stability. Civil society and democratisation will develop

---

[102] Chua Beng Huat, "Constrained NGOs and Arrested Democratization in Singapore", p. 175.

under a 'Singapore brand', with its own concept of illiberal but good governance. This is also likely to go hand in hand with the active participation in a civic society that supports the promotion of national development and social peace.

Think Questions

1. What is a civil society in the Singapore context?
2. Why is civic society more active than civil society in Singapore?
3. Can civil society thrive in Singapore?

Chapter Nine

Rise of New Issues in Singapore's Politics

> Nobody else but the government can build houses not just to achieve a housing objective, but to achieve a social goal — racial integration, community bonding, establishing and upgrading and maintaining a high quality living environment for the whole community … Singaporeans' aspirations have risen sharply. Finding a roof over our heads is no longer the pressing requirement. The HDB flat is not just a shelter, but also a key investment asset.[1]

Introduction

Many Singaporeans thought that the Republic would be ready to withstand any difficulty after being consecutively hit by the post-9/11 recession and SARS epidemic but few were prepared to witness the worst financial meltdown in history in 2008. Many investors lost their lifetime savings in financial products directly linked to the sub-prime housing mortgage crisis in the United States while businesses were hit by the slowdown in demand. Yet, when the economy had just begun to pick up, speculation on both the HDB flat and private property markets led to escalating property prices — to the disgruntlement of many Singaporeans. In addition, the emergence of a new elite — rich foreigners — increased resentment amongst home buyers who felt that these non-citizens were inflating property prices and displacing Singaporeans from homes that should rightfully be Singaporean-owned. This chapter focuses on five main interrelated topics that have been of increasing concern in the recent years: immigration, housing, income inequality, democracy, and the issue of race and religion.

---

[1] Statement made by Lee Hsien Loong, cited in "New Flats Will Stay Affordable: PM Lee", *The Straits Times*, 27 January 2010.

Immigration

The census report released in September 2015 showed that Singapore's population reached the 5.53-million mark, with foreigners making up 29.4%. The government plans to bring in more immigrants — official numbers have ranged from 100,000 more foreign workers, in order to increase the Singapore population to 6.5 million. The former CEO of HDB, Tay Kim Poh, even predicted that the quality of life in Singapore would not be heavily affected even if the population were to hit 7.5 million people.[2] Adding to the overcrowding is the 1.1 million tourists who set foot on the island every month.[3]

It is important to have a general distinction between two types of migrants, namely, the Foreign Talents (FTs) and the Foreign Workers (FWs). Based on skill level more than anything else, FTs are white-collar workers consisting of professionals, managers, executives and specialists that are highly sought after by various organisations. Foreign students who take up permanent residence upon graduation from universities also fall into this category. The FWs, on the other hand, consist of 'S' Pass holders — mid-skilled workers earning at least S$1,800 per month — and 'R' Pass holders and domestic workers — low-skilled or unskilled workers.

The reactions towards the presence of FWs have been mixed. On one hand, residents in middle-class Serangoon Gardens were petitioning against the building of a dormitory for foreign workers in their neighbourhood in 2006. The reasons given ranged from financial — "having the dormitory in close vicinity will decrease my property value" — to downright bigotry: "the construction workers will rob me if they live right across". When Prime Minister Lee Hsien Loong mentioned that 100,000 more FWs would be hired early in 2010, concerns arose again about whether they would be competing with Singaporeans for jobs. Other issues include overcrowding, the competition for housing, congestion on public transportation, including Mass Rapid Transit and more epistemological matters like nation building.[4]

On the other hand, it has been acknowledged that these FWs are easily exploited and work with very little welfare. Reports have surfaced online that these workers were living under miserable conditions[5] and had no recourse if their salaries were

---

[2] "S'pore Has Room for 7.5m People: Ex-HDB Chief", *Todayonline*, 9 September 2010, www.todayonline.com/Singapore/EDC100909-0000132/Spore-has-room-for-7,5m-people--Ex-HDB-chief.

[3] "No more the most open", *The Star Online*, 4 September 2010, thestar.com.my/columnists/story.asp?col=insightdownsouth&file=2010/9/4/columnists/insightdownsouth/6972260&sec=Insight%20Down%20%20South.

[4] See Transcript of Prime Minister Lee Hsien Loong's National Day Rally English Speech on 29 August 2010. Available at https://www.mfa.gov.sg/content/mfa/overseasmission/washington/newsroom/press_statements.html, accessed on 19 September 2016.

[5] "TOC Special Feature: Is Singapore Really Slum-Free?", *The Online Citizen*, 27 September 2009, theonlinecitizen.com/2009/09/toc-special-feature-is-singapore-really-slum-free.

withheld. The latter led to a rare protest consisting of 100 Bangladeshi migrant workers, who gathered outside the Ministry of Manpower demanding their overdue salary. The group was also unwilling to be deported — despite there being no jobs during the 2008 recession — as many of them had taken loans to finance their trip to Singapore.[6] Those that returned home before earning enough to finance their loan often ended up penniless. Partly in response to the FWs' plight, Non-Government Organisations such as TWC2 (Transient Workers Count Too) and HOME (Humanitarian Organisation for Migration Economics) have emerged as a reaction against this perceived injustice.[7]

On a macroeconomic level, the government has also acknowledged that a near-limitless supply of cheap labour provided by foreign workers has caused a stagnation in the productivity of Singaporean industries;[8] by relying on manual labour instead of investing in capital or infrastructure, companies produce less work per worker and hence, are less productive. Although foreign worker levies have been increased in a bid to push companies to invest in technology and innovation,[9] and the government has set aside a sizeable sum of money in skills upgrading programmes for locals — S$400 million will be spent on Workfare, for example — the official stance continues to be pro-immigrant.[10] The challenge for the government is to balance the need for more migrant workers to do low-skilled work and the simultaneous imperative of quelling the discontent from citizens.[11]

The FTs are not spared from the 'old' citizens and 'new' citizens debate. In sports, for example, table tennis FTs such as Feng Tianwei and Li Jiawei, who are both China-born, were controversial sports heroes. Despite winning the silver medal for Singapore in the 2008 Olympics, Li still drew flak for being 'not truly Singaporean', and drew accusations that she had been given citizenship only to compete under the Singapore flag. Similarly, the liberalisation of the financial sector in the late 1990s prompted the steady influx of foreign CEOs into the banking sector. The debate was reignited again in 2010, and former DBS (Development Bank of Singapore) and senior civil servant, Ngiam Tong Dow, responded that:

---

[6] "Jobless Migrant Workers Protest in Singapore Again", *Reuters*, 27 February 2009, in.reuters.com/article/idINIndia-38247620090227.

[7] "Legal Recourse for Foreign Workers", *The Online Citizen*, 16 June 2009, theonlinecitizen.com/2009/06/legal-recourse-for-foreign-workers/.

[8] "Singapore Budget 2010", www.mof.gov.sg/budget_2010/speech_toc/pc.html, last updated 24 February 2010.

[9] "Foreign Worker Levy to Rise", *Reuters*, 3 July 2010, www.straitstimes.com/BreakingNews/Singapore/Story/STIStory_54913.html.

[10] National Day Rally Speech, 2010.

[11] National Day Rally Speech, 2010.

> When I was at DBS, our colleagues and I believed in growing our own timber … Foreign talents are like instant trees — they collapse at the first sight of a storm. We have to grow our own timber even though it may take longer.[12]

Just as in the debate over FWs, the inflation prices of HDB flats in the resale market have been blamed on the FTs and Permanent Residents. Unlike the FWs, however, FTs hold employment passes that allow them to bring their family members; they are also not subject to levies.[13] Some have even speculated that it is perhaps the 'politics of gratitude' that has influenced the PAP's pro-immigration policies. Driven partially by resentment over the lowered scarcity of citizenship, these critics purport that the PAP brings in pro-establishment new citizens to boost its waning popularity during elections.[14]

Aside from the FWs and FTs, there has been another prominent class of wealthy foreigners entering the country. More specifically, with the opening of the Sentosa Cove properties marketed towards the ultra-rich, the foreigners who are fast-tracked to permanent resident status via the Financial Investor Scheme, have become a class of their own.[15] According to the Monetary Authority of Singapore (MAS), these applicants must possess a minimum of S$20 million in Net Personal Assets, and must also place at least S$5 million of assets in Singapore, including one Sentosa Cove bungalow and a minimum of S$3 million in financial assets.

Aside from anti-immigrant sentiments, there is also the challenge of nation building with such a huge influx of new Singaporeans. Using Benedict Anderson's definition of a nation as an 'imagined community', a nascent nation needs to have a stable population size, common language and culture. If the rate of immigration were to continue, it would be an uphill task to organically forge a common language (localised English) and a uniquely Singapore culture.

Public Infrastructure

With rapid population growth in a super-dense city-state such as Singapore, the blistering pace of urbanisation has led to a stretch in public infrastructure. Complaints about overcrowding in trains, for example, have prompted the government to spend an extra S$60 billion over the next decade to double the rail network. However, MRT

---

[12] "DBS Chief Reignites Debate on Foreign Talent", *The Straits Times*, 19 June 2010.

[13] Brenda Yeoh (2007), "Singapore: Hungry for Foreign Workers at All Skill Levels", www.migrationinformation.org/Profiles/display.cfm?ID=570, accessed 15 September 2010.

[14] Seah Chiang Nee, "Politics of Gratitude", *The Star Online*, 3 July 2010, thestar.com/my/news/story.asp?file=/2010/7/3/focus/6590708&sec=focus, accessed 7 July 2010.

[15] See "Financial Investor Scheme" as run by the Monetary Authority of Singapore, www.sentosacove.com/FIS%20Ts&Cs%20-%20Option%20B.pdf, accessed 20 July 2010.

commuters would only enjoy shorter waiting times — about a sixth quicker — in six years' time.[16] Flash floods that left parts of Orchard Road submerged, causing S$23 million worth of damage, also begged the question of whether Singapore was prepared to handle the effects of rapid urbanisation.[17] Transport and drainage problems aside, the key challenge to sustainable development in Singapore still lies in its acclaimed public housing model.

With 80% of all Singaporeans living in HDB flats, public housing is a pervasive extension of the state, to the extent that it forms an integral role in the PAP's political and social control, and hence, legitimacy. It can even be said that a key component of the Faustian bargain between the state and the society, is the promise that all citizens, regardless of income or race, should have a roof over their heads. Yet, in recent years, cracks have formed in this national myth of each citizen owning a 'stake' in their country via the possession of some form of property.

As part of the asset enhancement policy spearheaded by the then Minister for National Development, Mah Bow Tan, HDB flats were seen not only homes for their owners but also a form of investment. Though flat prices have been increasing steadily over the years in line with Singapore's economic development, HDB prices hit a record high in 2010. Cash-over-Valuations (COVs), that is, the amount paid in addition to the bank-approximated price of the resale flat, hit S$30,000.[18] This prompted MM Lee Kuan Yew to urge Singaporeans not to cast protest votes over rising flat prices.[19] Prime Minister Lee Hsien Loong too, had to assure the public that the government was committed to keeping the rising prices of new HDB flats in check, although it had less control in the resale market.[20] Unsurprisingly, some Opposition parties openly declared that they would contest in the Tampines GRC, where Minister Mah was then its key Group Representation Constituency member.[21]

Cooling measures, have, however, been introduced in stages to calm the HDB property market. On the supply side, there were promises to increase the number of HDB flats built and to expedite the completion of Build-To-Order (BTO) flats (that is, flats bought directly from the HDB, and not from the resale market). To decrease the chances for speculation, restrictions on property owners buying HDB resale flats

---

[16] "A Six-Year Wait — for Shorter Waiting Times", *Todayonline*, 3 September 2010, www.todayonline.com/Singapore/EDC100903-0000108/A-six-year-wait---for-shorter-waiting-times.
[17] "Model City Singapore Shows Symptoms of Urban Stress", *AFP*, 24 August 2010, www.google.com/hostednews/afp/article/ALeqM5jzAlHpBUkU-kAkHJbfLpjovDds9g.
[18] "They Paid $130,000 COV for Yishun Flat 14 Years Ago", *Asiaone*, 31 July 2010, business.asiaone.com/Business/My%2BMoney/Property/Story/A1Story20100729-229476.html.
[19] "Don't Cast Protest Vote over Rising Flat Prices: MM", *The Straits Times*, 28 January 2010.
[20] "New Flats Will Stay Affordable", *The Straits Times*, 27 January 2010.
[21] "A Minister Must Fall in the Process of Change", *The Online Citizen*, 28 February 2010, theonlinecitizen.com/2010/02/a-minister-must-fall-in-the-process-of-change-says-nsp-sec-gen.

were also tightened. This included a 70% cap on loan-to-property-value for second mortgages, increasing the minimum cash payment from 5–10% of the flat valuation and also raising the Minimum Occupation Period (MOP) for the resale of non-subsidised HDB flats from one and two-and-a-half years to three years in order to reinforce owner-occupation.[22] Accompanying the debate on immigration, S$10,000 of HDB subsidies will be withheld from households with permanent residents until they take up citizenship.[23]

Aside from the economics of public housing, the politicisation of public housing by political parties has also become more prominent in the national consciousness. While it was previously expected and even taken for granted that wards under the ruling party had priority in various block upgrading schemes, this privilege has been increasingly questioned by both the press and the public.[24] A Town Council Management Report published in mid-2010 which graded the condition of HDB constituencies throughout Singapore, saw coincidentally, the then only two Opposition wards, namely, Hougang and Potong Pasir, at the bottom end while the wards of Minister Mentor Lee Kuan Yew and Prime Minister Lee Hsien Loong emerged tops. This ignited accusation by politicians from both the ruling party and Opposition, on whether each side was politicising the survey, and whether such reports should be politicised in the first place.[25]

Lastly, reports of homeless Singaporeans camping at Changi Beach and Sembawang Park have, again, brought questions regarding the national myth that all Singaporeans, by right, should be housed. Debates, both online and offline, were abound, discussing whether the government should be responsible for Singaporeans who are unable to afford HDB flats. Possibly, in response, the HDB promised to increase the supply of rental flats (for low-income families) to 50,000 units. Combined with amendments to the eligibility rules, the HDB also promised to half the waiting time, to 12 months, for needy families to be allocated a rental flat.[26]

The Economy

According to veteran diplomat Professor Tommy Koh, economic inequality has regressed from 0.436 to 0.478 over the past 20 years.[27] Yet, it was only in the

---

[22] "Reinforcing Owner-Occupation among HDB Flat Owners", www.hdb.gov.sg/fi10/fi10296p.nsf/PressReleases/3806E948A258B7A4482576DD00216692?OpenDocument, accessed 30 July 2010.

[23] "Policy Changes to Support an Inclusive and Cohesive Home", www.hdb.gov.sg/fi10/fi10296p.nsf/PressReleases/C515273FA086DD58482576DD00169155?OpenDocument, accessed 30 July 2010.

[24] "Adviser over MP Raises Many Questions", *The Straits Times*, 22 October 2009.

[25] "Low, Chiam Dismisses Report", *The Straits Times*, 11 June 2010.

[26] "In HDB Living, 'Give and Take Is Often Necessary'", *The Straits Times*, 6 March 2010.

[27] "Basic Pay: Tommy Koh Weighs in", *The Straits Times*, 15 September 2010.

post-2008 crisis world that the social divide has become more apparent. While there are groups of people buying S$36-million-dollar houses on Sentosa Cove, there are also groups of families living in tents at parks and beaches. The line between the 'haves' and 'have-nots' is not only drawn in terms of the types of housing but also in terms of 'who controls the money'.

During the worst financial crisis in history, an estimated 10,000 investors bought S$501 million worth of structured financial products linked to American investment giant, Lehman Brothers' Holdings, which collapsed. Over 500 of these investors participated in a rally on 11 October 2008, demanding compensation.[28] Though the victims were eventually compensated, there was much speculation that the DBS in Singapore only responded to the protest demands after the Hong Kong branch compensated their own investors.[29] Marginalisation in this case, was marked by those who possessed financial know-how and the small-time investors who did not. In the same vein, news that Town Councils were investing their sinking funds and sometimes, making losses, also ignited debates on whether residents should have been consulted before such public funds were used for investment.[30] Together with news that sovereign wealth funds such as GIC (Government Investment Corporation) and Temasek Holdings were making high losses, issues of accountability and transparency were once again at the forefront of public discussion.[31]

Visible economic disparity combined with record inflation of 7.4% in 2008 amidst increasing unemployment during the downturn, brought questions towards the government's stewardship of the economy.[32] Arguably, good management of the crisis, diminished the amount of public disaffection felt, in comparison to other affected countries. Initiatives such as the Job Credit Scheme and SPUR (Skills Programme for Upgrading and Resilience) helped shore up overall employment.[33] To the shock of the international community, Singapore's economy bounced back in

---

[28] "Singapore Investors to Seek Compensation on Lehman Minibonds", *Bloomberg*, www.bloomberg.com/apps/news?pid=newsarchive&sid=asigYSI14dIM&refer=asia, accessed 30 July 2010.

[29] "Difference between Singapore and Hong Kong", *The Online Citizen*, 20 October 2008, theonlinecitizen.com/2008/10/structured-products-difference-between-spore-and-hong-kong/, accessed 30 July 2010.

[30] "Town Councils and Sinking Funds", *Singapore Daily*, singaporedaily.net/town-councils-sinking-funds/, accessed 30 July 2010.

[31] Rolf Jordan, "Singapore in Its Worst Recession for Years: The Effects of the Current Economic Crisis on the City-State's Economy", *Journal of Current Southeast Asian Affairs*, Vol. 28 No. 4, pp. 95–110.

[32] "S'poreans Happy with Govt, but Not about Rising Costs", *The Straits Times*, 7 August 2009; "Did the Poor Really Progress?", *The Straits Times*, 17 June 2009. Also see Ganesan Narayanan, "Singapore in 2008: A Few Highs and Lows while Bracing for the Future", *Asian Survey*, Vol. 49 No. 1, p. 219.

[33] "SPUR Significantly Cushioned Fallout from Economic Crisis: Gan", *Channel News Asia*, 27 July 2010; "Exercise Wage Flexibility Even in Times of High Growth: PM", *Channel News Asia*, 28 July 2010.

2010 with an estimated 13–15% GDP growth, making it one of the fastest growing economies in the world.[34] Although it was reported that the exports of biomedical products led the growth, it was tourism that dominated public discourse in post-financial crisis Singapore.[35]

Both integrated resorts, Marina Bay Sands (MBS) and Resorts World Sentosa (RWS), opened with much fanfare, even though the projects had previously been plagued by sudden increases in sand prices and reported shortages of labour and materials.[36] Initially estimated to cost US$3.2 billion,[37] the bill for MBS eventually came up to US$5.5 billion,[38] nearly two times more. This put pressure on the casino to recoup its losses — MBS declared that they would recover their costs within five years. In terms of economic value, it was reported that the Integrated Resorts had added S$470 million or about 0.3% of GDP to the Singapore economy in the first half of 2010.[39] Tourist arrivals to Singapore also grew 24.1% to reach 1,095,000 in July.[40] Yet, it was also reported that gambling addiction was a real problem — a Singaporean businessman lost S$26 million at RWS in three days.[41]

The 2010 Youth Olympic Games (YOG) was another initiative to increase Singapore's profile as a tourist destination. Like MBS, the YOG tripled its budget from S$104 million to S$387 million,[42] though according to Ministry of Community, Youth and Sports, S$260 million dollars' worth of contracts were awarded to local

---

[34] "Sing a Song of Singapore: Small Asian State an Economic Powerhouse", *International Business Times*, 14 August 2010, www.ibtimes.com/articles/43426/20100814/singapore-gdp.htm.

[35] "Singapore Expects Double-Digit 2010 Economic Growth", *Channel News Asia*, 14 July 2010, www.channelnewsasia.com/stories/singaporebusinessnews/view/1069259/1/.html.

[36] "Las Vegas Sands Says Singapore Casino Opening Delayed", *Asiaone*, 8 July 2009, www.asiaone.com/Travel/News/Story/A1Story20090708-153565.html.

[37] "Las Vegas Sands Is Chosen to Build Singapore Casino", *The New York Times*, 27 May 2006, www.nytimes.com/2006/05/27/business/worldbusiness/27casino.html?_r=1.

[38] "Las Vegas Sands Says Singapore Casino Opening Delayed", *Asiaone*, 8 July 2009, www.asiaone.com/Travel/News/Story/A1Story20090708-153565.html.

[39] "DBS Report: IRs Added $470m to Economy in First Half of 2010", *Todayonline*, 27 August 2010, www.todayonline.com/Business/EDC100827-0000077/DBS-report--IRs-added-$470m-to-economy-in-first-half-of-2010.

[40] "Visitor Arrivals to S'pore up 24.1% to Exceed 1 Million in July", *Channel News Asia*, 27 August 2010, www.channelnewsasia.com/stories/singaporelocalnews/view/1077518/1/.html.

[41] "Local Businessman Loses $26m at RWS Casino over 3 Days", *Todayonline*, 18 August 2010, www.todayonline.com/Business/EDC100818-0000040/Local-businessman-loses-$26m-at-RWS-casino-over-3-days.

[42] "Worth It Despite Tripled Budget", *Asiaone*, 16 August 2010, news.asiaone.com/News/The%2BNew%2BPaper/Story/A1Story20100816-232261.html.

companies and tourism receipts were estimated at S$57 million.[43] Reactions to the event were mixed and this was reflected in the polarised coverage of the mainstream and online media. While the former generally produced positive coverage[44] and defended the establishment against the onslaught of negative responses,[45] the latter produced reports of the YOG volunteers being mistreated[46] and YOG venues remaining empty of spectators.[47] A netizen was arrested for posting inflammatory comments on an anti-YOG Facebook group.[48]

Political Democracy a la Singapore

Singapore leaders have consistently and persistently argued that Western democracy is unsuitable for Singapore. This is based on grounds of history, social-cultural fault lines, especially between the Chinese and Malays as well as the general all-round vulnerabilities the largely successful but Chinese-dominated island city-state confronts in a largely Malay-dominated geography. Historically, Singapore has been described as an 'authoritarian state', a 'police state', a 'garrison state', a 'managed democracy', and more recently, an 'illiberal democracy' with a persistent 'culture of fear'. Still, there is no denying that the political climate in Singapore has changed for the better, with the state becoming less draconian, unless and until threats are posed to the very essence of its stability and existence. Surely, the state usually responds robustly to its critics and opponents, but rarely is this undertaken outside the framework of the legal system and, more importantly, varied spaces have been opened for its citizens to become politically active. The political leadership has also become more tolerant of critics and dissenters as long as they do not pose a threat to the national social fabric.

Nevertheless, to the credit of both the government and governed, an amicable 'social contract' has actually emerged in the city-state, based largely on a legalist

---

[43] "$387m on YOG Well Spent", *The Straits Times*, 26 August 2010, www.straitstimes.com/BreakingNews/Singapore/Story/STIStory_571284.html. The MCYS was later restructured into the Ministry of Social and Family Development (MSF) and the Ministry of Culture, Community and Youth (MCCY).

[44] "YOG Ushers in New Generation of Sports Stars in S'pore", *Channel News Asia*, 26 August 2010, www.channelnewsasia.com/stories/singaporelocalnews/view/1077287/1/.html.

[45] "Give Views on YOG in Gracious Manner", *Asiaone*, 1 September 2010, news.asiaone.com/News/Mailbox/Story/A1Story20100830-234683.html.

[46] Fann Sim, "Controversy over Meal Packs for YOG Volunteers", 13 August 2010, www.temasekreview.com/2010/08/13/controversy-over-meal-packs-for-yog-volunteers/.

[47] "YOG — What the Local Media Don't Show You", *The Online Citizen*, 17 August 2010, theonlinecitizen.com/2010/08/yog-what-the-local-media-don't-show-you/.

[48] "$387m on YOG Well Spent", *The Straits Times*, 26 August 2010, www.straitstimes.com/BreakingNews/Singapore/Story/STIStory_571284.html.

format that is buttressed by economic prosperity, law and order, and the hope of a better future. At the same time, political change and innovations have been continuously introduced and experimented with, which have increasingly, albeit slowly, expanded the public political spaces. Critics have described this as 'managed' or 'controlled' political change but the fact remains that the political system has been undergoing continuous change, with the most marked feature being the steady widening of political space and somewhat ironically, the constriction of the power of the dominant ruling elite. This is evident from the changes such as the Non-Constituency Member of Parliament, Nominated Member of Parliament, and even the Elected President as well as televising of parliamentary debates, inclusion of Opposition members in various parliamentary committees and the sanctioning of the Speakers' Corner. Greater political liberalisation was also evident from the exemption to apply for public entertainment licence for indoor lectures and later, the sanctioning of protests and demonstrations at the Speakers' Corner. Most critical in this regard was the changes announced by Prime Minister Lee in May 2009 that will eventually see a Parliament consisting, at the minimum, of 18 non-PAP members.

At the same time, there has been a proliferation of alternative perspectives on Singapore politics, both online and offline, signaling that political changes have been taking place and are clearly in the offing. While some critics, for whom, whatever change instituted by the PAP is never ever sufficient, will continue to describe these developments as a 'farce', 'phoney' or 'façade', yet, in reality, what is clearly discernible is the emergence of a 'New Singaporean', who is not apathetic but more importantly, politically informed and probably, in the coming years, increasingly active. Thus, the changes and innovations that have been introduced, albeit slowly, are and will be bearing fruits as the polity matures and active citizenry is one of the many features of this new political paradigm. The crucial question would be how the changes introduced and the unintended consequences of these changes will impact on the peace and stability in this highly fragile, near-artificial state, and whether the city-state will continue to be blessed with economic prosperity and stability.

While most of the political changes, especially those associated with political liberalisation are, by most counts, measured, the fact remains that the polity has been liberalising. This is partly due to the onset of new political leaders such as Goh Chok Tong and Lee Hsien Loong, with a slate of much younger Members of Parliament, especially in the PAP as well as the changed political circumstances and environment that the PAP finds itself in, both amongst the electorate in Singapore and the world, and around the Republic, especially in Southeast Asia. The presence of the new media has also played a critical role, and traditional control mechanisms are no longer as effective in 'silencing' alternative views, which usually tend to be critical of what is being projected in the mainstream media. What transpired in the 2011 General Elections clearly signposted the emergence of a new Singapore with all the complex challenges associated with an emergent democracy. While the 2015 General Elections represented a minor push back of the Opposition, still fundamentally there is a slow and steady opening of the political corridor in Singapore, representing its approach to political liberalisation and democratisation.

Race and Religion

The two inter-related permanent features of Singapore political and demographic landscape are its racial and religious make-up. While this calls for the celebration of its diversity, it is also where much care and caution is required in managing this near-permanent demographic fault line of what is essentially a 'Chinese Island' in a predominantly 'Malay Sea'. The past racial and religious-oriented conflicts, often bloody, are a constant reminder of what can happen if sensitive race relations are mismanaged. The first generation of the PAP leaders were literally schooled in racial and religious politics and decided on independence in 1965 never to indulge or allow anyone to indulge in politics of any kind that would involve race, religion and even language.

The consensus out of this compact was a series of policies that have defined Singapore's approach to race and religion. Adopting a strategy of inclusiveness and accommodation, the article of faith that defines Singapore is multiculturalism within which all races, religions and languages are given equal status. The key policies stemming from this consensus on race and religion are as follows:

Politics: minorities as Presidents/Heads of States every once a while; establishment of Presidential Council on Minority Rights; GRCs to ensure minority representation in Parliament

Education: Bilingualism, Mother Tongue Education and National Education

National/Official Languages: English as the administrative language with Malay as the national language and Mandarin and Tamil also as official languages

Mass Media: television and radio broadcasts and newspapers in all the official languages

Housing: no ethnic enclaves through a quota system

National Service: involvement of all citizens in national defence

Security: Maintenance of Racial Harmony Act; Sedition Act; Internal Security Act to ensure deterrence and if these fail, to discipline violators according to the rule of law

Social: Ethnic Self-Help Groups; Economic prosperity; Support for under-privileged

Community Engagement: Inter-Racial and Religious Confidence Circles to enhance cohesion

There are also the constant reminders of what the mismanagement of racial and religious issues can lead to. In this regard, one of the most important annual exercises is in schools where the Racial Harmony Day is commemorated. This is celebrated as a school event on 21 July to remind the young of what happened in July and September 1964 when Chinese and Malay clashes broke out, leading to many deaths. While the purpose of the commemoration is to celebrate ethnic and religious diversity, it is also a constant reminder of the importance of maintaining racial and religious peace in Singapore.

Notwithstanding these measures and policies, due to various factors, issues relating to race and religion will simply not go away. Two major developments have made the issue more urgent: the threat of Islamist extremism and terrorism, including Singapore being targeted for attacks; and the increasing ethno-nationalism worldwide with rising jaundiced views towards the minorities, including in Singapore, say towards the Indians and Malays. While there have been growing emphasis on racial cohesion and harmony through various bodies such as the Inter-Religious Organisation, there is also the attempt to institute minority representation in national political offices, from time to time. In an interview in September 2016, Prime Minister Lee Hsien Loong stated:

> I think we have come a long way. It's not a Chinese or Malay or an Indian nation. Everybody has his place, everybody is equal. Treated equally, equal standing, equal rights and status.[49]

However, when it came to political office, Prime Minister Lee Hsien Loong lamented what was a reality, stemming from ethnic and religious fault lines:

> For most people, if you ask them, they will say I will choose a candidate, I don't care what race he is. But if you ask them the question in a survey and it's anonymous, well, they'll tell you race does make a difference and a significant number will prefer somebody who's their own race and what it means in Singapore is that if a minority stands for an election as President, a Malay or an Indian, he will be at a disadvantage.[50]

It was due to this reality that Prime Minister Lee Hsien Loong proposed amending the criteria for the EP. He argued:

> If we want a minority to be a President from time to time, which I think is very important in Singapore, because the President represents all Singaporeans, he is the

---

[49] "Important for Minority to Be President from Time to Time: PM Lee", *Channel News Asia*, 4 September 2016, http://www.channelnewsasia.com/news/singapore/improtant-for-a-m.
[50] Ibid.

figure representing not just a state but the nation, all of us; then we must have a minority President from time to time, non-Chinese, a Malay one, an Indian or other minority, and then people see that "Yes, this is my country. Someone like me can become the Head of State, can represent the country".[51]

It is to ensure ethnic and religious peace that the government proposed institutionalising a system whereby an Indian, Malay or Eurasian can become a President and Head of State to symbolise Singapore as a multiracial state. The decision to amend the rules regarding the EP and the various measures to secure Singapore from extremist attacks are clear indications that after 50 years of independence, race and religion continue to remain important issues in national politics and if these are not managed and problems not mitigated, then Singapore could suffer, with its ethnic and social peace as well as the progress undermined, as did in many other small multiracial states such as Lebanon and Sri Lanka.

Think Questions

1. Has the issue of income disparity and inequality become more serious than inter-racial divide in Singapore?
2. How effectively have these new developments and issues been exploited by the Opposition in Singapore?
3. Which of these issues have been largely addressed by the government?

---

[51] Ibid.

Chapter Ten

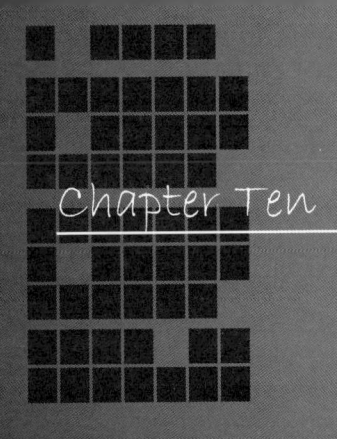

Elections in Singapore — Is the Hegemony Being Challenged?

> Parliament must play the crucial role of checking and pushing a powerful executive to make well-balanced policies and laws that protect and advance the people's interests.
> [Sylvia Lim, WP Chairman]

> I think people do trust us. They know we are not what as described by the PAP over the AHPETC saga. We are people of integrity. We've done the best that we could to serve the residents. Again, we could have done better and we would like to do better. But we have done our best nevertheless given the circumstances that we were in.
> [Low Thia Khiang, WP Secretary-General][1]

Introduction

As a concept, governance involves notions of those who govern and those who are governed. Good governance fundamentally involves a theory of representation whereby the governed has the right to be represented, and often by a candidate of their choice. Because elections and voting are positively correlated with, though not the sole prerequisites of representation and good governance, they are fundamental to the concept of democratic governance.

The functions of elections depend on the nature of the political system and on the institution for which the elections are carried out. In simple organisations such as the selection of a classroom representative, a simple show of hands may suffice, while in the election of parliamentarians, more complex and sophisticated mechanisms and procedures are required. Nonetheless, all elections serve several key functions which are crucial to the essence of democratic representation and the link in modern society between those who govern and those who are governed.[2] Firstly, elections are a

---

[1] "GE2015: PAP Vote Share Increases to 69.9%, Party Wins 83 of 89 Seats Including WP-Held Punggol East", *The Straits Times*, 12 September 2015.
[2] Andrew Heywood, *Politics* (London: Macmillan, 1997) pp. 212–213.

mechanism for political recruitment. As a rite of initiation, the aspiring politician must be identified and recruited by a political party and more importantly, fielded in an election whereby the candidate is deemed to be most suitable. The criterion of suitability may vary between level of education, ethnicity, voter identification and political connections but common to all is that most new faces to politics are introduced just before the election season.

Elections are important in the formation of governments because the result of the election determines the elites who are given the right to govern the polity. The composition of governments, whether made up of grand coalitions of political parties or a government where a single party clearly dominates Parliament, will no doubt have implications on the nature of governance. Some may argue that a more diverse Parliament with many opposing voices would be a good system of checks and balances but may not be an effective government as bills and legislations are often delayed or dismissed due to inter-party contestations within Parliament. On the other hand, an effective government could come about from a unanimous Parliament, often the result of overwhelming majority of a political party in Parliament but open to abuse as there are no checks within Parliament against excesses of the incumbent government.

In theory, elections provide the rights of representation to the masses. The individuals with voting rights are given a free hand to cast their votes for the candidates that they determine best represent their interests. As long as elections are free and fair, the electorate wields the ability to 'reward' and 'punish' political parties contesting in elections. If the incumbent government is viewed as performing to the voters' expectations, it may be reelected into power and if it did not make the mark, in theory, the electorate can vote the government out of power. The results of the elections do have an impact on policy matters. Successful parties may view that their policy platforms have been well-received and move towards that particular policy direction. Moreover, electoral results can be used as political leverage as parties weave in and out of policy coalitions to find like-minded partners in order to increase their influence in Parliament.

Elections and electoral process do contribute to the political education of the masses. As long as the elections and their processes are transparent and honest, and the elections held are free, fair and in frequent intervals, the electorate will be exposed to the system and in theory, be able to better understand the complexities of governance and be active participants in the entire process of governance. Since elections are generally about obtaining the votes of the masses, elections are important sources of securing legitimacy for those in power. As long as the elections are perceived to be free and fair, the victors of elections can derive their legitimacy in terms of obtaining the mandate to govern from the people. The importance of elections as a source conferring political legitimacy is recognised by all even in authoritarian and totalitarian states that conduct elections to portray a sense of legitimacy of the elites in power.

This leads to a caution that if elections are able to confer power, then they too can be abused to entrench elites both rightfully or wrongfully, because once elected, those in power are in a position to change the 'paths' to power, effectively locking out their opponents and perpetuating their dominance. It must be remembered that amongst the greatest tyrants in modern history, Adolf Hitler and the Nazi Party came to power by means of a free and fair election.

In Singapore, political elections have been held since the Legislative Council elections in 1948 (see Tables 10.1 and 10.2).[3] Prior to the Republic's independence in 1965, Singapore had a series of Legislative Assembly elections that contributed to the political education, experience and maturity of both the political parties and the electorate. It was during this period that Singapore saw the emergence and growth of many political parties. Upon independence in 1965, the Republic has conducted frequent general elections for parliamentarians, the latest in September 2015. Besides the parliamentary elections, be they for general elections or by-elections, Singapore has also carried out presidential elections since the introduction of the Elected Presidency (EP) in 1993.

The electoral process and procedures in place in Singapore were inherited from the Republic's former colonial masters, the British. Singapore adopted a first-past-the-post electoral system which granted the contested seat to the first candidate who received a simple majority of the popular votes. This form of electoral process favours disproportionate representation as the number of seats controlled by a political party is not proportionate to the overall number of popular votes it receives.

Table 10.1: Local Elections from 1948 to 1965

1948:	Legislative Council Elections
1951:	Legislative Council Elections
1955:	Legislative Assembly Elections
1957:	Legislative Assembly By-Elections
	Local Government (City Council) Ordinary Elections
1959:	Legislative Assembly Elections
1961:	Legislative Assembly By-Elections (April)
	Legislative Assembly By-Elections (July)
1962:	National Referendum on Merger with Malaya
1963:	Legislative Assembly Elections
1965:	Legislative Assembly By-Elections

Source: Author.

---

[3] Yeo Lay Hwee, "Electoral Politics in Singapore" in Aurel Croisant (ed.) *Electoral Politics in Southeast and East Asia* (Singapore: Friedrich-Ebert-Stiftung Office for Regional Co-operation in Southeast Asia, 2002) p. 203.

Table 10.2: Parliamentary Elections since Independence

1966:	Parliamentary By-Elections (January)
	Parliamentary By-Elections (March)
	Parliamentary By-Elections (November)
1967:	Parliamentary By-Elections
1968:	Parliamentary Elections
1970:	Parliamentary By-Elections
1972:	Parliamentary Elections
1976:	Parliamentary Elections
1977:	Parliamentary By-Elections (May)
	Parliamentary By-Elections (July)
1979:	Parliamentary By-Elections
1980:	Parliamentary Elections
1981:	Parliamentary By-Elections
1984:	Parliamentary Elections
1988:	Parliamentary Elections
1991:	Parliamentary Elections
1992:	Parliamentary By-Election
1997:	Parliamentary Elections
2001:	Parliamentary Elections
2006:	Parliamentary Elections
2011:	Parliamentary Elections
2012:	Parliamentary By-Election
2013:	Parliamentary By-Election
2015:	Parliamentary Elections
2016:	Parliamentary By-Election

Source: Author.

Voting is compulsory in Singapore and Singaporeans aged 21 years and above have the right to cast their votes during an election provided their names are on the list of registered voters prior to the elections. Failure to cast a vote will result in the individual's name being struck off the list of registered voters. Unless the individual is able to provide a credible explanation for not voting, a fine of S$50 will be imposed to reinstate the voter's name on the list.

The number of electoral seats in the Singapore Parliament has increased over time, from 25 in the 1955 Legislative Assembly elections, to 58 in the first post-independence elections, to 89 in 2015. Currently, Singapore's Parliament has two different types of electoral divisions, the Single Member Constituencies (SMCs) and the Group Representation Constituencies (GRCs), of which there are 13 and 16 respectively at

Table 10.3: Singapore — Single Member and Group Representative Seats in Parliament

Year	Number of SMCs	Number of GRCs
1988	42	13 [all were 3-member]
1991	21	21 [all were 4-member]
1997	9	15 [4 were 6-member] [6 were 5-member] [5 were 4-member]
2001	9	14 [5 were 6-member] [9 were 5-member]
2006	9	14 [5 were 6-member] [9 were 5-member]
2011	12	15 [2 were 6-member] [11 were 5-member] [2 were 4-member]
2015	13	16 [2 were 6-member] [8 were 5-member] [6 were 4-member]

Source: Compiled by Author.

present. In the present Parliament, the GRCs vary between four to six seats totaling 76 parliamentary seats. The number of SMCs and GRCs has been changing since the GRC system was first introduced in 1988 (see Table 10.3). In the latest general elections in 2015, the PAP was returned to power with 83 seats and the Opposition parties, namely, the Workers' Party (WP), held on to its single SMC ward in Hougang and a single GRC in Aljunied. At the same time, due to the introduction of two other categories of Members of Parliament (MP), namely, the Non-Constituency Member of Parliament (NCMP) and Nominated Member of Parliament, there are also seats allocated accordingly. Presently, the NCMP seats are held by three members of the WP, namely, Daniel Goh, Leon Perera and Dennis Tan, who emerged as the 'best winners' in the last general elections.

In the history of Singapore's elections, it is possible to disaggregate the electoral history into three distinct phases as follows:

Phase 1 (1948–1967) : Emergence of political parties and vibrant elections
Phase 2 (1968–1980) : PAP's total hegemony at the polls
Phase 3 (1981–current) : Reinvigorated Opposition

Each of these 3 phases displays distinct characteristics which have coloured the history of elections in Singapore.

Phase 1 (1948–1967) — Emergence of Political Parties and Vibrant Elections

The dawn of political parties in Singapore began in the period after the Second World War. The tumultuous years of war and the Japanese Occupation stirred political consciousness amongst the local population. With the desire of the British colonial masters to grant a certain degree of participation in Singapore, local elections were first held for a partially elected legislature in 1948. These local elections paved the way for increased participation leading to self-government and a fully elected legislature by 1959. In the early 1960s, Singapore held a crucial referendum on the desire to merge with the then Malaysia. An important event, the merger and eventual separation, has severely impacted the political development and political culture of the Republic in ways still evident to this day.

The political system which developed in Singapore greatly mirrored that of its colonial master. The political parties that emerged in the late 1940s and 1950s clearly developed identities along social class structures. From leftist political parties such as the banned Malayan Communist Party to left-leaning parties like the Labour Front and the more centrist party of the PAP, political parties in Singapore have their roots in typical ideology-based parties. While there were ethnic nationalist parties such as the *Persatuan Melayu Singapura* (Singapore Malay Association) in Singapore, the dominant parties which drew tremendous support tended to be those that were secular and had appealing ideologies to the post-war electorate. For example, in the Legislative Assembly elections of 1955, in which the Labour Front emerged as the leading political party with 10 out of 25 elected seats, the main issues were democracy, self-government, emergency regulations, education, housing and trade,[4] chief amongst which were the directions available for complete independence. The Labour Front's success and its ability to form a coalition with elements of the Alliance Party in Singapore warranted the invitation by the Colony's Governor to David Marshall to form the government.

In 1959, for the first fully elected Legislative Assembly in Singapore, the PAP emerged as the dominant political party. Winning 43 out of 51 seats, the PAP was in a commanding position to steer Singapore into the next stage of its desire for independence. The PAP, with a mix of English-educated intellectuals and left-leaning members had a combination of visionary leadership as well as the ability to mobilise, in particular, the Chinese-educated workers. While it was obvious that the English educated moderates in the PAP were uncomfortable with a sizeable pro-Communist element within the party, the PAP did not break apart as both factions understood the need for each other and moreover, both factions were bounded by the ideology and commitment to anti-colonialism.[5]

---

[4] Pugalenthi Sr., *Elections in Singapore* (Singapore: VJ Times, 1996) p. 10.
[5] Ibid., p. 39.

However, the cooperation between the moderates and the pro-Communist in the PAP was short-lived and by early 1961, the pro-Communist faction broke away from the PAP to form the *Barisan Sosialis* or the Socialist Front. This posed a great challenge to the PAP as the defections of left-leaning PAP assemblymen left the PAP with a single-seat majority in the Legislative Assembly. The PAP under the moderates held on to power by controlling 26 seats, while those opposing it led by the *Barisan* had 25 seats. Despite the odds against them, the PAP pushed forth their proposal for Singapore to merge with Malaysia. The left-leaning political parties were strongly against this proposal as it was mainly due to disagreement over merger that led to the breakup of the PAP in the first place. As Malaya had just successfully ended the Emergency, marking the Malayan government's 12-year struggle against the Communists, the *Barisan* understandably feared for its existence in Malaysia, as it was also labelled a pro-Communist organisation.

The victory in the merger referendum held in 1962 gave the PAP the mandate to steer Singapore into Malaysia, which it did in 1963. In that year, the PAP faced its strongest challenge by the *Barisan* in the Legislative Assembly elections. The PAP, despite numerous defections and loss of its machineries to mobilise — in particular, the Chinese working class — managed to return to office with 37 out of 51 seats and winning 47% of the popular votes.[6] The party's success in the 1963 elections was a boost to the party's morale and a huge relief to the party's leadership as it regained a firmer foothold in the legislature.

Although the PAP remained in office, merger with Malaysia was short-lived. By 1965, Singapore peacefully seceded from Malaysia and became an independent and sovereign state. The electoral contestation during this period was extremely vibrant and tough. Not only were political parties offering and contesting on different ideological platforms, the electoral contestation was not limited to a contest of words. Violence in the forms of political thuggery, riots and protests was part and parcel of the political scene. Nonetheless, it is to the credit of Singapore's early political framework and electorate that the results of the elections, though leaving many unsatisfied, were widely respected. Political parties at the losing end did not resort to non-constitutional means such as coups and revolts to delegitimise the electoral results. This period of electoral history is important as it marked the beginning of Singapore's political system. The tumultuous events during this period, ranging from racial riots, political extremism and the failure of merger left indelible marks on the polity and politics of Singapore which remain up to this day.

Phase 2 (1968–1980) — PAP's Total Hegemony at the Polls

The second phase of Singapore's electoral history saw the PAP consolidating its grip over politics in Singapore as a result of its complete and unbroken total control of

---

[6] Elections Department Singapore, GE 1963.

Parliament from 1968 to 1981. The PAP's total victories at the polls were not due to the absence of political Opposition but clearly something else which attracted the electorate to the PAP. The *Barisan* after the 1963 Legislative Assembly elections had moved towards a strategy to disengage the PAP in Parliament. This strategy culminated in the total boycott of the 1968 General Elections. The move, which aimed to bring the 'fight' out into the streets, was met with sufficient force of the law. However, the *Barisan*'s action to discredit the institution of elections and indirectly the PAP, was unsuccessful. Although the WP and some other independent candidates contested in the general elections, the Opposition's presence was barely felt as the PAP was returned to power on Nomination Day by winning 51 of 58 seats by walkovers.[7] The PAP secured approximately 87% of the popular votes for the remaining seven contested seats. Thus, this begun the PAP's total domination of Parliament for the next four general elections.

The 1972 General Elections proved to be more interesting. The Opposition parties only allowed the PAP walkovers in eight of the now expanded 65-seat Parliament on Nomination Day. The chief oppositional forces were the United National Front (UNF) and the WP which contested in 33 and 27 seats respectively.[8] The *Barisan* returned to electoral contestation by competing in 10 wards. However, despite the presence of a significant Opposition in the elections, the PAP was successful in keeping out the Opposition from Parliament by winning all seats with 69% of the popular vote.[9]

In the 1976 General Elections, the PAP managed to have total control of Parliament by winning all 69 seats, of which 16 were unopposed and gathered 72.4% of the popular vote.[10] The WP and the UNF were once again the leading Opposition political parties but they were unsuccessful in making inroads into Parliament. By the 1980 General Elections, the main issue during general elections moved away from ideologies and policy matters to the Opposition's plea to the electorate to end the PAP's complete control over Parliament. Once again, the PAP managed to retain its hold on Parliament by winning the 37 seats unopposed on Nomination Day and 38 seats on Polling Day, giving it a total of all 75 elected seats in Parliament. There were more Opposition parties competing in the 1980 General Elections but none were able to win any of the contested seats. The PAP received 77.7% of the popular votes while the closest Opposition party in terms of votes, the WP, only managed to obtain 6.2% of the total votes cast in the entire General Elections or 29.2% of the popular votes in the wards that they contested.

---

[7] Seats GE1968, SingaporeElections.com
[8] SingaporeElections.com
[9] SingaporeElections.com
[10] SingaporeElections.com

This period of electoral history that saw the parliamentary consolidation of the PAP gives rise to the fundamental question of what enabled the PAP to achieve such astounding victories. Was all this because of the *Barisan*'s failed attempt to delegitimise the 1968 General Elections that gave the PAP full control of Parliament and when in power, managed to engineer its subsequent successes? Or did the PAP, when given the complete power to govern Singapore in 1968, capitalised on the situation by providing effective, efficient and growth-oriented governance that won it the approval of the general electorate? While historical evidence tends to support the latter suggestion, it is undeniable that the PAP's incumbency facilitated its growth as a hegemonic political party and enriched its political capacity to bring about its subsequent victories at the general elections.

It must be noted that despite the PAP being in power, it did not use its powers to ban the Opposition. As evident in the electoral contestations, the political Opposition in Singapore was still vibrant though not as vibrant as that of the 1950s and 1960s. On the issues raised during elections, it was clear that issues became less ideological as the Opposition could not offer distinct policy alternatives. Arguably, this phase of the PAP's complete dominance of politics in Singapore enabled it to pursue its policies with no opposition. Policies and bills were able to be passed with ease in Parliament, and the constancy of the PAP in office enabled its leaders to follow through on policies to eventually achieve its desired goal. It was during this phase that Singapore underwent drastic transformation, and its economic growth and social stability can be traced to PAP's policies implemented in the late 1960s and early 1980s. As such, this period of electoral history remains as an important era to understand the Singapore's political evolution and progress.

Phase 3 (1981–Current): Reinvigoration of the Opposition?

From 1968 to 1980, the PAP had the luxury of enjoying total victories in four consecutive parliamentary general elections. The party's share of popular votes had been rising and it appeared that the challenge that was mounted by the Opposition began to wane as evident from the number of seats each political party was able to contest. However, the PAP's privilege of maintaining an exclusive membership in Parliament was about to end. The first instance of Opposition's presence came in the 1981 parliamentary by-election; and in subsequent general elections, Opposition parties have managed to maintain a token presence in Parliament.

The 1981 Anson by-election came about due to the resignation of Devan Nair as the MP for Anson. There was a three-cornered fight between the PAP, WP and United People's Front (UPF). Despite efforts by many senior PAP members such as the then Ministers Goh Chok Tong and Ong Teng Cheong assisting the PAP candidate Pang Kim Hin, the victory eventually went to long-time Opposition leader,

J. B. Jeyaretnam of the WP. The Anson seat was won by a slim margin of Jeyaretnam's 7,012 votes to Pang's 6,359 in the 14,512-voter constituency[11] but regardless, the former's success marked the end of the era of PAP's complete control of all seats in Parliament. While the ability of the Opposition to place one of its own in the ranks of Parliament was monumental, the PAP still had a firm grip over the politics of Singapore. Nevertheless, Jeyaretnam's victory proved to be the single event that invigorated the Opposition on the possibility of defeating the PAP at the polls. Jeyaretnam's demonstration-effect was a simple one; the PAP was, after all, not invincible!

The Opposition's new fervour was again rewarded in the 1984 General Elections. The WP managed to retain the Anson seat with incumbent Jeyaretnam obtaining 9,909 votes as compared to the PAP candidate's 7,533 votes.[12] The Singapore Democratic Party also won the Potong Pasir seat with Chiam See Tong defeating PAP's Mah Bow Tan with a majority of approximately 3,500 votes in the 17,915-voter constituency.[13] Additionally, the PAP's share of total popular votes decreased to 64.8%, a drop close to 13% from the previous general elections results.[14] The swing against the PAP could be attributed not only to a rejuvenated Opposition making a concerted effort in the elections but also to some unfavourable policies that the PAP had introduced, including the much debated 'graduate mother' scheme that rewarded children whose mothers were graduates, especially for entry into schools.

The inroads made by the Opposition further fueled its imagination and ambitions, and in the 1988 General Elections, the Opposition contested 70 seats, surrendering only 11 seats to the PAP on Nomination Day. However, the Opposition was to be disappointed as it lost in all contested seats except Potong Pasir. As a result, the Opposition became more careful in the following elections. The conclusion drawn by the Opposition was that while the electorate desired some Opposition in Parliament, it also preferred the PAP to be the government. Armed with this understanding, the Opposition adopted what was to be known as the 'by-election' strategy. Here, the Opposition deliberately conceded sufficient seats to the PAP to be returned as the government on Nomination Day. Following this, the Opposition called on the public to vote against the just-returned-to-power ruling party so that a viable Opposition presence could eventuate in Parliament. The rationale for this was that if the electorate was sufficiently convinced that the PAP would still be in power, then the discerning public would be more willing to vote for the Opposition to fill the other seats. This would allow the Opposition to make inroads into Parliament as fully-elected MPs and not merely as what was called the 'second-class'

---

[11] 1981 Parliamentary By-Election Results, Elections Department Singapore.
[12] 1984 Parliamentary Election Results, Elections Department Singapore.
[13] 1984 Parliamentary Election Results, Elections Department Singapore.
[14] SingaporeElections.com

NCMPs. This electoral strategy appeared to have some success in the 1991 General Elections as the Opposition made its best showing since 1963 by winning four of the 40 contested seats.

The 'by-election' strategy was utilised again in the 1997 and 2001 General Elections. However, the Opposition was not able to better or repeat its electoral performance of 1991. While the Opposition managed to retain its two SMC wards in 1997, it did not score any further upsets against the PAP. On the other hand, while being unable to counter the PAP's success, the presence of the Opposition had certainly reduced the PAP's share of popular votes, which hovered around 65% in the 1980s and 1990s. Though the PAP was able to increase its share of the popular vote to over 75% in the 2001 General Elections, this was predominantly due to the appeal made by Goh for the electorate to support the PAP as it was his final general elections as Prime Minister.

The 2006 General Elections proved to demonstrate that the Opposition political parties were still capable of organising themselves to effectively compete against the PAP. In the general elections, Lee Hsien Loong's first as Prime Minister, the Opposition decided not to pursue its 'by-election' strategy and opted to compete openly against the PAP. A move much welcomed by both political observers and the PAP itself, only 37 seats were conceded to the PAP by the Opposition on Nomination Day and 47 seats were contested on Polling Day.

To the credit of the Opposition, they were able to field a much more competent slate of candidates, even in the GRCs. Even in Aljunied GRC where the WP's candidate, James Gomez was accused of being 'dishonest', it was able to secure 58,593 votes against the PAP's 74,843 votes. This proved to be the Opposition's best losing performance and one of its member Sylvia Lim was later appointed as an NCMP.

However, the Opposition's best performance historically since the 1963 General Elections occurred in 2011. What has been described as a 'new normal' occurred on 8 May 2011 with Singaporeans waking up to a relatively new power structure for the first time. While the PAP still controlled the government, what was also clear was that the electorate was prepared to support an Opposition political party if it was credible. This was especially true with regard to the WP. On Nomination Day on 27 April 2011, of the 87 seats that were to be contested, only five seats were won by walkovers by the PAP, all belonging to the Tanjong Pagar GRC. What stood out on Nomination Day was the decision by Opposition incumbents, Low Thia Khiang and Chiam to contest a GRC with the *battle royale* focused on Aljunied GRC. On 8 May 2011, the PAP was returned to power for the 14th time, winning 60.14% of the votes, compared to 66.6% it won in 2006 (Table 10.4). However, it suffered on a number of counts. The electoral results represented a major game changer in Singapore politics, with most, including the PAP top leaders, believing that Singapore had entered a new era of politics.

While there was a similar expectation that the Opposition, especially the WP, would be able to strengthen its parliamentary position in the 2015 General Elections,

Table 10.4: 2011 General Elections Results

Party	Seats Won	Total Votes	Percentage of Votes
PAP	81	1,212,514	60.14
WP	6 [+2 NCMPs]	258,510	12.82
NSP	0	242,682	12.04
SDP	0	97,362	4.83
RP	0	86,294	4.28
SPP	0 [+1 NCMP]	62,639	3.11
SDA	0	55,988	2.78

Source: Compiled by Author.

Table 10.5: 2015 General Elections Results

Party	Seats Won	Total Votes	Percentage of Votes
PAP	83	1,576,784	69.85
WP	6 [+ 3 NCMPs]	281,697	12.48
SDP	0	84,770	3.76
NSP	0	79,780	3.53
RP	0	59,432	2.63
SFP	0	50,791	2.25
SPP	0	49,015	2.17
SDA	0	46,508	2.06
PPP	0	25,460	1.13

Source: Compiled by Author.

this was not to be. The 2015 elections were held on 11 September against the backdrop of the passing of Lee Kuan Yew, the Republic's 50th anniversary celebrations, and amidst a flood of government handouts to the people, including special assistance programmes for the elderly. The elections also saw the largest number of electoral wards, 89. The number of SMC and GRC had increased by one to 13 and 16 respectively, compared to the last general elections.

The PAP won 83 out of the 89 seats, securing 69.86% of the valid votes. This increased the PAP's seats in Parliament by two. More important, there was a 9.7% swing in favour of the PAP compared to the 2011 elections. The 2015 results were the best for the PAP since 2001 when it captured 75.3% of the valid votes. The PAP also won back Punggol East SMC, which it had lost to the WP in a 2013 by-election. All the Opposition parties suffered a dip in their results (Table 10.5), especially in comparison to the 2011 General Elections (Table 10.4).

By-Elections in Singapore

Overall, by-election results have mirrored the outcomes of general elections. Since independence in 1965, out of the 31 by-elections held, the PAP has lost only three, namely, in October 1981 in Anson, in May 2012 in Hougang, and in January 2013 in Punggol East (see Table 10.6). All the PAP's defeats were at the hands of the WP.

Table 10.6: Parliamentary By-Elections

Year	Constituency	Winner
Jan 1966	Bukit Merah	PAP
Mar 1966	Choa Chu Kang	PAP
	Crawford	PAP
	Paya Lebar	PAP
Nov 1966	Bukit Timah	PAP
	Joo Chiat	PAP
	Jurong	PAP
Feb 1967	Bukit Panjang	PAP
	Havelock	PAP
	Jalan Kayu	PAP
	Tampines	PAP
Mar 1967	Thomson	PAP
Apr 1970	Delta	PAP
	Havelock	PAP
	Kampong Kapor	PAP
	Ulu Pandan	PAP
	Whampoa	PAP
May 1977	Radin Mas	PAP
Jul 1977	Bukit Merah	PAP
Jan 1979	Geylang West	PAP
	Nee Soon	PAP
Feb 1979	Anson	PAP
	Mountbatten	PAP
	Potong Pasir	PAP
	Sembawang	PAP
	Telok Blangah	PAP
Oct 1981	Anson	WP
Dec 1992	Marine Parade GRC	PAP
May 2012	Hougang	WP
Jan 2013	Punggol East	WP
May 2016	Bukit Batok	PAP

Source: Compiled by Author.

Generally, voters tend to be less cautious in a by-election as there is already the PAP as the government. This has allowed for the Opposition to make inroads into Singapore politics via by-elections and accounts for their relative success in contesting such elections, as shown by the facts that the first ever Opposition parliamentary seat was won in a by-election and that the Opposition has won three out of the last five by-elections. Still, the PAP's victory in the 2016 Bukit Batok by-election where Murali Pillai resoundingly defeated veteran Opposition politician Chee Soon Juan of the SDP indicates that the PAP's dominance over politics in Singapore as a whole remains intact, regardless the type of election.

From the above general and by-election results, the period of renewed and rejuvenated Opposition does suggest that there is active politics in Singapore. As was argued by Chan Heng Chee, "politics has returned to Singapore".[15] In many ways, current areas of electoral contestation have moved away from ideology and towards particular issues. For example, the Opposition's main rallying cry tends to be 'greater democratisation' and 'voices in Parliament'. Additionally, only when the electorate is unhappy with the ruling party on specific issues does one see a fundamental swing in favour of the Opposition, which is usually more to protest against the government rather than to support the Opposition as was the case during the 2011 General Elections with the public's anger focused on migration-related issues. Despite this, it demonstrates that the spirit of electoral contestation is still alive in Singapore.

At the same time, those who have or were thinking of writing an obituary for the Opposition in Singapore should think again. The reason for the Opposition's continued relevance in Singapore is partly a response to PAP's continued hegemony and the various policies it has implemented as well as due to various international developments. In many ways, the continued relevance and even ascendancy of the Opposition in Singapore is due to the success of the PAP itself in creating a highly educated and discerning electorate. It is also due to the successful developmental policies that have been implemented since 1959. Therein lays one of the many ironies of PAP's success, which is having a blowback effect on its own hegemony in Singapore politics.

Though short, the electoral history of Singapore has had its share of excitement, vibrancy and tension. The PAP rose from the fringes of elections to come to power in 1959 and was once holding onto its political survival by a single seat. Faced with considerable challenges, the PAP was nonetheless able to secure complete control of all seats in the 1968 elections and since then, has managed at first to exclude and then marginalise the presence of the Opposition in Parliament. While electoral innovations are not unique to any nascent independent state, the electoral innovations in

---

[15] See Speech by Ambassador Chan Heng Chee as the Guest-of-Honour at the NUS Department of Political Science 50th Dinner Anniversary, Orchid Country Club, Friday, 30 March 2012. Available at https://www.mfa.gov.sg/content/mfa/overseasmission/washington/newsroom/press_st...

Table 10.7: Singapore's Electoral Power: 1948–2015

Year	Party	Seats Contested	Seats Won	% Votes
1948	SPP	6	3	49.5
1951	SPP	9	6	45.5
1955	LF	25	10	26.7
1959	PAP	51	43	53.4
1963	PAP	51	37	46.4
1968	PAP	58	58	84.4
1972	PAP	65	65	69.0
1976	PAP	69	69	72.4
1980	PAP	75	75	75.5
1984	PAP	79	77	62.9
1988	PAP	81	80	61.7
1991	PAP	81	77	59.3
1997	PAP	83	81	63.5
2001	PAP	84	82	75.3
2006	PAP	84	82	66.6
2011	PAP	87	81	60.1
2015	PAP	89	83	69.8

Source: Compiled by Author.

Singapore as examined in the previous chapters have shown to favour the incumbent PAP. Whatever explanations one puts forward to explain the status of political parties in Singapore, what is clear is that the PAP has been able to consistently out-distant the other parties and hence, entrench itself as the dominant and hegemonic party in Singapore. Even at a time when developed countries were great believers of the politics of 'checks and balances' and the need to constrain the rise of a hegemonic political party in a democracy, the PAP succeeded in securing almost 70% of the electoral votes in the 2015 General Elections (Table 10.7). Clearly, the one-party dominant system in Singapore is destined to survive. Short of an internal split, there appears to be no challenge on the horizon in the near future that can dismount the PAP from its hegemony.

Singapore's Presidential Elections

Since independence, Singapore has had seven presidents who are also the Heads of State. To date, Singapore's presidents can be categorised into two different types, namely, ceremonial and elected presidents. From 1965 to 1993, the first four presidents — Yusof Ishak, Benjamin Sheares, Devan Nair and Wee Kim Wee — were ceremonial presidents being appointed by Parliament. Since 1993, three presidents — Ong Teng Cheong, S. R. Nathan, and Tony Tan — have been elected presidents, coming to office as a consequence of an election even though the Republic's sixth president held office without having to contest in an election.

Following a constitutional amendment in 1991, the office of the president was transformed into one where the office holder was directly elected by the public with clearly stated custodial responsibilities. The rationale was to give the president the additional task of safeguarding the national reserves and the integrity of the public service. For anyone to contest for the presidency, stringent rules were put in place, including having experience in holding key government appointments, or having acted as chairman or chief executive officer of a major company with a paid up capital of at least S$100 million. The importance of the eligibility criteria was clearly evident when in the 1999 and 2005 presidential elections, Nathan won by a walkover as no one else was given the certificate of eligibility.

Since the concept of an EP was introduced, there had been four presidential elections, but only two had been contested (Table 10.8). The first was in 1993 when Ong a PAP's stalwart, won by garnering 58.69% of the votes. In the next two presidential elections, Nathan won uncontested. In the 2011 presidential elections, there was a four-way contest with Tony Tan winning by a narrow margin, garnering 35.2% of the votes compared to Tan Cheng Bock who succeeded in garnering 34.85% of the valid votes.

Since then, there have been many suggestions that the system of the elected presidency would be altered and this was publicly announced on 27 January 2016 to prepare for the next presidential elections that must be held on or before 26 August 2017. According to Prime Minister Lee Hsien Loong, a Constitutional Commission,

Table 10.8: Singapore's Presidential Election Results

Year	Polling Date	Votes Polled	Winner
1993	18 August 1993	Chua Kim Yeow: 670,358 (41.31%) Ong Teng Cheong: 952,513 (58.69%)	Ong Teng Cheong
1999	Walkover	S. R. Nathan: Uncontested	S. R. Nathan
2005	Walkover	S.R. Nathan: Uncontested	S. R. Nathan
2011	17 August 2011	Tony Tan: 745,693 (35.20%) Tan Cheng Bock: 738,311 (34.85%) Tan Jee Say: 530,441 (25.04%) Tan Kin Lian: 104,095 (4.91%)	Tony Tan

Source: Compiled by Author.

chaired by Chief Justice Sundaresh Menon, would look into three areas, namely, "to bring the eligibility criteria up to date, to strengthen the Council Presidential Advisors, and to ensure minority Presidents periodically".[16] Using the hiatus trigger approach, the government decided, following a debate in Parliament, that the next EP would be from the Malay community and that the elections would be held in Septembet 2017.

Think Questions

1. What has accounted for the emergence of a one-party dominant state in Singapore?
2. Is there a resurgence of the Opposition in Singapore? Will it be able to challenge the PAP's hegemony?
3. Is the presidential elections in Singapore important?

---

[16] See "PM Lee Hsien Loong Proposes Changes to NCMP, GRC and Elected Presidency Schemes: 8 Things about the Political Changes", *The Straits Times*, 27 January 2016.

Chapter Eleven

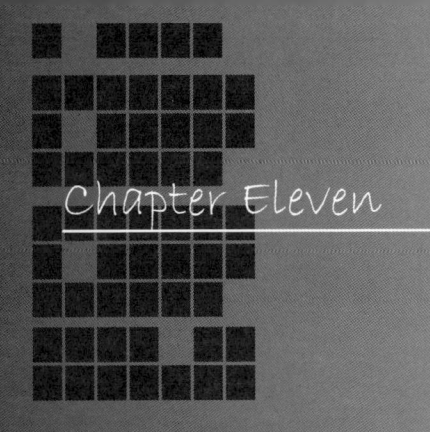

Singapore in the Post-Lee Kuan Yew Era

"Lee Kuan Yew kept an eagle eye on every aspect of Singapore. Yet he knew that he could not control everything personally and that even more so another Prime Minister would have to govern in a different way. This Cabinet Room was Mr. Lee's command tent, where issues were examined and debated, decisions were taken, instructions given, and progress tracked. So for nearly half a century, here in this room, we had a level of discussion and decision-making that would have been exceptional in any Cabinet room in the world … Now we are a new team, dealing with a changed world in new ways, but always inspired by Mr. Lee's example and his memory, and holding firm the ethos and the values that he stood and fought for. These will guide us as we, in turn, follow the rainbow that Mr. Lee himself chased all his life — to build an exceptional nation and to improve the lives of all Singaporeans".[1]

Introduction

An often heard cliché in Singapore since March 2015, when Lee Kuan Yew, the modern founding father of Singapore and architect of its success, died was that it is impossible for anyone 'to fit into his shoes'. Lee, who was born on 16 September 1923 and died on 23 March 2015, was very much an epitome of a driven and chosen person, who fought against all odds to create a nation out of the island's marshes and mangrove swamps. Today, there is hardly anything that the longest-serving Prime Minister in the world, who was a Member of Parliament (MP) from 1955 till his death and Prime Minister from 1959 to 1990, did not touch in Singapore, be it in politics, the economy, national defence, education, transport or the medical system and most important of all, the country's foreign policy. To

---

[1] "Lee Kuan Yew Made Huge Effort to Ensure Those Who Came after Him Succeeded: PM Lee", *The Straits Times*, 23 March 2016. See http://www.straitstimes.com/singapore/lee-kuan-yew-made-huge-effort-to-ensure-those-who-came-after-him-succeeded-pm-lee.

understand and appreciate what Singapore could be in the post-Lee era, it is first important to understand what was the Lee era.

The Lee Kuan Yew Era in Singapore

Lee dominated Singapore politics for 60 years. He won his first parliamentary seat in the Tanjong Pagar Constituency in April 1955 and remained its MP until his death. Following his legal studies in London, he returned to partake in colonial Singapore's turbulent labour world. He became adviser to many trade unions that were then engaged in conflicts with the colonial authorities or large colonial-linked corporations. In effect, his political career began in earnest when he became the legal adviser to the Postal and Telecommunications Uniformed Employees Union in 1952. According to one analyst, Lee was the "legal adviser to more than 100 unions and associations by the time the PAP was formed in 1954".[2] This also introduced him to the 'back-seat drivers' that were the 'brains' and provocateur's of these disputes, mainly the Communist Party of Malaya (CPM), either through its underground or open front leaders. While Lee became famous as a leading lawyer and one who was prepared to fight for nationalist causes, it also opened the door for him to enter into national politics. One of the cases that made him famous was the 'Fajar Trial' that involved sedition charges against eight students of the University of Malaya in Singapore and where the students were acquitted of the charges.[3]

Forming the PAP and Becoming Prime Minister

In November 1954, with like-minded socialist-oriented colleagues, he formed the PAP in a coalition with the left-wing groups, mostly Chinese-educated, who were strongly influenced by the CPM. Lee became the PAP's Secretary-General. On 5 June 1959, the PAP won resoundingly and Lee became Singapore's Prime Minister, a position he would hold for the next 31 years. He continued to remain in the Cabinet until 2011 — first as a Senior Minister and later, Minister Mentor. After the 2011 General Elections, at which his constituency was the only one uncontested, Lee remained a parliamentarian until his death. In other words, from the moment he first won a parliamentary election (then known as the Legislative Assembly) in April 1955 until his death in March 2015, he was one of the longest-serving parliamentarians in the world, chalking up a total of 60 years, almost his entire adult life. That partly explains the exceptionalism of the man and the state he came to dominate.

---

[2] Debby Lim, "Lee Kuan Yew's Legal Legacy". See http://www.lawgazette.com.sg/2015-08/1361.htm
[3] Lee Kuan Yew, *The Singapore Story: Memoirs of Lee Kuan Yew* (Singapore: Singapore Press Holdings, 1998) pp. 161–165.

The Transformation of Singapore

From the mud flat and swamp that it was in the 1950s, by 2015, Singapore had been transformed into a world-class metropolis city-state with one of the highest per capita income and standards of living. In almost every area, Singapore ranks high globally, be it in housing, education, transportation, urban planning, cleanliness, health care and corruption-free status. Today, its education system is world-class with the National University of Singapore ranked among the top 20 in the world. It is also one of the most attractive states for migration and investment, has a high level of internet penetration, and scores very well for business-friendliness. This has, however, come at a cost of increasing income disparities, political control through soft-authoritarianism and in the last decade or so, suffering backlash from its generally open-door policy towards foreign migrants that has made Singapore highly congested, with traffic jams now part of the state's ecology when it was not so in the past.

Lee's Passing and What Will Singapore Be in the Coming Years?

Lee's passing was a major political event that saw the nation united, and was met with the outpouring of grief on an unprecedented scale, the likes of which will probably never be seen again. Some 2 million people were believed to have paid their respects, out of a population of 5.5 million, and the government was compelled to extend the viewing of Lee's body at the national Parliament on a 24-hour basis, while many other tribute centres opened up all over Singapore. That itself was an amazing tribute to a man who came not just to dominate but also symbolise Singapore. For many, Lee was Singapore and Singapore was Lee.

Thousands queued for eight to 10 hours (many even up to 12 hours) to pay their respects. There was simply an astounding sense of endorsement, support, appreciation and gratitude from people of all walks of life. It was also, probably, the ruling party's best political rally in recent years. For many, despite criticisms of Lee and his party in recent years, especially from an intense political minority, the silent majority surfaced to show its support for Lee and his government. Such was the power of the man when he was alive, and even more so in his death. Lee united the nation through tough policies but most importantly, through successes never seen in a small state that was devoid of resources and yet located in an extremely dangerous geopolitical setting.

The big question in the minds of most Singaporeans and outsiders is — what will Singapore be like in the post-Lee era. In many ways, this is the first real political succession of politics being witnessed by Singapore as even though Lee stepped down from the position of Prime Minister in 1990, he was always around, spending another

21 years in cabinet as a Senior Minister/Minister Mentor and then four years as an elder statesman. This means that since March 2015, for the first time, Singapore and Singaporeans had to live with the reality that Lee or his direct influence was totally absent and that the founding father of modern Singapore was gone forever. Singapore has truly entered into the post-Lee era for good.

Post-Lee Kuan Yew's Singapore

Post-Lee Singapore is unlikely to totally diverge from Lee's Singapore, which was carefully crafted in the last 50-odd years since independence in August 1965 and another six years earlier when Lee led Singapore from 1959 to 1965 in colonial Singapore and then in Malaysia. The achievements and shortcomings of what is Singapore will greatly inform the kind of Singapore one can expect in the near future. Sure enough, Lee succeeded in building a nation out of disparate people. With colonial-oriented Malays, Chinese and Indians of the post-Second World War era and the 1950s, after 50-odd years of PAP's leadership, successful nation building has taken place even though this is still a work-in-progress.

Second, Lee succeeded in building a rich state and people. Singapore has minimum debt exposure, high reserves and immense all-round wealth. The Republic's people also have one of the highest per capita incomes in the world. Added to this, Singapore today boasts of a world-class infrastructure in almost every sector, with it becoming a key regional and global aviation and maritime hub. It also has one of the most highly educated and disciplined people. From a relatively weak and defenceless state, through adroit diplomacy and investment in military hardware, Lee also left behind a strong and highly secure nation. It has one of the best air forces in the region today, backed by a small but highly modern army and navy.

Unlike many developing countries, Lee's legacy must also include the bequeathing to the next generation of a highly disciplined and able political party that has remained united to this day. In fact, one of Lee's major learnings of Singapore's modern history is that since 1954, the biggest enemy of the ruling PAP has been the PAP itself and hence, the immense investment in strong party laws and leaders that excel in solidarity making. Finally, what Lee succeeded in crafting was an outward-looking people, craving to learn and excel, and a highly competitive workforce which has become part of the Singaporean national DNA today.

Over and above these successes, there is no running away from the fact that after more than 50 years, a different Singapore has also emerged. For many, the modern-day problems of Singapore stem from successes rather than failures, that is, due to the availability of higher education, access to the internet, etc. This for many is the classic Maslowian dilemma of 'higher needs'. Yet, this is not the full story. There has been growing discontent over rising property prices, widening income and wealth gap, and the 'mother of all issues' — the influx of foreigners who are often blamed for much of the Singaporean plight today. How to address and manage these issues in the post-Lee Kuan Yew era will also help to fashion the type of Singapore that emerges in the near future.

First and very poignantly clear, Singapore's 50th year of independence celebrations in August 2015 was the first National Day without Lee. While Lee ensured that Singapore was around to celebrate its 50th anniversary, will it be around to celebrate its 100th? In August 2013, Lee, publicly asked the question — will Singapore be around in 100 years? His answer: "I am not so sure. America, China, Britain, Australia — these countries will be around in 100 years. But Singapore was never a nation until recently". To make his point even clearer, he made it known that he was more worried about potential political changes at home, Lee said, "I am absolutely sure that if Singapore gets a dumb government, we are done for. The country will sink into nothingness". Whether Lee's prognosis is correct or not, or simply alarmist, the point is, this is essentially the key question about post-Lee's Singapore: what kind of Singapore will it be?

The answer to the type of nation Singapore will be in the post-Lee Kuan Yew era is one of both change and constancy. An exceptional man, Lee built an exceptional nation, Singapore. Lee helped create a strong Singapore with solid foundations. It has a functioning political, economic and social system, can almost be on autopilot, and is therefore unlikely to slide into chaos. This is due to Lee's abiding legacy of the rule of law. Singapore's political culture rejects violence and even street demonstrations as a means of political expression. For many critics, Lee's adherence to the rule of law was tantamount to brow-beating his political opponents into submission even though this had already become a thing of the past. Nevertheless, the chances are that moving forward, Singapore will continue in its way of doing things and continue to believe in the ways that things were done in the past. As Lee Hsien Loong, the current Prime Minister and the eldest son of Lee Kuan Yew said at the 'senior' Lee's funeral on 29 March 2015, "we come together to pledge ourselves to continue building this exceptional country". The broad-based policies politically, economically, socially and even in defence and foreign policy already in place will be largely continued to ensure not only Singapore survives but thrives exceptionally well.

Yet, there is no avoiding the signs that changes are on the horizon and will have to be embraced. In a way, Singapore has also always been about change and nothing remains static in the island republic. As a small state devoid of resources, a hinterland and a large population, Singapore has survived well by adapting to change and this will continue. While changes in Lee's Singapore have always been about adjustments to survive external political and economic changes, this time round, Singapore will have to deal with changes from within. In a way, with the passing of Lee, the PAP and Singapore have lost an extremely powerful, influential, intelligent and charismatic figure who, with an equally powerful team, succeeded in building Singapore. Lee's legacy has been to focus on building a strong team even though there may not be a powerful magnetic figure like him.

Finally, the passing of Lee also means that the city-state has lost a strong international figure who placed Singapore on the world map. This will be a loss that cannot be replaced and will definitely affect Singapore's future. In a way, with the loss of Lee, grinding political changes of recent years may be hastened and fast-forwarded. Wittingly or unwittingly, Singaporeans can brace themselves for a rebalancing of political power within the Republic, with the Opposition making further gains even though no one expects the ruling PAP to lose power. In the 2015 General Elections, the PAP won with 70% of the valid votes, one of its best performance after many years. The lacklustre performance of the Opposition, especially the Workers' Party, the leading Opposition party, does not give much hope for major shifts in the Singapore political terrain. The other related key question is whether the PAP will be able to maintain its internal unity or will factionalism inflict it as it has many political parties once a strongman leaves the scene. These are questions that are worth bearing in mind even though there are no clear signs of factions and splits in the PAP yet.

Conclusion

Lee departed Singapore, leaving behind an iconic nation that was the making of his iconic leadership. A strong political system, a strong world-class economy, a strong military-security infrastructure and a relatively strong united nation have been the key legacies of what one man achieved. Yet, there is no way of avoiding change in the post-Lee Kuan Yew era even though the type of changes and challenges remain to be seen. Whatever happens, presently, Singapore's approach is a simple one — 'if it ain't broke, don't fix it'. Singapore has strong foundations on most counts — politically, economically and social-culturally. Some of the changes that can be expected are — a more left-of-centre shift with focus on welfare programmes and addressing the woes of public issues like housing shortage, rising healthcare costs and breakdowns in the transport system rather than, as in the past, trying to justify why these failures are taking place. Other than that, there will be likely greater political openness, though gradually calibrated with increasing accountability, transparency and willingness to engage the public on key issues. Otherwise, Singapore will be, more or less, Lee Kuan Yew's Singapore in the short- to medium-term future.

Think Questions

1. What was the key impact of Lee Kuan Yew on Singapore politics?
2. What is the key negative impact on the PAP of Lee Kuan Yew's passing?
3. To what extent will the Opposition be able to take advantage of a political environment that is devoid of Lee Kuan Yew?

Chapter Twelve

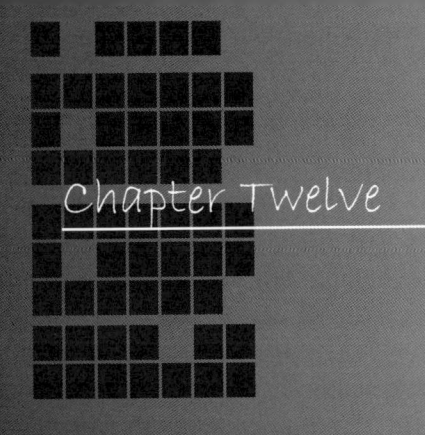

Linkage between Singapore's Domestic and Foreign Policy

> As a small state, Singapore's foreign policy is a balance between realism and idealism. We know we have to take the world as it is and not as we wish it to be. But we believe that we can and must defend ourselves and advance our interests ... the ASEAN bloc is the cornerstone of our foreign policy. [Relations with neighbours] are complex relationships. Problems will inevitably arise, and when they do, we aim to resolve them dispassionately without affecting our wider relationship.[1]

Introduction

Analysts have repeatedly argued that there is a very close link between a state's domestic and foreign policy. Scholars such as James Rosenau have long maintained that to understand a state's foreign policy, one must look deep into the domestic politics and imperatives of that state.[2] In the case of Singapore, in addition to this fact being articulated by policy makers, more clear is the manner domestic politics have impacted upon foreign policy and vice versa. The fact that few small states have survived successfully in international politics, all the more, that are characterised by sharp internal fault lines and surrounded or lying adjacent to big states, as is the case of Singapore, makes this fact almost self-evident in terms of the nexus between domestic and foreign policy.

---

[1] See "Singapore's Foreign Policy Balances Idealism and Realism: PM Lee", *Channel News Asia*, 27 November 2015. Available at http://www.channelnewsasia.com/news/singapore/singapore-s-foreign/2298768.html.

[2] James Rosenau, *Linkage Politics: Essays on the Convergence of National and International Systems* (New York: Free Press, 1969).

The Key Domestic Imperatives That Shape Singapore's Foreign Policy

Singapore's geography has played a key determinant of its foreign policy and especially security considerations as far as threats are concerned. A highly urbanised city-state with no strategic depth means that it is extremely vulnerable to internal and external threats. Totalling slightly more than 720 km^2, it is the smallest state in Southeast Asia. But it is its location that exudes particular vulnerabilities and makes it an attractive strategic target for acquisition. In particular, it is sandwiched between Malaysia to the north and Indonesia to the south. It also lies astride the important Strait of Malacca and is the most important connecting point between the Indian and Pacific oceans. It is in many ways a window to the world and hence, of great strategic value to almost everyone that is rich and powerful.

Its geographical vulnerability is worsened by the sharp domestic racial, religious and linguistic fault lines. Historically, Singapore has experienced bloodshed and conflicts due to these divisions, be it among the Chinese themselves and most dangerously, between the Chinese and Malays. The Hokkien-Teochew riots in 1854, the Maria Hertogh riots in 1950, and the Chinese-Malay racial riots in July and September 1964 are testimonies of what can transpire if racial and religious issues are not well-managed. Singapore's 75% Chinese majority literally confronts the 14% Malay minority, the original owners and 'sons of the soil' of Singapore. Yet, as a Chinese majority island state, Singapore is located in a 'Sea of Malays'. This creates a 'double minority' syndrome in Singapore. While the Chinese are a majority in Singapore, they are a definite minority in the region and where there is much antipathy towards the economically successful Chinese and in the past, who were mainly members and supporters of the communist movements in Malaysia, Singapore, Thailand, the Philippines and even Indonesia that posed a key security threat from the 1950s to the 1980s. The Malays in Singapore may be a clear minority but belong to the majority ethnic race in the region and where there are many who monitor and even speak up of the alleged persecution of Malays in Singapore. Hence, the demographic aspect of Singapore has a clear external dimension as far as foreign and security policies are concerned.

The economic realities confronting Singapore are also extremely important in terms of the domestic-foreign policy nexus. While Singapore is the richest state in Southeast Asia in terms of per capita and has one of the strongest and most successful economies in the Asia-Pacific region, it is also confronted by manifold vulnerabilities. It is almost totally without any major resource. Furthermore, it imports all of its raw materials and until recently, even bulk of its drinking water. It is also totally dependent on the world for its markets as well as foreign investments. The need to perform successfully economically compels a special need to maintain domestic peace while having a foreign policy that would be conducive to economic growth.

Singapore also needs to take cognisance of the geopolitics and geo-strategic importance of the Southeast Asia region. The region is one of the most important with the presence of all the key great powers of the world, including the United States, China, Japan, Russia and the European Union. These 'giants' have historically and continue to this date to have deep and abiding political, economic and strategic interests in the region. There are also critical land and territorial conflicts in the region, best exemplified by the competing claims over the South China Sea region. There are also racial- and religious-based insurgencies in Southeast Asia. Since 2001, the threat posed by Islamist extremism and terrorism has also increased, including to Singapore.

To all these imperatives must be added the nature of political system and government that has been in power for the last 50-odd years in Singapore. The PAP has been in power since 1959 and its experiences of challenges from within and without have greatly informed on how to perceive internal and external challenges. While the PAP is largely a non-ideological and extremely pragmatic-oriented government, the past continues to be relevant, some say, where the government may even become a 'prisoner' of its past experiences, that it continues to affect how it views the external world, including the manner it conducts its foreign policy.

How Domestic Imperatives Have Affected Foreign Relations?

There are a number of areas where the footprint of domestic politics is evident in Singapore's foreign policy. Singapore's relations with the great powers is clearly evident in this regard. While Singapore's relations with the West, especially the United States, are largely pragmatic and where the benefits have been evidently clear, this is not so with regard to the Asian powers. A major knock-on effect of Singapore being a Chinese-majority state is the historical allegation that it is nothing more than a 'third China', after the People's Republic of China and Taiwan. Singapore's need to defray and reject this perception has led to certain policies with regard to China. While Taiwan, though important, is too small a factor in international politics, 'communist China' in the past and especially today, is not. This was clearly evident, despite Singapore's close economic ties with China, that it announced a policy that it would be the last of the original five Association of Southeast Asian Nations' members [the other four members being Indonesia, Malaysia, Thailand and the Philippines] to establish diplomatic relations with China and only after its two Malay neighbours, Malaysia and Indonesia had done so. In the same vein, while India was not a significant trading or security partner in the past, relations were maintained on an even-keel, partly to assuage its domestic Indian population, despite its small size. Later, as

Singapore-Indian relations expanded, the presence of Singapore Indians was seen as an asset that would be able to facilitate the all-round growth, something that has been undertaken since the 1990s.

One area where domestic politics have played a part in foreign policy is the manner Singapore has devised its ties with Israel. Due to Israel's repressive policies towards the Palestinians and its wars with the Arabs since 1948, the Southeast Asian Muslim states, namely, Malaysia, Indonesia and Brunei, have not established diplomatic ties with Israel. There is also an intense negative racial and religious animosity towards Israel as a state that sponsors violence against Muslims in general, including through the support of Western states such as the United States. Yet, due to the manifold military and strategic assistance Israel has provided Singapore, close ties exist between the two states, with Singapore sticking out as the most friendly and pro-Israel state in the region. Even though Singapore's Muslim population are largely unhappy with this state of affairs, due to their minority status as well as the benefits Singapore accrues from its ties with Israel, the balancing of domestic politics and external foreign policy interest is clearly evident in Singapore-Israel relations.

Singapore's domestic architecture, especially in terms of its racial and religious structure, also had an impact on its ties with its immediate neighbours. This is mainly with regard to Singapore as an 'insensitive' Chinese neighbour and where it is seen to be adopting anti-Malay and even anti-Islam policies. In the past, many issues have surfaced, including the 'Tudung Issue' which many Malays in Malaysia and Indonesia viewed as being driven by the government's attempt to humiliate the Malays while undermining their religious practice.

While China, Israel and the perception of some Malay leaders in Malaysia and Indonesia towards the government policies on the minority Malay population in Singapore were the three areas where there appeared at times tensions between domestic political imperatives and foreign policy interests, since 2001, a new area and issue has surfaced, namely, terrorism. Historically, Singapore is no stranger to acts of terrorism. From the 1950s to the 1970s, the Chinese-based Communist Party of Malaya was the main perpetrator of acts of terrorism in Singapore. Additionally, Singapore experienced three external acts of terrorism. The first was in 1965 when Indonesian saboteurs bombed MacDonald House, killing three civilians. The second was in 1974 when four international terrorists, two who were members of the Japanese Red Army and two who were members of the Popular Front for the Liberation of Palestine, attempted to bomb an oil refinery and later hijacked a ferry. This crisis was resolved amicably without casualties. In 1991, four Pakistanis hijacked a Singapore Airlines plane en route from Kuala Lumpur to Singapore, demanding the release of some Pakistanis in Pakistan's prisons. The hijack ended with the death of the four hijackers.

Following the Al Qaeda-linked attacks on the United States' World Trade Centre in New York and the Pentagon in Washington, D.C., the threat posed by Islamist extremists has raised many folds. In December 2001, Singapore arrested 15 members of the pro-Al Qaeda *Jema'ah Islamiyah* who were planning to attack foreign embassies and government buildings in Singapore. In August 2002, another 21 members of the *Jema'ah Islamiyah* were arrested in Singapore. Since then, there have been regular arrests of Singaporeans who are members of the *Jema'ah Islamiyah* and since 2014, Singaporeans who believed to be supporters and members of the Islamic State have also been detained.

The rising threat posed by Islamist terrorism has the potential to affect inter-racial and inter-religious harmony within Singapore as well as Singapore's ties with its Malay neighbours. While terrorists anywhere are criminals intent on harming which ever society they are operating in, yet, the existence of such groups in Singapore and the terrorists' targeting of non-Muslims has the potential to undermine inter-racial and inter-religious harmony in Singapore. The unthinkable fear is that if the Islamists launched an attack, whether perpetrated by Singaporeans or non-Singaporeans, it could lead to a backlash against the Muslims in general, setting back hard-earned racial cohesion. Additionally, Singapore's pro-active policy of neutralising terrorist threats, especially Islamists that are operating in the Southeast Asia region, can have the potential of harming ties with its immediate neighbours with some interpreting this as nothing more than a cover to undertake anti-Malay and anti-Islam policies.

Think Questions

1. How has Singapore's demography affected Singapore's foreign and defence policy?
2. How has Singapore's location in Southeast Asia affected its domestic politics?
3. How has the threat of Islamist terrorism affected Singapore's politics?

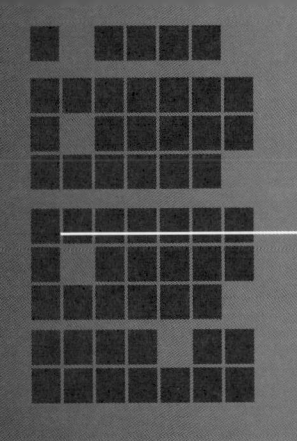

Conclusion: Whither Politics in Singapore?

> I'm not a great historian but look at Sparta and Athens, two city states in Greek history. Singapore is like Sparta … In the end, Sparta, a martial state known for being disciplines and strong crumbled … Athens survived … What legacy to leave for Singapore? … Is it to be a Sparta, a martial, well-organised, efficient society but in the end, very brittle, or an Athens, untidy, chaotic and argumentative but which survived because of its diversity of thinking?[1]

Introduction

For thinkers such as Aristotle, politics was described as the 'master science'. This was because almost every thing happened in the political arena and in turn, political decisions affected everything else in one way or another. Harold Lasswell, a renowned political scientist, described politics as the study "who gets what, when and how". No matter how one defines politics, all said and done, it involves the public sphere, power, and its use, distribution and delegation. Political decisions also greatly impact upon the private lives of anyone within the political entity. Hence, this raises the importance of understanding the politics of any system, and in this case, of Singapore. This study has tried to look at the 'bones' of Singapore politics and how, over time, the flesh has been added to make what has emerged as the 'Singapore Person'. Emphasis has been placed on the various political structures, the hardware of politics. At the same time, how this has affected the 'heart ware', especially in terms of nation building, civil society and electoral politics was also examined. An aspect of this study was also to discuss the growing importance of governance. Though not a new concept, it is not the same as government. It is much broader and more importantly, 'good government' is integral to good governance. A key question that needs to be

---

[1] Simon Tay S. C. (ed.), *A Mandarin and the Making of Public Policy: Reflections by Ngiam Tong Dow* (Singapore: NUS Press, 2006) pp. 28–29.

answered is how is Singapore faring as far as good governance is concerned. Most observers, including the World Bank, have rated the Republic high, stamping its approval of the direction the Republic and its politics is traversing.

Singapore's Achievements

Thus far, the successes far outweigh what might be regarded as failures or disadvantages. When the Republic was catapulted to the family of nations as an independent state, very few pundits gave it a chance of survival. If anything, the 'doomsday' soothsayers had a field day. Many believed that Singapore will eventually be compelled to 'crawl back to Malaysia on all fours'. This definitely did not happen; but Singapore advanced as a model of how a small state can emerge as a successful regional and global player. Examining the anatomy of Singapore politics, one cannot help but conclude that the odds against the Republic were tremendous and in many ways, these continue to haunt it. Yet, through brilliant political leadership and unity, social discipline and far-sightedness and most importantly, a pragmatic approach to problem solving, Singapore has demonstrated that success is highly possible. However, this has always involved choices. Often, some short-term 'pain' and attractions of what some would regard as a 'soft option' have to be sacrificed for the medium- to long-term good of society as a whole. Ultimately, it is about tough decision making in an environment of tough choices. This calls for tough leaders and at the same time, a tough populace that can weigh and see the long-term benefits of such policies. This, in essence, is the key to the operation of Singapore politics and its success.

Lee Kuan Yew, the founding father of modern Singapore, has written about the transformation of Singapore from a Third to a First World. In many ways, this encapsulates the achievements of the Republic within a generation, a rare feat in modern politics. Singapore is indeed a story of many stories. It is a story of successful decolonisation. It is a story of successful adjustment under different flags, from a British, Japanese, British again, Malaysian and finally, to Singapore's own flag as a sovereign state. It is a story of transforming a swampland into a modern metropolis. It is a story of relocating the majority of its populace into a modern housing environment. It is a story of effectively educating to its people. It is a story of providing modern health care. It is a story of providing personal safety and security. It is story of providing amenities, infrastructure and environment that all can identify as modern, clean and healthy. It is a story of creating modern trading, shopping and entertainment hubs. It is a story of being able to lead through brilliant ideas. In short, it is a successful story of rapid modernity and transformation, and where, almost unexpectedly, a modern beacon called Singapore emerged as an icon of what happens when a people and its leaders get their politics right. That is a short-hand for modern Singapore, something which even Sir Stamford Raffles would not have anticipated when he started the process of transforming a tiny fishing village into a regional emporium.

The international community is familiar with many of Singapore's successes. Its rapid economic growth is well known. Its international trade is more than four times the size of its gross national product. The Republic is the region's capital of multinational corporations. With a highly educated, trained and discipline workforce, Singapore has succeeded in having one of the highest per capita incomes in the world. Despite being without most resources, including sufficient drinking water, Singapore has been able to create niches in areas such as petrochemical refining and provision of health care. The Republic is characterised by political and social stability. It has world-class modern amenities and infrastructure in communications and transportation. There have been great advances in information technology. It has become a modern banking and financial hub. It has one of the world's best airports and seaports.

While these successes are well known, there are many other unsung achievements. Singapore and Singaporeans have been at peace with each other since the last racial riots broke out in 1964 and to some extent, 1969. What is important to note is that these riots broke out mainly as a result of Malaysian politics rather than something innate to Singapore. Today, despite the worldwide rise of ethno-nationalism, Singapore is an oasis of social peace and harmony. Despite the mosaic pluralism, multiracialism is the bedrock of Singapore's society. Singapore is corruption-free. It is a clean and healthy state. Some say too clean, resulting in a population whose natural immunity to diseases has been greatly reduced. Despite the rising cost of living, Singapore is a relatively affordable place to live. There are hardly any beggars and cheap food is accessible to all.

Challenges Confronting Singapore

Despite the tremendous successes that Singapore have made over the years, an understanding of its political anatomy reminds one of the manifold vulnerabilities and fragilities that continue and will continue to afflict it. In some ways, it has successfully lived on borrowed time. Devoid of resources, blessed by an excellent geographical location, good leaders and a hardworking population, the Republic has made its mark and grade. It has emerged as a peaceful, highly developed and wealthy state. Yet, these are impermanent attributes. Social peace can be easily wrecked by insensitive policies at home or developments in the region. The wealth of a nation, especially of a small state, can be quickly wiped out by tragedies such as war, long-term economic recession or poor policies of a government.

At the same time, there are new challenges that are emerging in the city-state. While there is tremendous ethnic peace, at the same time, ethnic and religious consciousness is also rising. While this is a worldwide phenomenon, the rise of ethnicity is fraught with danger if this is not moderated. If ethnic consciousness is manipulated for political purposes, it is bound to have a backlash, be it from the majority or minority communities. This will destroy the social fabric that has characterised modern Singapore. There is also a rising class consciousness in society. While poverty has literally been wiped out through effective economic policies, as far as distribution of wealth is concerned, this is extremely uneven. Hence, the simplistic (to some extent, erroneous) characterisation of Singapore as District 9, 10 and 11 versus Others, with the former being regarded as the enclaves of the rich. Increasingly, globalisation will further aggravate this divide. While many measures have been implemented to moderate this problem, it is something that will get worse, especially in a system where there are minimal subsidies and devoid of a national welfare system.

Challenges in the arena of ethnicity and economics are bound to impact Singapore politics. In particular, they will have an important bearing on the state of the political parties and electoral politics. With a thriving economy, educated population and an electorate exposed to international developments, there is a greater likelihood that increased participation and involvement in politics will develop. In short, civil society will expand and become active politically. In Maslowian terms, this is the phenomenon of hierarchy of needs, in this case, higher needs of political participation are sought once the basic economic ones have been satisfied. This will have a bearing on the role and place of the Opposition parties as well as the ability of the PAP to remain as the hegemonic guardian in a system that has been operating since 1959.

Within the region, Singapore's relationship with her neighbours remains fragile. Issues of race and religion within Singapore, particularly with regard to the Malay-Muslim community, will continue to affect how Singapore relates to its Malay-majority neighbours of Indonesia and Malaysia, as has been the case in the past. This problem will only intensify with the proliferation of terrorism and Islamist extremism in the region, which will require cooperation between Singapore and its ASEAN partners to combat. In addition to problems of demography, environmental issues such as the haze that has plagued the Southeast Asia region in recent years have emerged as an area of contention. As the blame for the haze shifts between the Indonesian government to Singaporean palm oil plantation owners, attempts at managing the issue have been fraught with finger-pointing with few solutions that productively tackle the issue. Therefore, in matters both physical and cultural, Singapore in the coming years will continue to be faced with the challenge of managing regional relations.

Internationally, Singapore also faces challenges. The loss of Lee meant the loss of a statesman who put Singapore on the world stage and gave the city-state global influence way above its station as a small island nation. Uncertainties surrounding trade partnerships with the rest of the world, as well as how Singaporeans and the Singapore government will respond to waves of democratisation all over the world in a time of new media only raise more questions for Singapore's place in a globalised world. Given the realities of the physical limitations Singapore is challenged with and given the pace of change, it has thus become especially imperative that the government helming Singapore is one well-equipped to deal with these changes.

Telescoping Ahead

Looking back, what eventually catapulted Singapore to its present state of development was the landmark split of the PAP in 1961, culminating in the victory of the moderates in the 1963 General Elections. This placed a particular group of individuals into power. The group was led by individuals such as Lee, Toh Chin Chye, Goh Keng Swee and S. Rajaratnam. Since that period, this group of individuals and adherents of that mould have remained in power. The Singapore of today is a continuation of the politics of 1963 and thereafter, rather than prior to that period. That was the paradigmatic change that fundamentally altered Singapore, its politics, economic outlook, social-cultural relations and even its foreign and defence policies. Sure enough, that group of individuals did not survive the Malaysian Federation, which has been considered as one of their major setbacks. That aside, the modern Singapore of today cannot be divorced from the leaders of the post-1963 period.

Having fundamentally succeeded in achieving all-round success, a key and legitimate question is what of the future? What will Singapore and its politics be like in the next 10 to 25 years? In many ways, the Singapore system is in place and as it is characterised by success and efficiency, this is likely to remain. The adage "why fix it if it isn't broken" would apply. At the same time, in view of national, regional and international changes, Singapore politics would have to come to terms with the 2Rs, namely, race and religion. This will increasingly play an important role in national politics and its management will determine what type of Singapore would emerge in the near future. As was argued by Lee in August 2005, "it is demography, and not democracy, that will be the critical factor in shaping growth and security in the 21st century".[2] Thus far, Singapore has avoided the disease that has afflicted many small states that are in similar positions. The Republic has avoided what the 'League of Tragic Sisters' such as Cyprus, Sri Lanka, Lebanon and Fiji have endured and destroyed what were often referred to as 'paradises' of their respective regions. They

---

[2] Channel News Asia, 31 August 2005. Cited at http://www.channelnewsasia.com/stories/singaporelocalnews/view/165842/1/html.

were destroyed and disabled by the politics of the 2Rs. Avoiding this will remain a key challenge.

Secondly, the Republic will remain embroiled in the 'battle of ideas'. There will be two levels of contestation worthy of note. First, will be the contestation within the polity. This will pit the PAP's ways and style of doing things versus the rest of the citizens. Second, will be the manner in which the PAP government is viewed internationally. As Singapore strengthens its presence globally and embraces globalisation, how will this impact the style and substance of PAP's rule in Singapore? Can the PAP's approach to political, economic and social management be sustained? How will the PAP respond to calls for 'loosening up' and greater 'tolerance' of contrarian views and perspectives? Must all who publicly raise political issues join political parties to do so? Will the PAP permit a 'freer' mass media to operate in Singapore? Will the PAP government loosen its control of the trade unions and grassroots organisations? Will civil society organisations be permitted to operate in the 'political market place'? How will the Opposition be treated? Will challenging the government remain a costly endeavour? Also, can the PAP's views on key issues such as good governance, role of the Opposition, importance of the government, changing behaviour electorate, just to mention a few, be sustained?

Closing Remarks

In the final analysis, the Republic's anatomy will perpetually haunt it. Essentially, Singapore politics is a function of its anatomy (geography, demography, economy) and how human ingenuity has added value to make it a model of envy. How is it possible that at a time of rising ethno-nationalism, the Republic continues to enjoy uninterrupted ethnic and religious harmony since 1965? How it is possible that a resourceless island state has emerged as one of the wealthiest states in the world, with a per capita higher than many developed Western European states? Also, how has it been able to accumulate one of the highest reserves in the world? The list of achievements is almost unending, be it in terms of technological successes, infrastructure development, banking facilities, excellent sea and air port services, and its emergence as a medical and education hub in the region. The answer lies in excellent political leadership, a highly hardworking and progressive populace, and the good fortune of geography.

While Singapore's achievements have become legendary, the challenges are by no mean insignificant. In many ways, history is Singapore's key enemy. The past is littered with failures and irrelevance of small states. While Singapore has been able to punch 'above its weight', this is something that is not easy to sustain. Also, the odds against the Republic will grow in commensurate terms as the populace becomes developed and more interested in luxurious living and as competition from the region and beyond intensifies. In this regard, a unique Singapore Paradox might surface: can a small state survive successfully in a highly competitive world? Will Singapore be able to defend itself from new, non-traditional threats that might impact upon its domestic politics? Does the present political system facilitate or hamper the Republic's ability to compete effectively in the international market place? In view of these challenges, Singapore politics and the future of the Republic will most likely be determined by the skills and capabilities of its leaders, the nature and character of the challenges, and most important of all, how the two Rs — race and religion — are managed.

Think Questions

1. What will remain and what will change in Singapore politics in the coming years?
2. What will be the key determinant that will alter Singapore politics?
3. How will external developments influence the directions of Singapore politics in the years to come?

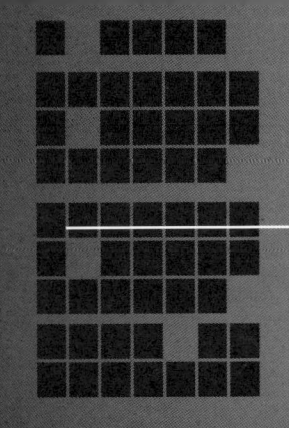

Select Bibliography

Primary Documents/Official Publications

1989 Singapore Elections: PAP Electoral Candidates, Singapore, 1989.

Balakrishna, V. R. *Brief History of the Singapore Trade Union Movement*, Singapore: National Trades Union Congress, 1976.

Constitution of the People's Action Party, 15 November 1982.

Fong, Sip Chee, *The PAP Story: The Pioneering Years (November 1954–April 1968)*, Singapore: Times Periodicals Pte Ltd for PAP, Chai Chee Branch.

Goh, Chok Tong, *Agenda for Action: Goals and Challenges, A Green Paper Presented to Parliament by Mr Goh Chok Tong First Deputy Prime Minister and Minister for Defence, 15 February 1988*, Singapore: Singapore National Printers, 1988.

National Trades Union Congress, *30 Years On: Strong Union, Cultivated Workforce*, Singapore: National Trades Union Congress, 1991.

PAP 45th Anniversary Celebrations Organizing Committee, People's Action Party, *For People through Action by Party*, Singapore: People's Action Party, 1999.

People's Action Party, *Elections Manifesto 1980*.

People's Action Party, *People's Action Party: 1954–1979*, Singapore: Central Executive Committee People's Action Party, PETIR 25th Anniversary Issue, 1979.

People's Action Party, *People's Action Party: 1954–1984*, Singapore: Central Executive Committee People's Action Party, PETIR 30th Anniversary Issue, 1984.

People's Action Party, *People's Action Party Youth Wing Fifth Anniversary Commemorative Volume*, Singapore: 1991.

Rosenau, James, *Linkage Politics: Essays on the Convergence of National and International Systems*, New York: Free Press, 1969.

Singapore 21 Secretariat, *Singapore 21: Together, We Make the Difference: Our Vision for the 21st Century*, Singapore 21 Secretariat c/o Prime Minister's Office, Public Service Division, 1999.

The Singaporean, Singapore National Trades Union Congress (ed.), *Devan: Nation Builder, People's President*, Singapore: Singapore National Trades Union Congress, 1981.

Transcript of Prime Minister Lee Hsien Loong's National Day Rally English Speech on 29 August 2010. Available at https://www.mfa.gov.sg/content/mfa/overseasmission/washington/newsroom/press_statements.html. Accessed on 19 September 2016.

Yeo, George, "Civic Society" edited by V. Mohan, *Inaugural NUSS Lecture at World Trade Centre Auditorium, 20 June 1991*, Singapore: National University of Singapore Society, 1991.

Young PAP 10th Anniversary 1996.

Books

Asher, Mukul G. and Nandy, Amarendu, *Singapore's Policy Responses to Aging, Inequality and Poverty: An Assessment*, Singapore: Lee Kuan Yew School of Public Policy, 2008.

Ban, Kah Choon, Pakir, Anne, and Tong, Chee Kiong (eds.), *Imagining Singapore*, Singapore: Times Academic Press, 1992.

Ban, Kah Choon, Pakir, Anne, and Tong, Chee Kiong (eds.), *Imagining Singapore*, 2nd edition, Singapore: Eastern Universities Press, 2004.

Chan, Heng Chee, *The Dynamics of One Party Dominance*, Singapore: Singapore University Press, 1976.

Chee, Soon Juan, *Dare to Change: An Alternative Vision for Singapore*, Singapore: The Singapore Democratic Party, 1994.

Choo, Carolyn, *Singapore: The PAP and the Problem of Political Succession*, Singapore: Asiapac Books and Educational Aids, 1985.

Chua, Beng Huat, *Communitarian Ideology and Democracy in Singapore*, London: Routledge, 1997.

Clammer, John, *Race and State in Independent Singapore, 1965–1990: The Cultural Politics of Pluralism in a Multiethnic Society*, Ashgate, 1998.

Fernandez, Warren, *Thinking Allowed? Politics, Fear and Change in Singapore*, Singapore: SNP International, 2004.

George, Cherian, *Singapore: The Air-Conditioned Nation: Essays on the Politics of Comfort and Control 1990–2000*, Singapore: Landmark Books, 2000.

Gillis, E. Kay, *Singapore Civil Society and British Power*, Singapore: Talisman Publishing Ltd, 2005.

Gomez, James, *Internet Politics: Surveillance and Intimidation in Singapore*, Singapore and Bangkok: Think Centre (Singapore and Thailand), 2002.

Gomez, James (ed.), *Publish and Perish: The Censorship of Opposition Party Publications in Singapore*, Singapore: National Solidarity Party, 2001.

Han, Fook Kwang, Fernandez, Warren, and Tan, Sumiko (eds.), *Lee Kuan Yew: The Man and His Ideas*, Singapore: Singapore Press Holdings [and] Times Editions, 1998.

Hill, Michael and Lian, Kwen Fee, *The Politics of Nation Building and Citizenship in Singapore*, London: Routledge, 1995.

Koh, Gillian and Ooi, Giok-Ling (eds.), *State-Society Relations in Singapore*, Singapore: Institute of Policy Studies and Oxford University Press, 2000.

Lau, Albert, *A Moment of Anguish: Singapore in Malaysia and the Politics of Disengagement*, Singapore: Times Academic Press, 1998.

Lee, Kuan Yew, *The Singapore Story: Memoirs of Lee Kuan Yew*, Singapore: Singapore Press Holdings, 1998.
Lee, Kuan Yew, *From Third World to First: The Singapore Story: 1965–2000 Memoirs of Lee Kuan Yew*, Singapore: Times Media Private Limited and The Straits Times Press, 2000.
Lim-Ng, Been Eng, *Chronology of Trade Union Development in Singapore, 1940–1984*, Singapore: NTUC, 1985.
Lingle, Christopher, *Singapore's Authoritarian Capitalism: Asian Values, Free Market Illusions, and Political Dependency*, Barcelona: Edicions Sirocco, S. L., 1996.
Lo, Joseph and Huang, Guoqin (eds.), *People Like Us: Sexual Minorities in Singapore*, Singapore: Select Publishing, 2003.
Low, Donald and Sudhir, Thomas Vadaketh (eds.), *Hard Choices: Challenging the Singapore Consensus*, Singapore: NUS Press, 2014.
Low, Linda (ed.), *Singapore: Towards a Developed Status*, Singapore: Centre for Advance Studies, National University of Singapore and Oxford University Press, 1999.
Mahizhnan, Arun and Lee, Tsao Yuan (eds.), *Singapore Re-Engineering Success*, Singapore: Institute of Policy Studies and Oxford University Press, 1998.
Mauzy, K. Diane and Milne, R. S., *Singapore Politics under the People's Action Party*, London: Routledge, 2002.
Mutalib, H., *Parties and Politics: A Study of Opposition Parties and the PAP in Singapore*, Singapore, Marshall Cavendish Academic, 2nd edition, 2004.
Mutalib, H., *Singapore Malays: Being Ethnic Minority and Muslim in a Global City-State*, London: Routledge, 2012.
Ong, Jin Hui, Tong, Chee Kiong, and Tan, Ern Ser (eds.), *Understanding Singapore Society*, Singapore: Times Academic Press, 1997.
Open Singapore Center, *Elections in Singapore: Are They Free and Fair? An Open Singapore Centre Report on the Conduct of Parliamentary Elections in Singapore*, Singapore, 2000.
Pang, Cheng Lian, *Singapore's People's Action Party*, London: Oxford University Press, 1971.
Pugalenthi, Sr., *Elections in Singapore*, Singapore: VJ Times International Pte Ltd, 1996.
Quah, S. T. Jon, Chan, Heng Chee, and Seah, Chee Meow, *Government and Politics of Singapore*, Oxford: Oxford University Press, 1985.
Quah, S. T. Jon (ed.), *In Search of Singapore's National Values*, Singapore: Times Academic Press for The Institute of Policy Studies, 1990.
Rodan, Garry, *Singapore Changes Guard: Social, Political and Economic Directions in the 1990s*, Melbourne: Longman Cheshire; New York: St. Martin's Press, 1993.
Rodan, Garry (ed.), *Singapore*, Burlington, VT: Ashgate, 2001.
Rodan, Garry, *Transparency and Authoritarian Rule in Southeast Asia: Singapore and Malaysia*, London: Routledge Curzon, 2004.
Schak, David C. and Hudson, Wayne (eds.), *Civil Society in Asia*, Burlington, VT: Ashgate, 2003.
Sim, Soek-Fang, *Obliterating the Political: One-Party Ideological Dominance and the Personalization of News in Singapore 21*, Working Paper No. 119, Perth, Western Australia: Murdoch University, 2005.
Singam, Constance, Tan, Chong Kee, Ng, Tisa, and Perera, Leon (eds.), *Building Social Space in Singapore: The Working Committee's Initiative in Civil Society Activism*, Singapore: Select Publishing, 2002.

Singam, Constance *et al.*, *The Future of Civil Society in Singapore*, Singapore: Association of Muslim Professionals, 1997.

Singh, Bilveer, *Whither PAP's Dominance? An Analysis of Singapore's 1991 General Elections*, Malaysia: Pelanduk Publications (M) Sdn Bhd, 1992.

Singh, Bilveer, *Quest for Political Power: Communist Subversion and Militancy in Singapore*, Singapore: Marshall Cavendish, 2015.

Tae, Y. Nam, *Racism, Nationalism, and Nation-Building in Malaysia and Singapore: A Functional Analysis of Political Integration*, Meerut: Sadhna Prakashan, 1973.

Tan, Y. L. Kevin and Lam, Peng Er (eds.), *Managing Political Change in Singapore*, London: Routledge, 1997.

Tay, Simon S. C. (ed.), *A Mandarin and the Making of Public Policy: Reflections by Ngiam Tong Dow*, Singapore: NUS Press, 2006.

Vasil, Raj, *Governing Singapore: Democracy and National Development*, Singapore: Allen & Unwin, 2000.

Vasil, Raj, *A Citizen's Guide to Government and Politics in Singapore*, Singapore: Talisman Publishing Pte Ltd, 2004.

Yap, Mui Teng, Koh, Gillian, and Soon, Debbie (eds.), *Migration and Integration in Singapore: Policies and Practice*, New York: Routledge, 2015.

Journal Articles

Barr, Michael D., "The Bonsai under the Banyan Tree: Democracy and Democratisation in Singapore", *Democratisation*, Vol. 21, No. 1, September 2012.

Chalmers, Ian M., *Weakening State Controls and Ideological Change in Singapore: The Emergence of Local Capital as a Political Force*, Working Paper No. 13, Murdoch, W. A.: Asia Research Centre, Murdoch University, 1992.

Chan, Heng Chee, "The Role of Parliamentary Politicians in Singapore", *Legislative Studies Quarterly*, Vol. 1, No. 3, August 1976.

Chang, W. David, "Nation-Building in Singapore", *Asian Survey*, Vol. 8, No. 9, September 1968.

Chong, Terence, *Civil Society in Singapore: Reviewing Concepts in the Literature*, ISEAS Working Paper, Social and Cultural No. 1 (2005), Singapore: Institute of Southeast Asian Studies, 2005.

Ganesan, Narayan, "Singapore: Entrenching a City-State's Dominant Party System", *Southeast Asian Affairs 1998*, Singapore: Institute of Southeast Asian Studies, 1998.

Hart-Hamilton, Natasha, "The Singapore State Revisited", *The Pacific Review*, Vol. 13, No. 2, 2000.

Ho, Khai Leong, "Citizen Participation and Policy Making in Singapore: Conditions and Predicaments", *Asian Survey*, Vol. 40, No. 3, May–June 2000.

Huxley, Tim, "Singapore and Malaysia: A Precarious Balance", *Pacific Review*, Vol. 4 No. 3, 1991.

Huxley, Tim, "Singapore in 2000: Continuing Stability and Renewed Prosperity Amid Regional Disarray", *Asian Survey*, Vol. 41, No. 1, A Survey of Asia in 2000, January 2001.

Huxley, Tim, "Singapore in 2001: Political Continuity Despite Deepening Recession", *Asian Survey*, Vol. 42, No. 1, A Survey of Asia in 2001, January 2002.

Jones, Martin David, "Democratization, Civil Society and Illiberal Middle Class Culture in Pacific Asia", *Comparative Politics*, Vol. 30, No. 2, January 1998.

Jones, S. David, "Performance Measurement and Budgetary Reform in the Singapore Civil Service", *Journal of Public Budgeting, Accounting & Financial Management*, Vol. 13, No. 4, Winter 2001.

Jordan, Rolf, "Singapore in Its Worst Recession for Years: The Effects of the Current Economic Crisis on the City-State's Economy", *Journal of Current Southeast Asian Affairs*, Vol. 28, No. 4.

Kuo, C. Y. Eddie, "Multilingualism and Mass Media Communications in Singapore", *Asian Survey*, Vol. 18, No. 10, October 1978.

Kuruvilla, Sarosh, "Linkages between Industrialization Strategies and Industrial Relations/Human Resource Policies: Singapore, Malaysia and the Philippines, and India", *Industrial and Labor Relations Review*, Vol. 49, No. 4, July 1996.

Lee, Hsien Loong and Ngiam, Moses, "The FP Interview: Singapore's Big Gamble", *Foreign Policy*, No. 130, May-June 2002.

Lee, Lai To, "Singapore in 1998: The Most Serious Challenge since Independence", *Asian Survey*, Vol. 39, No. 1, A Survey of Asia in 1998, January 1999.

Lee, Lai To, "Singapore in 1999: Molding the City-State to Meet Challenges of the 21st Century", *Asian Survey*, Vol. 40, No. 1, A Survey of Asia in 1999, January 2000.

Lee, Terence, "The Politics of Civil Society in Singapore", *Asian Studies Review*, Vol. 26, No. 1, March 2002.

Leifer, Michael, "Singapore in Malaysia: The Politics of Federation", *Journal of Southeast Asian Studies*, Vol. 6, No. 2, September 1965.

Mauzy, Diane K., "Leadership Succession in Singapore: The Best Laid Plans", *Asian Survey*, Vol. 33, No. 12, December 1993.

Meagher, Patrick, "Anti-Corruption Agencies: Rhetoric versus Reality", *The Journal of Policy Reform*, Vol. 8, No. 1, 2005.

Milne, R. S., "Singapore's Exit from Malaysia: The Consequences of Ambiguity", *Asian Survey*, Vol. 6, No. 3, March 1966.

Milne, R. S., "Technocrats and Politics in the ASEAN Countries", *Pacific Affairs*, Vol. 55, No. 3, Autumn 1982.

Narayanan, Ganesan, "Singapore in 2008: A Few Highs and Lows while Bracing for the Future", *Asian Survey*, Vol. 49, No. 1.

Nathan, K. S., "Malaysia-Singapore Relations: Retrospect and Prospect", *Contemporary Southeast Asia*, Vol. 24, No. 2, August 2002.

Ortmann, Stephen, "Political Change and Civil Society Coalitions in Singapore", *Government and Opposition*, Vol. 50, No. 1, November 2013.

Ramesh, M. "The Politics of Social Security in Singapore", *The Pacific Review*, Vol. 13, No. 2, 2000.

Rigg, Jonathan, "Singapore and the Recession of 1985", *Asian Survey*, Vol. 28, No. 3, March 1988.

Rodan, Garry, "The Internet and Political Control in Singapore", *Political Science Quarterly*, Vol. 113, No. 1, Spring 1998.

Rodan, Garry, "Singapore in 1997: Living with Neighbours", *Asian Survey*, Vol. 38, No. 2, A Survey of Asia in 1997: Part II, February 1998.

Rodan, Garry, "Asian Crisis, Transparency and the International Media in Singapore", *The Pacific Review*, Vol. 13, No. 2, 2000.

Shee, Poon Kim, "Singapore in 1991: Endorsement of the New Administration", *Asian Survey*, Vol. 32, No. 2, A Survey of Asia in 1991: Part II, February 1992.

Tae, Yul Nam, "Singapore's One-Party System: Its Relationship to Democracy and Political Stability", *Pacific Affairs*, Vol. 42, No. 4, Winter 1969.

Tan, Kenneth Paul, "Democracy and the Grassroots Sector in Singapore", *Space & Polity*, Vol. 7, No. 1, 2003.

Tan, Kenneth Paul, "Meritocracy and Elitism in a Global City: Ideological Shifts in Singapore", *International Political Science Review*, Vol. 29, No. 1, 2008.

Yeoh, Brenda S. A., "Cosmopolitanism and Its Exclusions in Singapore", *Urban Studies*, Vol. 41, No. 12, November 2004.

Newspapers Articles

"15 Years of Tracking Politics", *The Straits Times*, 19 August 2006.

"$387m on YOG Well Spent", *The Straits Times*, 26 August 2010, www.straitstimes.com/BreakingNews/Singapore/Story/STIStory_571284.html.

"A Minister Must Fall in the Process of Change", *The Online Citizen*, 28 February 2010, theonlinecitizen.com/2010/02/a-minister-must-fall-in-the-process-of-change-says-nsp-sec-gen.

"A Question of Loyalty: The Malays in Singapore", *The Straits Times*, 30 September 1999.

"A Six-Year Wait — for Shorter Waiting Times", *Todayonline*, 3 September 2010, www.todayonline.com/Singapore/EDC100903-0000108/A-six-year-wait---for-shorter-waiting-times.

"Adviser over MP Raises Many Questions", *The Straits Times*, 22 October 2009.

"Basic Pay: Tommy Koh Weighs in", *The Straits Times*, 15 September 2010.

"Bloggers with a Cause", *The Straits Times*, 28 May 2006.

"Change Unlikely as Singapore Votes, but the Young Chafe", *International Herald Tribune*, 6 May 2006.

Channel News Asia, 31 August 2005, http://www.channelnewsasia.com/stories/singaporelocalnews/view/165842/1/html.

Channel News Asia, "Feedback Unit to Officially Launch Blogs in First Half of 2007", 6 December 2006, http://www.channelnewsasia.com/stories/singaporelocalnews/print/245630/1/.html, accessed on 11 December 2006.

Charissa Yong, "Parliament: 2017 Presidential Election Will Be Reserved for Malay Candidates, Says PM Lee", *The Straits Times*, 8 November 2016.

"Civil Service to Permit Teleworking", *The Business Times*, 29 August 2000.

"Closing One Eye, the Civil Service Way", *The Straits Times*, 12 January 2001.

"Cooking, Scotching Rumours — All in a Day's Work for New PAP Candidates", *The Straits Times*, 23 November 1996.
"Cyberspace Challenge Facing Reality, Singapore Rethinks Thought Control", *The Asian Wall Street Journal*, 1 September 1999.
"Cyberspace — Wired Singapore: Island State Finds the Net a Two-Edged Sword", *Far Eastern Economic Review*, 27 July 1995.
"David Marshall: Praise as Well as Criticise Govt", *The Straits Times*, 18 January 1994.
"DBS Chief Reignites Debate on Foreign Talent", *The Straits Times*, 19 June 2010.
"DBS Report: IRs Added $470m to Economy in First Half of 2010", *Todayonline*, 27 August 2010, www.todayonline.com/Business/EDC100827-0000077/DBS-report--IRs-added-$470m-to-economy-in-first-half-of-2010.
"Did the Poor Really Progress?", *The Straits Times*, 17 June 2009.
"Difference between Singapore and Hong Kong", *The Online Citizen*, 20 October 2008, theonlinecitizen.com/2008/10/structured-products-difference-between-spore-and-hong-kong/, accessed 30 July 2010.
"Don't Cast Protest Vote over Rising Flat Prices: MM", *The Straits Times*, 28 January 2010.
"Elected Presidency: Amendments to Constitution Passed in Parliament", *Channel News Asia*, 9 November 2016, http://www.channelnewsasia.com/news/singapore/elected-presidency-amendments-to-constitution-passed-in/3271856.html.
"Exercise Wage Flexibility Even in Times of High Growth: PM", *Channel News Asia*, 28 July 2010.
"FACTBOX — Defamation Suits a Staple of Singapore Politics", *Reuters News*, 27 April 2006.
"Fair Play: Respect for Rules or Equal Treatment of All Parties?", *The Straits Times*, 5 May 2006.
Fann Sim, "Controversy over Meal Packs for YOG Volunteers", 13 August 2010, www.temasekreview.com/2010/08/13/controversy-over-meal-packs-for-yog-volunteers/.
"Flirting with the Other Suitor?", *The Straits Times*, 5 May 2006.
"For SDP, Writing Is on the Wall; Default Judgment Passed against Party Which Must Pay Damages to Stay Alive", *Today (Singapore)*, 8 June 2006.
"Foreign Worker Levy to Rise", *Reuters*, 3 July 2010.
"Forum for Free Speech", *Financial Times*, 4 May 2006.
"From Light to Lighter, to No Touch?", *The Straits Times*, 17 June 2006.
"FT.Com: Inequality Is Centre Stage in Singapore's Election", *Financial Times*, 3 May 2006.
"FT.Com Site: Observer from Singapore", *Financial Times*, 7 May 2006.
"GE2015: PAP Vote Share Increases to 69.9%, Party Wins 83 of 89 Seats Including WP-Held Punggol East", *The Straits Times*, 12 September 2015.
"Getting Heard in Cyberspace", *The Straits Times*, 29 August 2006.
"Give Views on YOG in Gracious Manner", *Asiaone*, 1 September 2010, news.asiaone.com/News/Mailbox/Story/A1Story20100830-234683.html.
"Going the Distance to Cast Ballots", *The Straits Times*, 7 May 2006.
"Government Will Not Stand in the Way of Entrepreneurs — DPM Lee", *Channel News Asia*, 10 March 2004.
"Govt-Labour Ties Started with Founding of NTUC", *The Straits Times*, 7 August 1993.
"Govt Won't Let Reputation for Integrity Be Tarnished: MM", *The Straits Times*, 29 April 2006.

"Grassroots Job Same, But No Gangsters Now", *The Straits Times*, 4 October 2004.
"Grassroots Movement Politicised? Not True", *The Straits Times*, 10 March 2006.
"Grassroots Veteran Rose through Party Ranks", *The Straits Times*, 12 April 2006.
"GRCs Make It Easier to Find Top Talent: SM", *The Straits Times*, 27 June 2006.
"GRCs Needed to Get Minorities, Women into House", *The Straits Times*, 30 April 2006.
"If I Were Not Lee Kuan Yew's Son …", *The Business Times*, 10 July 1999.
"In HDB Living, 'Give and Take Is Often Necessary'", *The Straits Times*, 6 March 2010.
"Indonesia Bans Exports of Sand to Singapore", *The Straits Times*, 24 January 2007.
"Internet Regulations to Start on Monday", *The Straits Times*, 12 July 1996.
"It's a Very Strong Mandate", *The Straits Times*, 7 May 2006.
"Jobless Migrant Workers Protest in Singapore Again", *Reuters*, 27 February 2009, in.reuters.com/article/idINIndia-38247620090227.
"Join PAP? Up to Grassroots Leaders, says Kan Seng", *The Straits Times*, 21 February 2006.
"Keeping the Civil Service Clean — A Matter of Principles", *The Straits Times*, 7 June 1998.
Kevin Sinclair, "Reins to be Loosened: Chok Tong", *The Straits Times*, 23 June 1990.
"KL and Spore File Notices at ICJ on Island Row", *The Straits Times*, 25 July 2003.
Koh Buck Song, "The 1000 PAP 'Cardinals' Who Appoint the 'Pope'", *The Straits Times*, 4 April 1998.
"Labour MP's Ties with Govt: How It All Began", *The Straits Times*, 29 January 1994.
"Las Vegas Sands Is Chosen to Build Singapore Casino", *The New York Times*, 27 May 2006, www.nytimes.com/2006/05/27/business/worldbusiness/27casino.html?_r=1.
"Las Vegas Sands Says Singapore Casino Opening Delayed", *Asiaone*, 8 July 2009, www.asiaone.com/Travel/News/Story/A1Story20090708-153565.html.
"Lee Kuan Yew Made Huge Effort to Ensure Those Who Came after Him Succeeded: PM Lee", *The Straits Times*, 23 March 2016, http://www.straitstimes.com/singapore/lee-kuan-yew-made-huge-effort-to-ensure-those-who-came-after-him-succeeded-pm-lee.
"Legal Recourse for Foreign Workers", *The Online Citizen*, 16 June 2009, theonlinecitizen.com/2009/06/legal-recourse-for-foreign-workers/.
"Let Politics Ride This Animal; It's Hard to Tame, Impossible to Muzzle but Worth Befriending", *TODAY (Singapore)*, 7 June 2006.
"Light of Reason", *The Straits Times*, 20 September 1991.
Lim Siong Guan, "Letter — Graft — Not Just Stats Alone", *The Straits Times*, 16 June 1998.
"Lively Debate at NUS Forum", *The Straits Times*, 27 April 2006.
"Local Businessman Loses $26m at RWS Casino over 3 Days", *Todayonline*, 18 August 2010, www.todayonline.com/Business/EDC100818-0000040/Local-businessman-loses-$26m-at-RWS-casino-over-3-days.
"Low, Chiam Dismisses Report", *The Straits Times*, 11 June 2010.
"Malaysia Tells Singapore to Stop Provocative Claims", *New Straits Times*, 18 August 2008.
"MM Lee on Lawyers, Politicians and S'pore's Future", *The Straits Times*, 9 August 2006.
"Model City Singapore Shows Symptoms of Urban Stress", *AFP*, 24 August 2010, www.google.com/hostednews/afp/article/ALeqM5jzAlHpBUkU-kAkHJbfLpjovDds9g.
"Net and Politics: Fired up When Wired up?", *The Straits Times*, 19 August 2006.
"Net Was Abuzz with Politics during Poll Period", *The Straits Times*, 9 May 2006.

"New Flats Will Stay Affordable", *The Straits Times*, 27 January 2010.
"New Parliament's Terrific Three", *The Straits Times*, 2 June 2006.
"No Reason to Want to Curb Opposition's Rights: PM", *The Business Times*, 20 June 2006.
"Opposition Politician Freed but Barred from Leaving Singapore", *Agence France Presse*, 8 May 2006.
"PAP Has a Track Record of Delivering on Promises: PM", *The Straits Times*, 30 April 2006.
Peh Shing Huei, "S'pore Must Preserve Its System of Govt: MM", *The Straits Times*, 16 September 2006.
"People's Association and PAP Linked or Not? Minister Refutes NCMP Steve Chia", *TODAY*, 10 March 2006.
"Pillay Pays Tribute to Role of Civil Service in Rise of Modern S'pore", *The Straits Times*, 28 August 1996.
"Politics Enter Cyberspace", *The Straits Times*, 20 January 1996.
"Politics Is about Solving Residents' Woes: Khaw", *The Straits Times*, 6 May 2006.
"Relative Unknown in Major Role in Singapore Vote", *Reuters News*, 5 May 2006.
Reme Ahmad, "Khairy's Use of Race Card Raises Eyebrows", *The Straits Times*, 26 August 2006.
Sandra Davie, "4 Still Wearing *Tudung* as Deadline Approaches", *The Straits Times*, 30 January 2002.
"SDP Headed for Disappointing End", *The Straits Times*, 3 May 2006.
Seow Bei Yi, "Shanmugam on qualities of next PM", *The Straits Times*, 22 January 2017.
"Sing a Song of Singapore: Small Asian State an Economic Powerhouse", *International Business Times*, 14 August 2010, www.ibtimes.com/articles/43426/20100814/singapore-gdp.htm.
"Singapore Court Dismisses Opposition Complaint", *Reuters News*, 23 June 2006.
"Singapore Expects Double-Digit 2010 Economic Growth", *Channel News Asia*, 14 July 2010, www.channelnewsasia.com/stories/singaporebusinessnews/view/1069259/1/.html.
"Singapore Film Maker Gets Police Warning", *Reuters News*, 7 August 2006.
"Singapore's Foreign Policy Balances Idealism and Realism: PM Lee", *Channel News Asia*, 27 November 2015, http://www.channelnewsasia.com/news/singapore/singapore-s-foreign/2298768.html.
"Singapore: 'Founding Father' Lee Kuan Yew Defends Media Curbs", *BBC Monitoring Media*, 23 December 2004.
"Singapore Founding Father Lee Kuan Yew to Mentor Son's Cabinet", *Agence France Presse*, 10 August 2004.
"Singapore: Freedom of Blog Speech Depends on Who They Insult", *Inter Press Service*, 18 November 2005.
"Singapore General Turned PM Wins Strong Mandate in Polls", *Agence France Presse*, 7 May 2006.
"S'poreans Happy with Govt, but Not about Rising Costs", *The Straits Times*, 7 August 2009.
"S'pore Has Room for 7.5m People: Ex-HDB Chief", *Todayonline*, 9 September 2010, www.todayonline.com/Singapore/EDC100909-0000132/Spore-has-room-for-7,5m-people--Ex-HDB-chief.
"S'pore High Court Rules against Opposition Party — Paper", *Reuters News*, 8 June 2006.

"Singapore Investors to Seek Compensation on Lehman Minibonds", *Bloomberg*, www.bloomberg.com/apps/news?pid=newsarchive&sid=asigYSI14dIM&refer=asia, accessed 30 July 2010.
"Singapore's Lee Kuan Yew Defends Media Rules in City-State", *Associated Press Newswires*, 21 December 2004.
"Singapore's Lee Kuan Yew: High Salaries Curb State Graft", *Dow Jones International News*, 28 April 2005.
"Singapore's Lee Kuan Yew 'No Longer in Charge', Son Says", *Dow Jones International News*, 16 August 2004.
"Singapore's Lee Kuan Yew Pays Tribute to Outgoing PM Goh", *AFX International Focus*, 12 August 2004.
"Singapore's Lee Kuan Yew Slams Foreign Media Criticism", *Agence France Presse*, 29 April 2006.
"Singapore's Lee Kuan Yew Still a Power on 80th Birthday", *Agence France Presse*, 16 September 2003.
"Singapore Needs More Babies and Immigrants", *Reuters News*, 20 August 2006.
"Singapore Opposition Charged for Speaking without Permit", *Reuters News*, 20 June 2006.
"Singapore Opposition Figure Seeks to Void Election", *Reuters News*, 23 May 2006.
"Singapore Opposition Firebrand Vows IMF Protest", *Reuters News*, 31 August 2006.
"Singapore Opposition Leader Charged Over Trip", *Reuters News*, 10 October 2006.
"S'pore Opposition Party Files No Defence in Defamation Suit", *Reuters News*, 17 May 2006.
"Singapore's Opposition to Contest More Than Half of Parliament Seats", *Kyodo News*, 27 April 2006.
"Singapore's PAP Denied Automatic Return to Power", *Agence France Presse*, 27 April 2006.
"Singapore Plans Purge of Net Politics", *The Guardian*, 27 July 2001.
"Singapore — Politics", *Hilfe Country Report*, 17 November 1999.
"Singapore Politics: PAP Seeking Clean Sweep", *Economist Intelligence Unit*, 3 May 2006.
"Singapore Politics: PAP Victory Masks Signs of Dissent", *Economist Intelligence Unit — Viewswire*, 8 May 2006.
"Singapore Posts Restrictions on the Net — Content and Access Providers to Be Accountable for Pornography, Politics", *The Asian Wall Street Journal*, 6 March 1996.
"Singapore: Singapore Ruling Party Wins Elections by a Landslide", *Thai News Service*, 9 May 2006.
"Singapore: Singapore's Younger Lee Shows Business Sense", *Thai News Service*, 9 May 2006.
"Singapore Slingshot", *Malaysian Business*, 16 June 2006.
"Singapore: The New Generation — Gently Does It: Younger Leaders Want More Debate — Within Limits", *Far Eastern Economic Review*, 22 April 1999.
"Singapore to Have First Fully Contested Election in Decades", *Financial Times*, 28 April 2006.
"Singapore to Keep Protests Indoors at World Bank Meeting", *Reuters News*, 28 July 2006.
"Singapore Trade Union Congress Launches Islamic Fund", *BBC Monitoring Asia Pacific*, 26 May 2005.
"Singapore Trade Union Official Sacked for Opposition Political Ties: Report", *Agence France Presse*, 5 December 2002.

"Singapore: Two Junior Ministers Promoted to be 'Full Ministers'", *BBC Monitoring Asia Pacific*, 28 March 2005.

"Singapore's Young Challengers Beg to Differ", *International Herald Tribune*, 6 May 2006.

"Some Hard Questions at NUSS Forum", *The Business Times*, 27 April 2006.

"Soo Sen on Why Opposition MPs Are Not for CDCs", *The Straits Times*, 28 April 1997.

"SPUR Significantly Cushioned Fallout from Economic Crisis: Gan", *Channel News Asia*, 27 July 2010.

"Straits Under Strain: Why Inequality Is Centre Stage in Singapore's Election Asia: A Model Combining an Open Economy with Stern Political Control Has Brought Gains but Is under Pressure from Globalization: Writes John Burton", *Financial Times*, 4 May 2006.

"Students Today, Leaders Tomorrow?", *Today (Singapore)*, 25 May 2006.

"Taiwan Official All Praise for Singapore's Civil Service", *The Straits Times*, 12 September 1996.

Tham Yuen-C and Charissa Yong, "Shaping Singapore's 4th-Gen Leadership", *The Sunday Times Insight*, 4 October 2015.

"The Battle with the PAP Giant; The Workers' Party Might Have Lost, but They Are Not Disheartened", *Today (Singapore)*, 7 May 2006.

"The 'Chilli Padi' Packs a Punch", *The Straits Times*, 27 April 2006.

"The Fairer Side of Singapore Politics: A Bumper Crop of 22 Women Contested in the GE, Giving Females a Louder Voice", *Today (Singapore)*, 2 June 2006.

"The Internet — The New Political Ward", *The Straits Times*, 29 November 2003.

"The Line between Defamation and Debate: Defence of Reputation, Free Speech Calls for a Delicate Balance of Interests", *Today (Singapore)*, 24 May 2006.

"The Litmus Test in Singapore Polls — Singapore — The Furor over an Opposition Candidate's Electoral Form Is Threatening to Turn Singapore's General Election into a 'Gomezgate', but Will Not Be a Deciding Factor for Voters in Saturday's General Election, Political Analysts Say", *Manila Bulletin*, 4 May 2006.

"The Opposition and Its Future: What's in Store for Its Mount Ophir and Mount Kinabalu?", *Today (Singapore)*, 18 May 2006.

"The Price of Opposition", *The Straits Times*, 7 May 2006.

"The Young and the Restless (But Not Reckless)", *The Straits Times*, 12 May 2006.

"They Paid $130,000 COV for Yishun Flat 14 Years Ago", *Asiaone*, 31 July 2010, business.asiaone.com/Business/My%2BMoney/Property/Story/A1Story20100729-229476.html.

"Time to Go Back to Three-Member GRCs?", *The Straits Times*, 7 July 2006.

"TOC Special Feature: Is Singapore Really Slum-Free?", *The Online Citizen*, 27 September 2009, theonlinecitizen.com/2009/09/toc-special-feature-is-singapore-really-slum-free.

"Town Councils and Sinking Funds", *Singapore Daily*, singaporedaily.net/town-councils-sinking-funds/, accessed 30 July 2010.

"Update 3 — Exclusive — Lee Kuan Yew to stay in Singapore Cabinet", *Reuters News*, 27 July 2004.

"Visitor Arrivals to S'pore up 24.1% to Exceed 1 Million in July", *Channel News Asia*, 27 August 2010, www.channelnewsasia.com/stories/singaporelocalnews/view/1077518/1/.html.

"Voters Likely to Take Long-Term View and Play Safe", *The Straits Times*, 29 April 2006.

Walter Woon, "MPs as Directors — Where to Draw the Line", *The Business Times*, 26 February 1991.

"Worth It Despite Tripled Budget", *Asiaone*, 16 August 2010, news.asiaone.com/News/The%2BNew%2BPaper/Story/A1Story20100816-232261.html.

"YOG Ushers in New Generation of Sports Stars in S'pore", *Channel News Asia*, 26 August 2010, www.channelnewsasia.com/stories/singaporelocalnews/view/1077287/1/.html.

"YOG — What the Local Media Don't Show You", *The Online Citizen*, 17 August 2010, theonlinecitizen.com/2010/08/yog-what-the-local-media-don't-show-you/.

Electronic Media

http://www.pap.org.sg/
http://www.wp.org.sg/
http://www.spp.org.sg/
http://www.singaporedemocrat.org/
http://www.nsp.sg/
http://www.amp.org.sg
http://www.feer.com/
http://www.littlespeck.com/content/
http://www.thinkcentre.org/
http://www.singapore-window.org/index.html
http://www.singapore-elections.com/
http://www.newsintercom.org/
http://www.asiaobserver.com/singapore.htm
http://www.asiamedia.ucla.edu/
http://www.tomorrow.sg/
http://www.mrbrown.com/
http://www.yawningbread.org/
http://mysingaporenews.blogspot.com/
http://i-speak.blogdrive.com/
http://tribolum.com/
http://www.politicaldiscussions.blogspot.com/
http://singabloodypore.blogspot.com/
http://miyagi.sg/
http://commentarysingapore.blogspot.com/
http://singaporegovt.blogspot.com/
http://singaporeelection.blogspot.com/
http://singaporemind.blogspot.com/
http://www.singaporeangle.com/2006/07/flowing-river-of-history-social-class.html
http://thinkhappiness.blogspot.com/
http://www.mediawatchsg.blogspot.com/

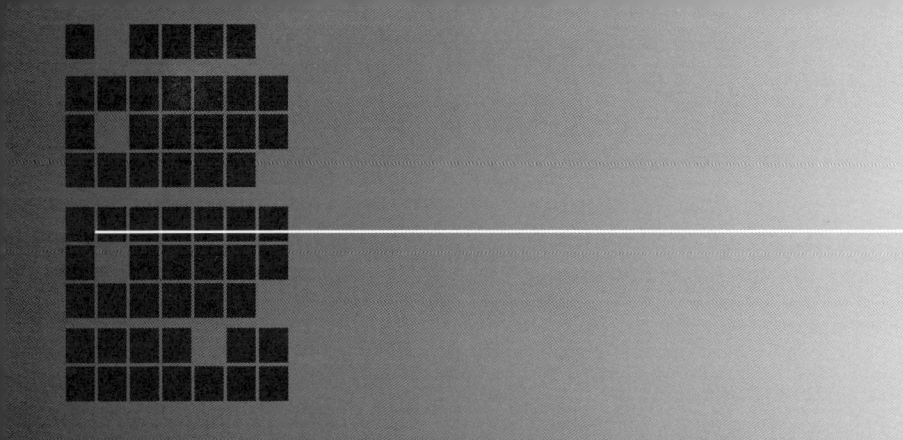

Index

Adnan, Saidi, xv
Al Qaeda, xliii, 15, 157
Aljunied GRC, x, xiv, xviii, 30, 37, 131, 137
Alliance Party, 13, 17, 132
Allied Forces, xvi, xxvii, 12
Anglo-Dutch Treaty, xv, 12, 14
Anson By-Election, viii, xviii, 135, 139
Anti-British League, vii
Anti-Corruption Branch, xxiii
ASEAN, xviii, xxiii, xxvii, 9, 153, 155, 162
Asian Wall Street Journal, xxiii
Assistant Secretary General, xi
Association of Muslim Professionals, xxiii
Association of Women for Action and Research, xxiii, 107
Athens, 159

Badawi, Abdullah, xliii, 19
Ban Kah Choon, xli
Barisan Sosialis, ix, xiv, xvi, xvii, xxiii, 16, 34, 47, 76, 133-135
Batam, 4
Bedok GRC, 30
Bengal, xv, 12,
Bishan-Toa Payoh GRC, vii-viii
Bonaparte, Napoleon, 75
British Colonial Office, xv, 12
British Military Administration, xv, xxiii, 13
Built-to-Order, xxiii, 117
Bukit Batok Constituency, 139

Bukit Merah Constituency, 139
Bukit Panjang Constituency, xiv
By-elections, 130, 139–141

Cash-Over-Valuations, xxiii, 117
'Catherine Lim Affair', 102–103
Causeway, xv
Central Executive Committee, ix, xi–xii, xxiii
Central Provident Fund, xxiii, 68–69
Chan Chun Sing, xii, xix, 89
Chan Heng Chee, xli, xliii, 140
Chee Hong Tat, xii–xiii, 89
Chee Soon Juan, xix, 38–39, 140
Chen, Bernard, 90
Cheng San GRC, 30
Chia, Steve, 39
Chiam See Tong, vii, xvii–xviii, 136–137
Chief Minister, vii, x, xvi, xxvii
Chinese Development Assistance Council, xxiii, 62
Choa Chu Kang Constituency, 139
Chua Kim Yeow, 27
Citizens' Consultative Committees, xxiii
Civil Aviation Authority of Singapore, xxiii
Civil Service, 42–46
Civil Society, 93–112
Civil Society Organisation, xxiii, 110
Choo, Desmond, xviii
Communist Party of Malaya, xxiii, 146

179

Community Centres, 46
Community Centres Management Committees, 46
Community Clubs, 46
Community Development Councils, xxiii, 46
Consumer Association of Singapore, xxiii
Coordinating Minister for National Security, xi
Corrupt Practices Investigation Bureau, xxiii, 43–44
Council of Presidential Advisers, xxiii
Crawford Constituency, 139
Criminal Investigation Department, xxiii
Crown Colony, xv, xxvii, 12
Customs, Immigration and Quarantine, xxiii, 18
Cyprus, 163

Danziger, James, 22, 31
Delta Constituency, 139
Democratic Action Party, viii
Democratic Progressive Party, 33
Deputy Prime Minister, xi–xii, xvii–xviii
Development Bank of Singapore, xxiii, 115
Dutch, xv, 12

East India Company, xv, xxiii, xl, 12, 14
Economic Development Board, xxiii
Economy Drive Committee, xxiii
Elected President, xvii, xix, xxiii, 23, 26–29, 37, 124–125, 141–143
Emeritus Senior Minister, viii
Ethnic Self-Help Groups, 123
Eurasians, 63
Excellence through Continuous Enterprise and Learning, xxiii

'*Fajar* Trial', 146
Far Eastern Economic Review, xxiii
Farquhar, William, xv
Feedback Unit, xxvii, 104–105
Fiji, 163

Fong Swee Suan, 76
Foo Seck Guan, 91
Foreign Talent, xxiii, 7, 114, 116
Foreign Worker, xxiii, 114–116
Formula One, xviii

Gan Kim Yong, xix
General Elections, 1968, xvii
General Elections, 1972, xvii
General Elections, 1976, xvii
General Elections, 1980, xvii
General Elections, 1984, viii, ix, xvii
General Elections, 1991, x
General Elections, 1997, viii
General Elections, 2001, xvii
General Elections, 2011, ix, x, xiii, xxi, 138
General Elections, 2015, viii–x, xiii–xiv, xxi, 138
Geylang West Constituency, 139
Giam, Gerald, 91
Goh Chok Tong, viii–ix, xi, xvii–xviii, 38, 83, 135
Goh, Daniel, 90, 131
Goh Keng Swee, viii, 13, 81
Goh Report, viii
Gomez, James, 137
Government Investment Corporation, xxiii, 119
Government-Linked Company, xxiii
Grassroots Organisations, 46–50
Group Representation Constituency, xi, xxi, 23, 25–26, 130–131, 137–138

Havelock Constituency, 139
He Ting Ru, 90
Head of State, xi
Heng Swee Keat, xiii, 89
Heywood, Andrew, 31
Hitler, Adolf, 75
Hock Lee Bus Riots, ix
Hong Lim Park, xvii
Hougang Constituency, x, xviii, 118, 131, 139

Housing and Development Board, xxiii, 67–68, 113–114, 116–117
Humanitarian Organisation for Migration Economics, xxiii, 115
Hussein, Sultan, xv

Ibrahim, Anwar, xliii
Immigration, 114–116
Indian Mutiny, xv
Indonesia, xvi, xliii, 1
Infocomm Technology Committee, xxiii
Inland Revenue Authority, xxiii
Inter-Racial and Religious Confidence Circles, xxiii, 123
Internal Security Act, xxiii
International Herald Tribune, xxiii
International Monetary Fund, xxiv, 109–110
International Court of Justice, xviii, xxiii, 3
Islamic State, 157
Israel, 156

Jalan Kayu Constituency, 139
Jamaluddin, Khairy, 19
Japan, xv–xvi, 13, 155
Japanese Red Army, xi
Japanese Occupation, 11, 13, 16, 43
Jema'ah Islamiyah, xvii, xxix, 4, 15, 157
Jeyaretnam, J. B., viii, xvii, xliii, 38, 136

Kampong Glam, xi
Kampong Kapor Constituency, 139
Kapur, Basant, xli
Keppel Corporation, xiii
Knowledge-Based Economy, xxiii, 105
Koh Poh Koon, xix
Koh, Tommy, 118
Konfrontasi, xvi–xvii, 156
Kreta Ayer Constituency, viii
Kwa Geok Choo, xviii

Labour Front, 132, 141
Labour Movement 2011, xxiii

Labour Party, x
'Laju Incident', xi
Lasswell, Harold, 159
Lebanon, 163
Lee Hsien Loong, ix, xi–xii, xiv, xviii, xlii, xliv, 149
Lee Li Lian, xix, 91
Lee Kong Chian, 75
Lee Kuan Yew, vii–ix, xii, xvi–xix, 5, 13, 145–151, 163
Lee Siew Choh, 77
Lee Tsao Yuan, xlii
Legislative Assembly, ix, xvi, 21, 129
Legislative Council, xvi, 129
Leifer, Michael, xli
Lim Chin Siong, ix, 56, 77
Lim Hng Kiang, xlii
Lim Hwee Hua, xviii
Lim, Michael, 88
Lim Swee Say, xlii
Lim, Sylvia, 127, 137
Lim Yew Hock, 76
Loh, Cheryl, 90
Low, Linda, xlii
Low Thia Khiang, x, xviii, 127, 137

MacDonald House, xvi, 156
Mah Bow Tan, 117, 136
Mahizhnan, Arun, xlii
Maintenance of Racial Harmony Act, 123
Majelis Ugama Islam Singapura, xxiii
Majulah Singapura, xvi, 71
Malacca, xv
Malay Regiment, xv
Malay World, xxxvii, 4, 8
Malayan Chinese Association, xxiii, 17–18
Malayan Communist Party, ix, xvi, xxiii, 16, 55, 132
Malayan Forum, viii, xii
Malayan Indian Congress, xxiii, 17
Malaysia, xvi, xviii, xix, xliii, 1, 3, 21
Malaysian Malaysia, 14
Maria Hertogh Riots, xvi, 154

Marina Bay Sands Casino, xxiii, 120
Marine Parade GRC, xiv, 139
Marsiling-Yew Tee GRC, xiii
Marshall, David, vii, xvi, 13, 132
Maslow, Abraham, 162
Mass Media, 50–54
Mass Rapid Transit, 116
Mauzy, Diane K., xlii, 80
Member of Parliament, xxiii
Mendaki, 60–61
Menon, Sundaresh, 143
Meritocracy, 63–64
Milne, R. S., xli–xlii
Minimum Occupation Period, xxiii, 118
Minister Mentor, ix, xiii, xxiii, 117, 146, 148
Ministry of Community, Youth and Sports, xxiii
Ministry of Culture, Community and Youth, xxiii
Ministry of Information, Communications and the Arts, xxiii
Ministry of Social and Family Development, xxiii
Mohammed, Mahathir, 19
Monetary Authority of Singapore, xi, xiii, xxiii
Mountbatten Constituency, 139
Multiculturalism, 59–63
Mussolini, Benito, 75

Nair, Devan, vii, xvi–xvii, 56, 99, 135, 142
Najib Tun Razak, xviii, xliii, 19
Nathan, S. R., xi, xvii–xix, 27, 73, 83, 142
National Anthem, xvi
National Education, 4, 8, 66–67, 123
National Education Committee, xxiii
National Service, xvii, xxiii, xxx, 69–70
National Solidarity Party, xxiii, 33, 39, 138
National Trades Union Congress, vii–viii, xii-xiii, xxv, 17, 54, 57, 99
National Wages Council, xxv, 57

Nature Society of Singapore, xxiii, 107
Nee Soon Constituency, 139
Newspapers and Printing Presses Act, xxiii
Ngiam Tong Dow, 115
Nominated Member of Parliament, xxiii, 23–25, 29–30
Ng Chee Meng, xiii, 89
Non-Constituency Member of Parliament, xxiii, 23–24, 29–30, 131, 137–138

Ong, David, xix
Ong Teng Cheong, xvii, 27, 73, 135, 142
Ong Ye Kung, xiii, xix, 89
Operation Coldstore, 38, 77
Opposition, viii, 31–40, 127–143
Orang Laut, x
Our Singapore Conversation, xvi
Out-of-Bound Markers, xxv, 18, 102, 109

Pakir, A., xli
Palestine, 156
Palmer, Michael, xix
Pang Kim Hin, viii
Parliament, viii, x, xvii
Pasir Panjang Constituency, x
Paya Lebar Constituency, 139
Peceival, Arthur E., 13
Pedra Branca, xviii, xxx, 3, 18
Penang, xv
Persatuan Melayu Singapura, 132
People's Action Party, vii–ix, xi, xvi–xviii, xlii, 32–40, 127–143
People's Association, xxv, 46–48
People's Front for the Liberation of Palestine, xi
People's Power Party, 138
People's Republic of China, xx
Perara, Leon, 91, 131
PERDAUS, xxv, 61
Pertubuhan Ulama dan Guru-Guru Agama Islam Singapura, xxv
Pillai, Murali, xix, 140
Plato, xxxix

Png Eng Huat, xviii, 91
Post-Lee Kuan Yew Singapore, 145–151
Postal and Telecommunications Uniformed
    Employees Union, 146
Potong Pasir Constituency, vii, 118, 139
Presidential Advisory Committee, xxv
Presidential Council for Minority Rights,
    xvii
Presidential Election Committee, xxv
Principal Private Secretary, xii–xiv
Privy Council, viii, 15
Prophet Mohammad, x
Pulau Batu Putih, 18
Punggol East By-Election, xix
Punggol East SMC, 138–139
Pulau Bukom, xi

Quah, Jon, xli, xliii

Racial Harmony Day, 124
Racial Riots (1964), x, 154
Radin Mas Constituency, 139
Raffles, Stamford, xv, xl, 1, 6, 12
Rahman, Abdul (Tunku), xv–xvi, 13
Rajaratnam, S., 13, 81, 163
Razak, Abdul, xii
REACH, 105
Reform Party, ix, xxv, 138
Rendel, George, xvi, 13
Republic of Singapore Air Force, 18
Republic of Singapore Navy, xi
Rosenau, James, 153

Sabah, xvi, 13
Sarawak, xvi, 13
Seah Chee Meow, xli, xliii
Second World War, vii, 4, 75
Secretary General, ix
Security Intelligence Department, xi
Sedition Act, 123
Sembawang Constituency, 139
Sembawang GRC, xiii
Senior Minister, xi, xvii–xviii, 146, 148

Sentosa Development Board, x
Severe Acute Respiratory Syndrome, xviii,
    xxv, xlii, 113
Shanmugam, K., 90
Shanmugaratnam, Tharman, xi
Sheares, Benjamin, 73, 142
Singapore, vii, ix–x, xv
Singapore Armed Forces, xi–xiii, xxv, 9,
    20
Singapore Association of Trades Union, xxv,
    56
Singapore Chinese Chambers
    of Commerce, 61–62
Singapore Democratic Alliance, vii, xxv, 33,
    138
Singapore Democratic Party, xvii, xxv, 33,
    138, 140
Singapore First Party, 33, 138
Singapore Indian Development Association,
    xxvi, 62
Singapore People's Party, vii, 33, 138
Singapore Progressive Party, xvi, 138, 141
Singapore Straits, 3
Singapore Tourism Board, x
Singapore Trades Union Congress, xxvi
Singapore Workforce Development Agency,
    xiii
Singh, Pritam, 90–91
Single Member Constituency, xxi, xxvi, xliv,
    130–131, 138
Sintercom, 106
Sitoh Yih Pin, xix
SG 50 Steering Committee, xiii
South China Sea, 3, 155
Sparta, 159
Speaker's Corner, xvii
Sri Lanka, 163
State of Emergency, xvi
Straits of Malacca, 1, 154
Straits Settlements, xv, xxvi, 1, 12
Suez Canal, xv
Suharto, xliii
Syonan-to, xv

Tan Cheng Bock, xviii, 142
Tan Chuan-Jin, xiv
Tan, Dennis, 91, 131
Tan Kah Kee, 75
Tan Kong Soon, 90
Tan, Ron, 90
Tan, Tony, viii, 73, 142
Tanjong Pagar Constituency, xii, xvii–xviii, 137, 146
Tanjong Pagar GRC, 137
Taiwan, 2, 155
Telok Blangah Constituency, 139
'Third China', 155
Toh Chin Chye, xii, 79, 81, 163
Tong Chee Kiong, xli
Trade Unions, 54–58
Transient Workers Count Too, 115

Ulu Pandan Constituency, 139
United Malays National Organisation, xvi, xliii, 14, 18
United National Front, 134
United Nations, 9
United Nations Conference on the Law of the Sea, 9
United People's Front, 135

United States, xviii, 2, 113

Vietnam War, 2

Weber, Max, 74
Wee Kim Wee, 73, 142
Westminster Parliamentary System, v, 20, 22, 30
White Paper on Competitive Salaries for Competent and Honest Government, 87
White Paper on the EP, 28
Wok, Othman, x
Wong, Lawrence, xiii, 89
Wong, Y. Y., xlii
Workers' Party, viii, xvii, 32–34, 37, 134–138, 150
World Bank, xxvi, 109–110

Yamashita, Tomoyuki, 12
Yaw Shin Leong, xviii
Yeo, George, xviii, 101–102
Youth Olympic Games, 120–121
Yusof bin Ishak, xvi, 73

Zulkifli, Masagos, xix